Fighting for Justice

The History and Origins of Adversary Trial

John Hostettler is a solicitor, legal biographer and historian whose subjects have included Sir James Fitzjames Stephen, Sir Edward Coke, Sir Matthew Hale, Thomas Erskine and Lord Halsbury. He has written widely for the legal press, including as a regular contributor to the leading UK weekly journal *Justice of the Peace*. A former magistrate himself, he played a leading role in the abolition of flogging in British colonial prisons. He has also served as chair of Social Security Appeals Tribunals. He holds the degrees of BA, MA, LLB (Hons), LLM and PhD (London) and is a member of the Royal Society of Literature.

Fighting for Justice
The History and Origins of Adversary Trial
John Hostettler

Published 2006 by
WATERSIDE PRESS
Domum Road
Winchester SO23 9NN
United Kingdom

Telephone or Fax 01962 855567 UK Local-call 0845 2300 733
E-mail enquiries@watersidepress.co.uk
Online catalogue and bookstore www.watersidepress.co.uk

ISBN 1 940 380 29 8

Classifications Crime, Criminal law, Law, Lawyers, Legal history, Evidence, Criminal procedure.

Cataloguing-in-Publication Data A catalogue record for this book can be obtained from the British Library.

Printing and binding CPI Antony Rowe, Chippenham and Eastbourne.

Cover design ©2006 Waterside Press. Cover image from a 100 years old aquatint.

Sole North American distributors International Specialised Book Services (ISBS), 920 NE 58th Ave, Suite 300, Portland, Oregon, 97213-3786, USA
Telephone 1 800 944 6190; Fax 1 503 280 8832; website: www.isbs.com; email: orders@isbs.com

Fighting for Justice

The History and Origins of Adversary Trial

John Hostettler

WATERSIDE PRESS

Acknowledgements

I would like to acknowledge the great insight shown by my publisher, Bryan Gibson, in considering both the content and context of the predominant thesis of this book and I am most grateful for his invaluable help in its production. I am also indebted to Dr Richard Vogler, Senior Lecturer in Law at the University of Sussex, who read the text and helped me to get to grips with the genesis of the adversary tradition and the consequent procedural revolution in the criminal law.

I thank the staff at the Library of the University of Sussex, the British Library and the London Library for their courtesy and help during the research necessary for the writing of the book.

Also of kind assistance in locating the situation of Sir William Garrow at the Honourable Society of Lincoln's Inn were its Librarian, Jo Hutchings, and Assistant Librarian, Frances Bellis.

Needless to say, any mistakes are entirely my responsibility.

Preface

It is commonly believed that something like the same antiquity can be ascribed to adversary trial in our criminal courts as to parliament and trial by jury. In reality, however, the opposite is true with adversary trial emerging in England only in the eighteenth century. Moreover, its origins have been totally unrecognised by lawyers and jurists until the last 30 years or so. Even now, there is considerable dispute as to how and why adversary trial came into existence and little connection has been made with the fact that its birth contributed to the genesis of a modern recognisable doctrine of human rights which, under the influence of the common law, has become diffused across the developed world.

As a consequence, a large part of this book concentrates on the birth and meaning of adversary trial. It also endeavours to assess how deep-rooted is the notion of conflict in the common law and the English psyche generally. After all, the adversary system of trial, with counsel as the forensic champions of hostile parties, is so well established in the modern public mind as to present a serious challenge to any would-be reformers.

Adversary trial is usually contrasted with the inquisitorial system operating in countries like France where the *juge d'instruction* controls the proceedings prior to and during the hearing of the case. This system was considered by the British Royal Commission on Criminal Justice (1991-93) which disliked its lengthy pre-trial detention of many defendants and the close involvement of judges with prosecutors and the police. In contrast, on 21 March 2006 the then Home Secretary, Charles Clarke, told the House of Commons Home Affairs Committee, "I think that a supervisory system and investigating magistrates' regime is very superior to the system that we have in this country." He added that he did not think the adversary system had been a particularly effective means of securing justice.

Was the Home Secretary 'flying a kite' for further changes to undermine lawyers and juries in a move away from the ingrained conflict philosophy or was he supporting restorative justice, or both? The present Government has not been slow to challenge the judiciary and the legal profession and, as juries have become more democratic, there have been numerous moves to restrict their powers. Furthermore, restorative justice, as a means of giving assistance to victims of crime, is a commitment of the Government in its rehabilitative agenda. This can be a positive approach as with the use of community sentences in situations that do not merit custodial sentences, and also within prisons where restorative approaches are also now spreading with a degree of enthusiasm.

On the other hand, it can involve dangers. For instance, on 24 April 2006, under a pilot scheme, the Old Bailey and Crown Courts in Birmingham, Cardiff, Manchester and Winchester were given a new historic role in their proceedings. For the first time, the relatives of victims of murder and manslaughter were able to address the court after a guilty verdict, but before sentence. This now opens the door to emotional pleading to influence sentences and secure revenge and may produce scenes hitherto foreign to English courts. How many will restrain their feelings and remember the rules of evidence? And what if there are multiple victims, as with the Shipman murders? Moreover, what is the purpose when there already exists a right of families to address the court in writing through a victim impact assessment which goes to the judge and which he can read out and use in sentencing? Programmes identified with restorative justice include assisting relatives of victims but there is no obvious need for this to be done in court to the potential detriment of justice.

But none of this is to say that we should not find better ways of treating victims and witnesses who often say that they find the criminal justice process a burden – and occasionally inhibiting to the extent that they do not wish to pursue a complaint originally made to the police. It is worth remembering also that our entire system has grown out of a historical line of development that sought to protect both victims and offenders, that began when blood money, or bot or botgeld became an alternative to outright self-help, retaliation and revenge. The adversary system is, in essence, a rule of law-friendly version of this and we should always remember the value that is inherent in a method that allows the individual to directly challenge any allegation made by or on behalf of the State.

As justice and the rule of law are all-important it is to be hoped that this book may prove to be an aid both to understanding adversary trial and its contribution to human rights and the scales of justice. I hope that it might also prove to be an enjoyable insight into the life, times and until now not too well documented contribution to these developments made by Sir William Garrow and his erstwhile contempories.

John Hostettler
Rustington-on-Sea
2006

Fighting for Justice
The History and Origins of Adversary Trial

Contents

Books by John Hostettler

The Politics of Criminal Law: Reform in the Nineteenth Century (1992) Barry Rose

Thomas Wakely: An Improbable Radical (1993) Barry Rose

The Politics of Punishment (1994) Barry Rose

Politics and Law in the Life of Sir James Fitzjames Stephen (1995) Barry Rose

Thomas Erskine and Trial by Jury (1996) Barry Rose

Sir Edward Carson: A Dream Too Far (1997) Barry Rose

Sir Edward Coke: A Force for Freedom (1997) Barry Rose

At the Mercy of the State: A Study in Judicial Tyranny (1998) Barry Rose

Lord Halsbury (1998) Barry Rose

The Red Gown: The Life and Works of Sir Matthew Hale (2002) Barry Rose

Law and Terror in Stalin's Russia (2003) Barry Rose

The Criminal Jury Old and New: Jury Power from Early Times to the Present Day (2004) Waterside Press

With **Brian P. Block**

Hanging in the Balance: A History of the Abolition of Capital Punishment in Britain (1997) Waterside Press

Voting in Britain: A History of the Parliamentary Franchise (2001) Barry Rose

Famous Cases: Nine Trials that Changed the Law (2002) Waterside Press

CHAPTER 1

Introduction

WHAT IS ADVERSARY TRIAL?

It is intrinsic to the nature of adversary trial that it is rights-based. It emerged in
early eighteenth century England as the right of prisoners to engage counsel to
assist in their defence in felony trials. Once established it quickly spread to
countries where the common law had been introduced—usually English
colonies, including those in North America.

It contrasts with the Roman-canon inquisitorial system in operation in other
parts of the world, particularly Europe. Differing from the battle between
opposing counsel in adversary trial, the continental system imposed on the judge
a duty to inquire into the circumstances of the case with a view to uncovering the
truth. In fact, his powers were so extensive that his authority had to be limited by
evidentiary strictures under which, according to Stephan Landsman:

> he could convict a criminal defendant in only two circumstances: when two eye
> witnesses were produced who had observed the gravamen of the crime, or when the
> defendant confessed. Circumstantial evidence was never sufficient in itself to warrant
> conviction. These evidentiary rules made it impossible to obtain convictions in many
> cases unless the defendant was willing to confess. Roman-canon process authorized
> the use of torture to extract the necessary confessions. Thus, torture became a tool of
> judicial inquiry and was used to generate the evidence upon which the defendant
> would be condemned.[1]

This system was adopted on the continent following the abolition of trial by
ordeal by the Lateran Council in 1215.[2] At that time in England Henry III was an
infant and, lacking strong leadership from the King's council, the judges
hesitated before finally, in 1219, they turned the presenting jury into a jury of fact
finders who could determine guilt or innocence. They thereby avoided both the
all-powerful judge and the use of torture.[3]

Over succeeding centuries, the criminal trial jury in England changed its
character but remained a fact-finding body whilst criminal law procedure made
the parties responsible for producing all the evidence on which the jury would
base its verdict. In time, it was the conflict between the parties that was the basis
on which the procedure of adversarial trial would be built. But this did not come
about until lawyers were permitted to examine and cross-examine witnesses in a
manner in which, as will be seen, they came to dominate the courtroom.[4]

As Landsman has written elsewhere, '[t]he fundamental expectation of an
adversarial system is that out of a sharp clash of proofs presented by litigants in
a highly structured forensic setting will come the information upon which a

neutral and passive decision maker can base a satisfying resolution of the legal dispute.'[5] And, in its nature it is based upon a clash which must be rights-based. That was, of course, not the traditional method in England before the eighteenth century, when the judge dominated the trial and prisoners' rights were almost non-existent.

Landsman identifies the essence of the adversary system when he outlines three modern elements that are fundamental to it. First, 'the decision-maker remains neutral and passive during the trial'. Secondly, the parties must produce the evidence and proof. Finally, there must be 'an elaborate set of rules to govern the trial and the behaviour of the advocates ...' He adds that, 'no one set out to build the adversary system. It was neither part of a grand governmental design nor the scheme of an ingenious legal philosopher.'[6] Nor, he might have added, of ingenious judges or practising lawyers.

Nevertheless, in summing up the advantage of the process Sydney Smith aptly said, 'justice is found, experimentally, to be most effectually promoted by the opposite efforts of practiced and ingenious men presenting to the selection of an impartial judge the best arguments for the establishment or explanation of truth.'[7]

As to the impact adversary trial made on contemporaries in the eighteenth century, we have the words of the well-known criminal barrister, John Adolphus, who described the excitement aroused by his first experience of it when attending court,

> I cannot describe the effect produced on my mind by the first hearing of an impassioned address, quick taunt, convincing reply, and above all the *viva voce* examination of witnesses and the comments on their evidence.[8]

So different was it from the earlier mode of trial that he added that from that day he became, 'early and constant in my attendance'[9] at court.

It must be recognized, however, that there is some questioning of adversary trial and opponents ask if it is a search for the truth or a 'game of bluff, suspense and surprise?'[10] They prefer the continental inquisitorial system where, instead of a battle between parties to establish guilt or innocence, there is an attempt to establish the truth by a long investigation process conducted by the judge. Unlike adversary trial, there is no presumption of innocence and the witnesses are called by the pro-active judge, not by the parties' lawyers. Defence counsel and juries play a far less prominent role than in the common law system. Whether or not this is superior to adversary trial will be considered in what follows in this book, particularly in the concluding chapter.

LAWYER-FREE TRIALS

So well established today is the English adversary system of trial, with counsel at its centre, that it is hard to believe it is historically of fairly recent origin. Both trial by jury and trial by barristers have existed in England since the thirteenth century. Yet from early in the thirteenth century until the eighteenth century, *by law,* following a landmark case in the reign of Edward I (1273-1307),[11] prisoners in trials of treason and felony were not allowed to have counsel appear for them, even though the sentence for treason and felony was capital. At first, as lawyers were not yet upon the scene (except in civil suits), this prohibition meant the exclusion of helpful friends and relatives acting as counsellors. The ban took in lawyers only after they began to appear in 1235[12] and may be one reason why they continued to act mainly in civil cases.

Equally, it seems likely that since early criminal trials were usually of short duration, members of the Bar would have found them neither sufficiently interesting nor remunerative enough to wish to act as prosecutors and England had no system of public prosecution. Instead, both the accuser and the defendant each told their own story, often inadequately, and the judge and members of the jury were actors in the trial joining in with questions and comments at will. In that sense, although not in its consequences for those convicted, a criminal trial was a freewheeling affair.

The only exception to the exclusion of defence counsel was on points of law,[13] but these were rare and although they could be raised by the judge, a juror or even the prisoner, they had to be certified as such by the judge before they could be pleaded.

The rule prohibiting counsel did not apply to the prosecution and this left defendants at a severe disadvantage for centuries to come, particularly in trials for treason, where the Crown was always represented. The logic of the rule, says J. H. Langbein, was to pressurize the accused to speak in his or her own defence[14] but the idea that this was an advantage to a prisoner will be questioned later when the reasons given for the rule will be considered.

To make matters worse, accused persons were also not allowed to subpoena witnesses, nor, if they appeared voluntarily, could defence witnesses give evidence on oath, which placed them at a lower level than prosecution witnesses whose credibility was enhanced by testimonial evidence.[15] The rationale for this last rule will be examined in the next chapter but it is already clear that prisoners suffered from a serious handicap in presenting a defence and were often saved from the gallows only by the mercy of juries or, in some cases, the judge.

JURY OR TORTURE

Jury trial replaced trial by ordeal in England in 1219[16] and at first jurors were witnesses, or in contact with witnesses, from the community where the alleged crime occurred. This gave them a discretionary power and there is a good deal of evidence to show that they used it to acquit accused persons if the crime were not premeditated or too severe.[17] As a consequence, in early homicide trials the great majority of those guilty of non-premeditated killings were acquitted and only about 50 per cent of those convicted of murder were sent to the gallows.[18] In fact, in cases of homicide, these early juries distinguished between unpremeditated killing and murder long before the difference between manslaughter and murder was legally established.

With the reigns of the Tudors and Stuarts there came a change. In response to the divisions in the country during the Wars of the Roses, the Tudors had set about establishing a strong central government and a nation state.[19] This included exercising more control over the criminal justice system than monarchs had in earlier times and as part of its search for strong government, the Crown was well-disposed towards the continental canon law and the exercise of torture, with the central, and dominating, role of the judge.

In many European countries, the rules of law and procedure were more precise than in England. Western Europe, long closer than England to Rome and its influences, developed the principles of the canon law by 'means of glosses and commentaries and treatises upon the text of Justinian's books.'[20] Roman forms of proof were adopted 'which exalted the probative power of sworn eye-witness testimony and of the accused's confession, often coerced by torture.'[21] In this way 'the law encouraged and, indeed, often required, the torture of the accused in order to produce a confession, which was considered of particularly high evidentiary value.'[22] It is in this period that torture was also practised in England, although under the royal prerogative and not at common law.[23] Nevertheless, despite the fact that the majority of English cases involving torture between 1540 and 1640 were crimes of state, more than a quarter of torture warrants issued were for cases of murder, robbery, burglary and horse stealing.[24] However, the crucial point is that torture did not become regularized in English criminal procedure.[25] At the same time, juries were by now being drawn not from the locality where the crime was committed but from the wider county. They were also acting more judicially as they ceased to be self-informing and started to evaluate evidence.[26]

DEFENCE IMPEDIMENTS

Under the Tudors, the Marian bail and committal statutes of the 1550s meant that magistrates temporarily ceased to be judicial officers and, by taking depositions and binding over witnesses to appear at trial, became agents of the King. As such they were required to ensure effective prosecutions of accused felons,[27] and in many cases they obtained evidence for the prosecution. It also meant that the justices of the peace assisted the prosecutor in preparing his case and as the justices could also send an accused person to gaol pending trial, some prejudice towards the prisoner who had been held in custody might surface in the courtroom. Moreover, whilst witnesses for the prosecution were bound over to appear at trial, the accused could not compel the attendance of witnesses and could not know the exact nature of the indictment against him or her, or have access to the depositions of the prosecution witnesses.[28] With these difficulties added to the denial of counsel it is not surprising that criminal trials in England at the time have been described as 'nasty, brutish, and essentially short.'[29]

During the Interregnum (1649-1659) the problems were to some extent recognized and it was proposed by the Hale Commission, chaired by Sir Matthew Hale,[30] that prisoners should have counsel to act for them fully in all cases where the prosecution was represented and that defence witnesses should be able to give evidence on oath.[31] However, Cromwell's law-reforming zeal was stalled by his infrequent parliaments and nothing was done to implement these suggestions before the Restoration of Charles II put paid to them.

In the late seventeenth century, under the later Stuarts, judges held office at the King's pleasure and at times were subjected to extreme pressure to ensure that they executed royal commands. Probably at no time had the English judiciary been more intimately associated with politics.[32] Those judges who failed to do what the King required were abruptly dismissed, including 12 in four years during the reign of James II.[33] Among those remaining were the two most well-known and notorious hanging judges in English history, George Jeffreys and William Scroggs, who were prominent in treason trials arising from the Popish Plot (1678-81), the Rye House Plot (1683) and the Monmouth Rebellion (1685). These resulted in the execution of prominent Whig leaders, who became martyrs and inspired their followers to help trigger the Glorious Revolution of 1689 and subsequent changes in criminal procedure.

THE FIRST BREACH IN THE 'NO-COUNSEL' RULE

The Whig politicians and grandees, in power after the Glorious Revolution and in the process of creating a new party,[34] emphasized the growing importance of the individual in society and enshrined some rights in the *Bill of Rights* of 1689.[35] In an early manifestation of the modern concept of human rights, this provided, *inter alia*, for the free election of MPs; the right to trial by jury and the empanelling of jurors fairly; that excessive bail should not be required nor excessive fines be imposed; and that no cruel and unusual punishments be inflicted.

The Whig leaders also introduced the radical Treason Trials Act of 1696,[36] a landmark statute which had an unwitting and powerful effect on the birth of adversary trial. It gave prisoners on trial for treason the right to have counsel act for them in all respects, including addressing the jury on the facts as well as on questions of law. As Beattie says, 'It flowed from the Revolution of 1689 as a means of redressing a wrong the now-dominant Whig political class had suffered in the previous decade–the use of charges of treason to destroy political opponents.'[37] It was also a response to lawyer-driven prosecutions.

It was thought at the time that the formal reasons for the Act—namely that in treason trials two witnesses to an overt act were required and, of greater significance, that the Crown always employed counsel to prosecute—were not applicable to felony trials and that similar legislation for such trials was not necessary. As Serjeant Hawkins wrote, 'Experience' has shown 'great Disadvantages [to defendants] from the want of Counsel, in Prosecutions of High Treason against the King's Person, which are generally managed for the Crown with greater Skill and Zeal than ordinary Prosecutions.'[38]

Nevertheless, the conduct of felony trials themselves was changing. With the incidence of crime appearing to increase, Associations for the Prosecution of Felons were formed in large numbers throughout the country to meet the growing demand for prosecuting counsel and to spread the cost of investigating crime and paying legal fees. At the same time the government sponsored a bounty system which encouraged reward-seeking thief-catchers. These, together with Crown witnesses induced to turn King's evidence and testify against their co-accused to save their own necks, were increasingly creating more perjury which could injure innocent defendants who were threatened with the death penalty even for trivial offences.

Accomplice evidence was not only widespread but also officially encouraged. Some people argued that it tainted the criminal justice system and reduced its authority.[39] Others believed that immunity for accomplices was an important weapon against crime. There was a 'widely held view that advertised rewards were an indispensable instrument for the discovery of all serious crime, and the Home Office followed a consistent policy of encouraging all victims to offer them.'[40] At the same time, 'the injured parties, in their turn, came to regard the official promise of impunity almost as a right. To refuse them this form of assistance, even if it appeared to be contrary to "the ends of public justice" might act as a discouragement.'[41] But it had a dangerous downside. As Joseph Chitty wrote:

> The law confesses its weakness by calling in the assistance of those by whom it has been broken. It offers a premium to treachery, and destroys the last virtue which clings to the degraded transgressor. Still, on the other hand, it tends to prevent any extensive agreement among atrocious criminals, makes them perpetually suspicious of each other, and prevents the hopelessness of mercy from rendering them desperate.[42]

This system, and its resulting widespread perjury, appears to have led some judges to believe that the scales were weighted too heavily against prisoners charged with capital offences in felony trials. As a consequence, a few of them allowed counsel to appear for defendants but it was a slow process although it gradually led to counsel, and not the judges, establishing adversariality.

EARLY STEPS TOWARDS ADVERSARY TRIAL

It was in the 1730s, and without legislation, that such judges by slow degrees began sporadically to permit prisoners to engage counsel. However, barristers were not allowed to examine their clients and the judges limited their role to examination and cross-examination in order to retain the situation whereby the unsworn defendant in person told the jury his or her side of the story unembellished. What they did not envisage was that in spite of this limitation the lawyers would capture the courtroom and reduce the previously active role of the prisoner, as well as those of the judge and jury who respectively became solely umpire and fact finders.[43]

In this development a pivotal role was played by William Garrow who appeared in many hundreds of cases at the Old Bailey and established an aggressive style of questioning in cross-examination. As will be seen, this was vital in securing adversary trial and also helped lead to the introduction of rules of evidence, such as the 'best evidence' rule, the rule against accomplices' evidence and the hearsay rule,[44] all of which suited the purposes of defence counsel. Indeed, although Langbein argues that the judges introduced these evidential rules, with motives he does not explain and as if of their own volition, this is not the view of Beattie who considers that they flowed from the involvement of defence lawyers. He says,

> It seems certain ... that it was the insistent questioning by defense counsel that raised as matters of immediate urgency many of the issues whose resolution by the judges in their post-circuit meetings at Serjeants' Inn helped to form what amounted to a law of evidence in criminal trials.[45]

Stephan Landsman goes even further in seeing the new rules of evidence as one of the impetuses for the lawyers taking over the criminal trial. Other impulses, he says, included 'the rise of dynamic individualism and the growth of a market economy.'[46] He concludes that '[t]he adversary system with its emphasis on the action of individual litigants was well suited to the economic and social needs of such a time.'[47] It should also be added that, together with the rule of law, it is sometimes an important factor in securing the proper functioning of the market economy.

ORIGINS OF ADVERSARY TRIAL DISPUTED

As a consequence of counsel being allowed a restricted appearance for prisoners, the adversarial system was slowly brought into existence in the course of the eighteenth and nineteenth centuries in what amounted to a 'crucial formative period for English criminal justice.'[48] Its origins, however, were for long unknown and are now disputed. Criminal barristers practising in the Old Bailey and Crown

Courts today do not appear to be greatly concerned with where their power in the courtroom comes from and academic lawyers cannot agree on how adversary trial arose. As Langbein, who has carried out a great deal of research on the subject over 25 years and seeks to remedy the situation, acknowledges, 'although the importance of this transformation from lawyer-free to lawyer-dominated trial has been remarked in the historical literature, not much has been known about how and why it occurred.'[49]

There is considerable academic dispute as to whether adversary trial was consciously introduced over time by the judges or resulted from the tactics of the defence barristers in the courtroom. Langbein himself, Beattie, Landsman, Vogler and May have all written on the subject and their views will be considered and discussed.

Furthermore, it will be argued that Langbein's conclusions that adversary trial is seriously flawed have been accepted too uncritically. Moreover, in his book Langbein refers to the 'trickster William Garrow'[50], although none of the quotations he takes from Garrow's advocacy justifies such a description. Indeed, Brougham testified to Garrow's discretion, judgment and self-command when he wrote that on an occasion when defending a prisoner on a charge of murder, Garrow 'sat in court during the whole trial and of course watched each word, look, and gesture of each witness, as well as of the prosecuting counsel, and the judge, and the jury, with the eyes of an eagle, and never once uttered a word from the beginning to the end of the proceeding.'[51] He acted in a similar manner in a trial at the Old Bailey in 1786. Again the prisoner was charged with murder, and Garrow sat through the trial, asked only two questions and allowed the prosecution witnesses to lie and contradict each other. At the end of the case the jury found the prisoner 'guilty of manslaughter but not of murder' and she was burnt in the hand and discharged.[52]

Nevertheless, as Garrow, more than any other lawyer, was responsible for the extensive growth of adversarial criminal trial, his role will be examined in detail and it will be considered more fully later whether Langbein's assessment is warranted. Counsel, of course, act in the interests of their clients, and it will be considered how far Garrow went to the limits of the burgeoning, but by modern standards primitive, Bar etiquette.

In the meantime it can be noted that Garrow could sometimes be curt and rude and was not as polite to witnesses as his contemporary and rival, Thomas Erskine. According to one writer, Erskine was noted for his 'unfailing courtesy in the courtroom' and 'gentlemanlike' examination of witnesses.[53] On the other hand, Garrow is described by Beattie as tenacious, insistently and doggedly determined, and with a capacity for sarcasm.[54] As will be seen, he was sometimes criticized by judges and jurors for his harsh cross-examination of witnesses but he was foremost at the Bar in changing criminal procedure dramatically and advancing adversariality. To a large extent it was to his aggressive and combative approach that could be credited the establishment of so many due process rights that would have been impossible without men like him.

In any event, Garrow always endeavoured to act with professional propriety in his advocacy and he and Erskine quite often acted together in trials. Indeed,

Erskine said of him that, 'he knows more of the real justice and policy of everything connected with the criminal law than any man I am acquainted with.'[55] Above all, he may with justice be called the father of adversary trial.

PRISONERS' COUNSEL

By the nineteenth century counsel for the prosecution and for the defence were appearing quite regularly in criminal trials and the refusal to allow counsel to address the jury was more commonly seen as the anomaly it was. Early in the century various efforts were made to change the position by legislation but they all failed.[56] As a consequence, when Lord John Russell was Home Secretary three years after the Great Reform Act of 1832, he sought the support of the criminal law commissioners, who had been appointed by Lord Chancellor Brougham in 1833 to codify the criminal law, by asking them to examine and report on the question of permitting prisoners to have counsel act for them fully.[57]

The commissioners quickly responded entirely favourably and their report assisted in securing the enactment of the Prisoners' Counsel Act of 1836[58] which was a vital step in guaranteeing adversary trial in England and elsewhere. The members of the Bar had largely opposed the Bill[59] but soon found a vastly increased source of income which also had the effect of greatly increasing their numbers. For example, the Law List of 1800 showed 598 barristers and by 1900 the figure, including non-practising barristers, was 9,457.[60] Indeed, within that period the *Law Review* claimed that whilst in 1809 there were only 456 practising barristers, by 1846 the number was 3,000. At no period of its history, said the journal, had the Bar ever been so numerous.[61] Of course, not all would have been criminal lawyers but many, including Garrow and Erskine, acted in both civil and criminal cases.

Nevertheless, the early opposition to the Bill by barristers arose in part because, at the same time, they were losing some of their monopolies to the rising profession of solicitors. Indeed, the *Law Review* strongly urged that it was 'unwise to encourage the establishment of any "inferior order of advocates."'[62] The Bar was fighting for its professional life with most of its members more concerned to survive than indulge in political reform movements. Subsequently, after a considerable increase in work, the Bar's campaign to preserve its monopolies became absorbed in the dramatic expansion of adversarial trial.

CONCLUSION

The 'no defence counsel' rule was a serious blemish on the face of English criminal procedure for centuries. To some extent, it was tolerated because, although the situation of prisoners in felony trials was perilous, the dangers they faced were modified by jury nullification and the benefit of clergy which meant that some of them suffered reduced sentences or no penalty at all, apart from branding. As a consequence, the demand for reform was to some extent stifled.

For the prisoner in the dock charged with felony and weighed down by rules that, unless the jury showed mercy or he had 'clergy', meant his life was in serious danger, the change to adversary trial was a momentous transformation. The prime purpose of this book is to examine the development of adversary trial, and the procedural revolution it inspired, in order to show how and why it arose and the conditions in which it could flourish and have an impact on criminal procedure around the globe. The crucial role of Sir William Garrow in that development will be illustrated from the trials in which he appeared as defence counsel at the Old Bailey.

Langbein insists that adversary trial arose from the judiciary correcting the leanings of a trial system that favoured prosecutors. Nevertheless, this view of the role of the judges is open to serious question and the dispute that exists around it requires further clarification and will be discussed in later chapters. In any event, it does not explain why it was adopted so widely and so quickly in some other countries.

Adversary trial was born around the time of striking changes that were altering both the physical face of England and its customs and culture—namely the Industrial Revolution and the Enlightenment. The destruction of the medieval legal world was finally coming to its conclusion. Following the American and French Revolutions there was also a growing awareness of rights, outlined in their public Declarations. These momentous upsurges in national life, and the intellectual ferment they aroused, together with the philosophy of John Locke and the English *Bill of Rights* of 1689, foreshadowed human rights becoming an integral part of the legal, moral and political fabric of civilized society in which today the courts play 'a leading role in resolving human rights controversies and developing human rights norms.'[63]. It is relevant to ask whether, and if so how far, adversary trial was linked with this development of a theory of human rights and this will be examined later in the book.

ENDNOTES for *Chapter 1*

[1] S. Landsman. (1983) 'A Brief Survey of the Development of the Adversary System.' 44 (1) *Ohio State Law Journal*. p. 724.

[2] J. Hostettler. (2004) *The Criminal Jury Old and New: Jury Power from Early Times to the Present Day.* Winchester, Waterside Press. p. 21.

[3] Ibid. pp. 21-2.

[4] J. H. Langbein. (2003) *The Origins of Adversary Criminal Trial*. Oxford, Oxford University Press. p. 311.

[5] S. Landsman. (1990) 'The Rise of the Contentious Spirit: Adversary Procedure in Eighteenth Century England.' New York, *Cornell Law Review*. Cornell Law Association. p. 499.

[6] Ibid. p. 500.

[7] Cited by S. Rogers. (1899) 'The Ethics of Advocacy'. 15 *Law Quarterly Review*. London, Stevens & Sons, Ltd. p. 259.

[8] A. N. May. (2003) *The Bar and the Old Bailey, 1750-1850*. Chapel Hill, University of North Carolina Press. p. 78.

[9] Ibid.

[10] *Time* magazine. 30 September 1966.

[11] Year Books. 30 and 31. (Rolls Series) pp. 529-30.

[12] A. Harding. (1973) *The Law Courts of Medieval England*. London, George Allen & Unwin Ltd. p. 78.

[13] S.C.F. Milsom. (1981) *Historical Foundations of the Common Law*. London, Butterworths. p. 413.

[14] J.H. Langbein. (2003) *The Origins of Adversary Criminal Trial*. Oxford, Oxford University Press. p. 2.

[15] G. Fisher (1997) 'The Jury's Rise as Lie Detector.' New Haven, 107 *Yale Law Journal*. p. 603.

[16] J. Hostettler. (2004) *The Criminal Jury Old and New. Jury Power from Early Times to the Present Day*. Winchester, Waterside Press. p. 21.

[17] Ibid.

[18] See T.A. Green. (1985) *Verdict According to Conscience: Perspectives on the English Criminal Trial Jury 1200-1800*. Chicago, University of Chicago Press. p. 34.

[19] J.D.Mackie. (1992) *The Earlier Tudors 1485-1558*. Oxford, The Clarendon Press. p. 562.

[20] Sir W. Holdsworth. (1966) *A History of English Law*. London, Methuen & Co. vol. iv. p. 221.

[21] G. Fisher. 'The Jury's Rise as Lie Detector.' Op. cit. p. 587.

[22] B. J. Shapiro. (1983) *Probability and Certainty in Seventeenth-Century England. A Study of the Relationships between Natural Science, Religion, History, Law and Literature*. New Jersey, Princeton University Press. p. 174.

[23] See D. Jardine. (1836) 'A Reading on the Use of Torture in the Criminal Law of England Prior to the Commonwealth.' Delivered at New Inn Hall, London, Michaelmas Term. Published in 67 *Edinburgh Review*. (1838).

[24] J. H. Langbein. (1977) *Torture and the Law of Proof: Europe and England in the Ancien Regime*. Chicago, University of Chicago Press. pp. 73-4.

[25] Ibid. p. 4.

[26] J. H. Langbein. (1973) 'The Origins of Public Prosecutions at Common Law.' 17 *The American Journal of Legal History*. North Carolina University Press. pp. 313-14.

[27] 1 & 2 P. & M. c. 13, and 2 & 3 P. & M. c. 10. (1554-5)

[28] J.M. Beattie. (1991) 'Scales of Justice: Defence Counsel and the English Criminal Trial in the Eighteenth and Nineteenth Centuries.' 9 (2) *Law and History Review*. University of Illinois Press. pp. 222-3.

[29] J. S. Cockburn. (1972) *A History of the English Assizes 1558-1714*. Cambridge, Cambridge University Press. p. 109.

[30] Hardwicke Papers. British Library, *Add. MSS.* 35863.

[31] J. Hostettler. (2002) *The Red Gown – The Life and Works of Sir Matthew Hale*. Chichester, Barry Rose Law Publishers. p. 42.

[32] A. F. Havighurst. (1950) 'The Judiciary and Politics in the Reign of Charles II.' 66 *The Law Quarterly Review*. London, Stevens & Sons. pp. 62-78.

[33] Havighurst. (1953) 'James II and the Twelve Men in Scarlet.' *The Law Quarterly Review*. London, Stevens & Sons. p. 522.

[34] Sir G. Clark. (1955) *The Later Stuarts 1660-1714*. Oxford, The Clarendon Press. p. 101.

[35] 1 W. &. M. s. 2. c. 2.

[36] 7 Will. 3. c. 3.

[37] J.M. Beattie. 'Scales of Justice' Op. cit. p. 224.

[38] Serjeant W. Hawkins. (1716) *Treatise of the Pleas of the Crown*. London, J. Walthoe. vol. ii. p. 402.

[39] P. Rawlings. (1999) *Crime and Power: A History of Criminal Justice 1688-1998*. Harlow, Addison Wesley Longman Ltd. pp. 18-19.

[40] L.Radzinowicz. (1956) *A History of English Criminal Law and its Administration from 1750*. London, Stevens & Sons Ltd. vol. ii. p. 50.

[41] Ibid.

[42] J. Chitty. (1826) *A Practical Treatise on the Criminal Law etc.* (2nd edn.) vol. 1. p. 769. Cited by Radzinowicz. Ibid. p. 54.

[43] J. Hostettler. (1992) *The Politics of Criminal Law: Reform in the Nineteenth Century*. Chichester, Barry Rose Law Publishers. Chap. 4.

[44] J. H. Langbein. *The Origins of Adversary Criminal Trial*. Op. cit. p. 178.

[45] J.M. Beattie. 'Scales of Justice.' Op. cit. p. 233.

[46] S. Landsman. 'The Rise of the Contentious Spirit.' Op. cit. p. 602.

[47] Ibid. note 548.

[48] P. Handler. (2005) Review of Allyson N. May's *The Bar and the Old Bailey, 1750-1850.* London, 26 *The Journal of Legal History.* p. 111.

[49] J. H. Langbein. *The Origins of Adversary Criminal Trial.* Op. cit. p. 253.

[50] Ibid. p. 332.

[51] H. Brougham. (1845) 'Mr. Baron Garrow.' 1 *Law Review.* London, p. 322.

[52] OBP Online. (oldbaileyproceedingsonline.org, 10 February 2005) 26 April 1786. Trial of Frances Lewis. Ref: t17860426-84.

[53] D. Lemmings. (2002) *Professors of the Law. Barristers and English Legal Culture in the Eighteenth Century.* Oxford, Oxford University Press. p. 307.

[54] J.M. Beattie. (February 1991) 'Garrow for the Defence.' London, *History Today.* History Today Ltd. p. 51.

[55] A. Aspinall. (1963) (ed) *The Correspondence of George, Prince of Wales: 1770-1812.* London, Cassell. vol. 7. p. 268.

[56] J. Hostettler. *The Politics of Criminal Law.* Op. cit. Chapter 4.

[57] Parliamentary Papers. (1836) xxxvi. 183.

[58] 6 & 7 Will. 4. c. 114.

[59] Allyson N. May. (2003) *The Bar and the Old Bailey, 1750-1850.* Chapel Hill, The University of North Carolina Press.

[60] W. B. Odgers. (1901) *A Century of Law Reform.* London, Macmillan and Co. Ltd. p. 30.

[61] 3 *Law Review.* (August 1845-May 1846). pp. 348-9.

[62] 9 *Law Review.* (Nov. 1848-Feb. 1849).

[63] Steiner & Alston. (1996) *International Human Rights in Context: Law, Politics, Morals.* Oxford, Clarendon Press. pp. v-vi.

CHAPTER 2

No Counsel for Prisoners

INTRODUCTION

In English criminal law indictments for felony have always been taken in the name of the monarch and, in early times, it was considered *lèse majesté* for those indicted to be allowed counsel against the King or Queen.[1] Later, jurists such as Coke and Hawkins sought other explanations for the 'no-counsel' rule and held that a prisoner could better express the truth in person than through the medium of lawyers. In addition, the judge would act as his or her counsel.

Prisoners and their witnesses were also not permitted to give evidence on oath since following the precedent set by trial by ordeal, the result of a trial by jury was believed to bear a 'divine Imprimatur'[2] and a conflict of oaths between the parties was considered blasphemous and inappropriate. As a consequence only the prosecution, in the name of the monarch, could call upon witnesses to give evidence on oath which, of course, greatly strengthened their credibility and the impact of their evidence. This severely prejudiced defendants when the judges failed to assist them, as was shown in numerous cases and the example used in this chapter will be that of Stephen Colledge, charged with treason in 1681.[3]

These were some of the problems for prisoners that required solution in the late seventeenth century, by which time England and parts of the rest of the world were changing rapidly. Although the larger picture was to a great extent unremarked at the time, technology was commencing to transform the agricultural and industrial fabric of England alongside the final ending of the 'divine right' of monarchy and the enactment of the *Bill of Rights* following the Glorious Revolution. Later, the American and French Revolutions ended many types of privilege, some tyrannies and a great deal of religious persecution. Institutions and fundamental aspects of social structure that had been taken for granted were found to be artificial and amenable to change. The revolutions and the Enlightenment set in motion a range of new forces and ideas in politics and economics[4] and elicited a new awareness of the rights of the individual.

HISTORIC REASONS FOR DENIAL OF COUNSEL TO THE DEFENCE

According to Pollock and Maitland, '[i]n the *Leges Henrici* (1118) it is already the peculiar mark of an accusation of felony that the accused is allowed no counsel, but must answer at once; in all other cases [i.e. trespass or misdemeanours] a man may have counsel.'[5] Misdemeanours were minor offences and although a defendant accused of such could have counsel, in the early twelfth century this meant communal and not professional help. But it also meant that those accused of felony and likely to be sentenced to death could have no counsel at all, either before or after 1235 when lawyers came on the scene.[6]

Then, in the reign of Edward I, by which time lawyers were established as a profession, the judges formally confirmed the exclusion of defence counsel in trials for felony. It was laid down judicially in a case of rape[7] that prisoners on indictment in treason and felony trials were not permitted to have counsel appear for them except on points of law, and then only at the direction of the court.[8] As for the reason, in the leading case the court told the prisoner that he could not have counsel 'because the King is party in this case, and sues *ex officio*, for which reason it is not proper that you should have counsel against the King … if a woman acts against you, you shall have counsel against her, but not against the King.'[9] This meant, of course, that lawyers could not speak out against the Crown in treason or felony trials and this may well have been accepted by them since otherwise their careers and possibly their lives might well have been at risk.[10] Even after counsel were allowed in treason trials by the Treason Trials Act of 1696, in the first case under the Act defence counsel, Sir Bartholomew Shower, was at pains to disassociate himself from the sentiments alleged against his client, even though he conducted a robust defence.[11]

In consequence of the rule, every prisoner brought to trial for treason, murder, arson, rape, robbery, burglary, and most other forms of theft, had to defend himself or herself in court. As Langbein puts it, 'English criminal procedure was for centuries organized on the principle that a person accused of having committed a serious crime should not be represented by counsel at trial.' Furthermore, 'when the surviving sources first allow us to see something of how criminal trials were conducted, we see the judges resolutely enforcing this prohibition on defence counsel, despite persistent complaint from defendants.'[12]

Indeed, it was pointed out with some alarm by a judge in a case in 1602, that if counsel were allowed, 'every prisoner would want it.'[13] And, in the trial of John Mordant in 1658, 'when the prisoner asked to have representation of counsel, the court responded, "You have alleged nothing [i.e. no legal issue]: you are now upon matter of fact."'[14] On the other hand, even Lord Chief Justice Jeffreys told Thomas Rosewall on a charge of high treason in 1684,

> I think it is a hard case that a man should have counsel to defend himself for a two-penny-trespass, and his witnesses examined on oath; but if he steal, commit murder or felony, nay, high treason, where life, estate, honour, and all are concerned, he shall neither have counsel, nor his witnesses examined upon oath.[15]

According to Langbein, 'the main purpose of the trial was to give the accused the opportunity to speak in person to the charges and the evidence adduced against him,' and he calls this style of proceeding the 'accused speaks' trial.[16] There was no room, he says, for defence counsel to intermediate between the accused and the court. The logic of the rule (denying defence counsel) was to pressure the accused to speak in his or her own defence. 'Part of what motivated the rule was the fear (fully justified in hindsight) that defence counsel would interfere with the court's ability to have the accused serve as an informational source'.[17] What hindsight really appears to show, however, is that often the accused—incarcerated in conditions of appalling squalor,[18] frequently ill, illiterate, in awe of the trappings of the court, in fear of their lives and with no resources to prepare a defence—could not take advantage of Langbein's 'accused speaks' style of trial and were frequently sentenced unheard. Even if they could speak, they were not permitted to give sworn evidence.

At the time of the lustre and vibrant spirit of the Elizabethan Age, when Sir Edward Coke (1552-1634) was exercising an extraordinary influence on English common law, most crimes remained felonies and continued to attract the death penalty.[19] Not surprisingly, to modern eyes the refusal of counsel, then and later, appears to be barbaric but so eminent an authority as Coke, and others, sought to justify the practice.

EARLY MODERN ENGLAND: THE BAN ON COUNSEL

The reasons given by Coke for the denial of counsel to the defence were first, that in cases where life was at risk the evidence and proofs should be so clear that they could not be contradicted, and, secondly, that the judge should exercise the function of counsel for the prisoner.[20] How a lawyer so experienced in the practice of the courts could pronounce these beliefs is hard today to comprehend but it should be remembered that at the time (the sixteenth century) criminal law continued to bear many feudal attributes which, in other respects Coke was endeavouring to eliminate. And, even in 1678, in the case of *R. v. Coleman*, Chief Justice Scroggs still spoke in similar terms when he said, 'the proof belongs to [the Crown] to make out these intrigues of yours; therefore you need not have counsel, because the proof must be plain upon you, and then it will be in vain to deny the conclusion.'[21] Interestingly, this attempt to justify the denial of counsel led even Scroggs into an early example of the presumption of innocence with the burden of proof on the prosecution.

What the judges of a different disposition from that of Scroggs could do in those days was to ensure that a trial was conducted in a seemly manner. Baker has shown that in an Old Bailey case in 1616, 'although there are no arguments by counsel ... the judges nevertheless concerned themselves all the time with legal and procedural refinements.'[22] And, in the trial in 1663 of John Twyn for treason, Chief Justice Hyde told him, 'the court ... are to see that you suffer nothing for your want of knowledge in matter of law; I say, we are to be of counsel with you.'[23] But such refinements were not what prisoners really needed, nor were they always what they got. In a curious example of his understanding of that role Hyde told the jury to believe the prosecution witnesses, saying, 'I presume no man among you can doubt but the witnesses have spoken true; and for answer you have nothing but his [Twyn's] bare denial.'[24] Vigorous cross-examination of the witnesses might have revealed an entirely different picture.

JUDGE AS COUNSEL

All this was small compensation for a defendant particularly if (as was likely) he or she was not learned in the law or the procedures of the court. Moreover, as is clear and as Blackstone pointed out, the entitlement of the defendant to have the judge act as their counsel was limited to questions of law. As he put it, 'the judge shall be counsel for the prisoner; that is, shall see that the proceedings against him are legal and strictly regular.'[25] In other words, more legal and procedural refinements. In reality, however, judges were often pro-active in court and frequently bore down on prisoners and witnesses if they doubted the truth of their evidence. As Beattie says, the idea of the judge as counsel for the prisoner, 'perfectly expresses the view that the defendant should not have counsel in the sense that we would mean.'[26]

A startling example of the flawed nature of the second wing of Coke's argument was seen in 1699 in the celebrated trial of barrister Spencer Cowper for the alleged murder of a Mrs Stout. Cowper was the younger brother of William Cowper, the Lord Chancellor and grandfather of the poet, William Cowper. At the conclusion of what had been a long trial, at a time when felony trials could not be adjourned, the judge was so fatigued as to be incapable of properly summing up the evidence or even commenting upon it. After saying to the jury that he could not sum up the case fully he concluded his short address to them by saying, 'I am sensible I have omitted many things; but I am a little faint, and cannot repeat any more of the evidence.'[27] Fortunately, the jury found Cowper not guilty and Fitzjames Stephen remarked that, 'the rule which prevailed then and long afterwards of finishing all criminal trials in one day must often have produced cruel injustice.'[28]

Again, there was a case heard at the Old Bailey on 18 April 1787 which lasted from 5.15 p.m. to 7.30 a.m. the next day.[29] Of the three defendants, the first two were barristers and the third the owner of a gin shop. They were charged with perverting justice by committing perjury and were defended by Erskine and another, with Garrow as one of the prosecuting counsel. After more than 14 hours of trial, when he came to address the jury, the judge, the recorder of London, preceded his summing up by saying, 'I am afraid it will not be in my power to state to you the law, and the material observations of so long a cause, with that distinctness and precision, which justice would require.' Notwithstanding this defect in administering justice the defendants were found guilty. Priddle was sentenced to two years' imprisonment, Holloway and Stephens received 18 months each and for some reason all three were also fined six shillings and eightpence.

NO BREAK FOR JURIES

Where trials were lengthy this affected not only judges but also jurors who had to sit throughout and retire without 'meat, drink, fire or candle' until they unanimously agreed on a verdict.[30] In a trial in 1588 jurors were fined when they were found to have 'figs and pippins in their pockets, though they did not eat them.'[31] The consequences for many defendants of such lengthy trials were appalling. As Sir Leslie Stephen put it after studying the state trials:

> The case might go on by candlelight, and into the early hours of a second morning, till even the spectators, wedged together in the close court, with a pestilential atmosphere, loaded, if they had only known it, with the germs of gaol fever, were well-nigh exhausted; till the judge confessed himself too faint to sum up, and even to recollect the evidence; till the unfortunate prisoner, browbeaten by the judge and the opposite counsel, bewildered by the legal subtleties, often surprised by unexpected evidence ... could only stammer out a vague assertion of innocence.[32]

Furthermore, if a jury had not arrived at a decision by the time the itinerant judges were due to leave the assize town they could be carried round the circuit from town to town in a cart.[33] The rule might well have brought about hasty verdicts as voiced in Alexander Pope's couplet in *The Rape of the Lock:*

> The hungry Judges soon the Sentence sign,
> And Wretches hang that Jury-men may Dine.[34]

The falsity of Coke's approach was expressed by Garrow in a charge to a grand jury in 1827 when he was himself a judge. 'It has been said, and truly said,' Garrow told the grand jury,

> that in criminal courts, Judges were counsel for the prisoners. So undoubtedly they were, as far as they could to prevent undue influence being excited against prisoners; but it was impossible for them to go farther than this; for they could not suggest the course of defence prisoners ought to pursue.[35]

SERJEANT HAWKINS

Coke's reasoning on the refusal of counsel to prisoners was followed by other judges and jurists, including Serjeant William Hawkins in his influential *Treatise of the Pleas of the Crown,* published in 1716. Despite the fact that Hawkins' work was written in a period when there was a large increase in the number of crimes made capital, he went further even than Coke when he urged that denial of defence by counsel was actually an advantage to an innocent person. Although admitting that many had complained that the rule was very unreasonable, Hawkins believed that, 'the very speech, gesture and countenance, and manner of defence of those who are guilty, when they speak for themselves, may often help to disclose the truth, which probably would not so well be discovered from the artificial defence of others speaking for them.'[36] From which he concluded that the absence of counsel helped the jury convict the guilty.[37]

He also thought that everyone could speak to a matter of fact as if he or she were the best lawyer. 'The simplicity, the innocence, the artless and the ingenious of one acquitted by his conscience,' he wrote, 'has something in it more moving and convincing than the highest eloquence of persons speaking in a cause not their own.' From his own perspective, Langbein also argues that Hawkins foresaw that the intervention of counsel would sometimes hinder the truth.[38] But, even if this view is justified, and this is not apparent, it seems a small point against the major disadvantages of the rule.

Such views were hardly likely to be shared by illiterate wretches in prison awaiting trial and probable death. According to J. M. Beattie,

> men not used to speaking in public who suddenly found themselves thrust into the limelight before an audience in an unfamiliar setting—and who were for the most part dirty, underfed, and surely often ill, did not usually cross-examine vigorously or challenge the evidence presented against them.[39]

In effect, they were presumed to be guilty and were often entirely overwhelmed by the atmosphere of the courtroom.

RESTRICTIONS ON DEFENCE WITNESSES

It is widely believed that in felony trials it only became openly possible for the defence to produce witnesses following *Tyndal's Case* in 1632 (where a number of witnesses were called for the defence), although even then they were not permitted to take the oath.[40] Yet Coke in his *Third Institute,* written at the end of the sixteenth century but not published until after his death, had mentioned a statute[41] which allowed witnesses on oath re the accused in certain trials for felony, 'for the better information of the consciences of the jury and justices.' To which he added, 'To say the truth, we never read in any act of Parliament, ancient author, book, case, or record that in criminal cases the party accused should not have witnesses sworn for him, and therefore there is not so much as *scintilla juris* against it.'[42] Notwithstanding that, as Sir Matthew Hale wrote after *Tyndal's Case,* 'Regularly the evidence for the prisoner in cases capital is given without oath, though the reason thereof is not manifest ... neither is counsel allowed him to give evidence to the fact, nor in any case, unless matter of law doth arise.'[43]

Further, in the days of Coke and Hale the defence laboured under another serious disadvantage in that whilst the prosecution could compel the attendance of its witnesses the prisoner could not.[44] How often a potential witness would wish to avoid the inconvenience and expense of travelling what was often a long distance to court, not to mention the ordeal of giving evidence, can only be conjectured but it may well have been frequently.

These eminent jurists could not explain the restrictions on defence witnesses but it has recently been argued that the system forbade a conflict of oaths in capital cases in order to ensure that a verdict of guilt bore as divine an imprimatur as the decision of the Almighty in the earlier trial by ordeal.[45]

In some cases witnesses were denied altogether, as in the trial of Sir Nicholas Throckmorton[46] in 1554 for high treason. In this state trial a defence witness, John Fitzwilliam, was peremptorily removed from the courtroom without being allowed to speak. 'The court have nothing to do with you', said the judge who revealingly added, 'probably you would not be so ready in a good cause.'[47] And, when Puritan minister John Udall was tried at Croydon assizes in 1590 his witness was not allowed to give evidence, 'against the Queen.'[48]

Of course, these were political cases and there were substantial differences between state trials and ordinary trials for felony. Langbein has argued forcibly that in any event there was not a rule forbidding defence witnesses in felony trials.[49] Indeed, he cites Dalton as saying as early as 1618 that assize judges 'will often hear Witnesses and Evidence which goeth to the clearing and acquittal of the Prisoner, yet [the judges] will not take [it] upon oath, but do leave such Testimony and Evidence to the Jury to give credit to or think thereof, as they shall see and find cause.'[50] However, that was before *Tyndal's Case,* and it is certainly clear that there was indeed no rule forbidding defence witnesses as Coke indicated before Dalton's case was heard. But the objection to their taking the oath was real, as Dalton confirms, no doubt for the reasons indicated by Fisher.[51] And, it was not until the early eighteenth century that the idea of the jury as a lie-detector was being replaced by the concept that skilful defence lawyers could draw out the truth by their cross-examination of witnesses.

As for the ban on defence counsel, Leveller leader John Lilburne asked for the assistance of counsel in his trial in 1649 but this was denied.[52] Moreover, the presiding judge, Mr Justice Keble, having heard the prosecution case but not Lilburne's defence, told the jury, 'I hope the Jury hath seen the Evidence so plain and so fully, that it doth confirm them to do their duty, and to find the Prisoner guilty of what is charged upon him.'[53] After hearing Lilburne's defence he went further and told the jury, 'you will clearly find that never was the like treason hatched in England.'[54] After Keble had so acted as his 'counsel', the jury ignored his advice and found Lilburne not guilty.[55]

But even in early times the ban was not always absolute. Hawkins cited a case from the *Year Books*[56] where a serjeant-at-law offered his opinion to the court during a murder trial and was not reprehended for it. Furthermore, by leave of the court, prisoners had sometimes been indulged the assistance of counsel to stand by them at the Bar, so long as they did not prompt them on matters of fact or assist them with papers.[57] And by 1724, at the Surrey assizes a solicitor was allowed to represent a prisoner who was deranged.[58] When in 1771, a prisoner charged with mail robbery was unwell, the judge allowed his counsel to state the defence case to the jury, although it did not help him and he was found guilty and sentenced to death.[59] But while these few cases illustrate that the whim and politics of the judge might occasionally have an effect, the oppressive general rule forbidding counsel was consistently used over centuries, as contemporaries testify.

THE PROTESTANT JOINER

For instance, when Stephen Colledge was prosecuted for treason in 1681,[60] Lord Chief Justice North refused him counsel and kept from him all his papers including counsel's advice on the examination of witnesses. Freed by a grand jury in London, Colledge was taken to Oxford where a royalist grand jury decided he should stand trial. Colledge's skill as a joiner had brought him the friendship of many prominent people, as a result of which his sense of self-importance had swollen. As a consequence, he wrote a number of tracts against the papists although it was fatuously alleged in court that he was one himself.

Prosecuting for the state were, among others, Robert Sawyer, the Attorney-general and, at the personal request of the King, Sir George Jeffreys–later the notorious Hanging Judge. At the trial the judge observed that to let Colledge have his papers would be 'to give you counsel in an indirect way'–or, as Jeffreys intervened to put it, 'by a side wind.'[61] Defending the denial of counsel, Roger North, himself a lawyer, declared that defendants in criminal trials, 'should not have any assistance in matters of fact, but depend upon plain truth, which they know best, without any dilatories, arts or evasions.'[62]

Furthermore, when Colledge stated that papers he had brought to court for his defence had been taken from him and requested that they be restored, he was told by Chief Justice North that he must trust to public justice and the judges would be counsel for him. As for his papers, the Lord Chief Justice asked how he came to have any since they were not permitted under an accusation of high treason. He ignored the fact that prior to the trial the King in council had made an order on 11 August 1681 that several friends and relations and a solicitor might visit Colledge in the Tower of London where he was held.[63] Indeed, in court the prisoner's solicitor, Aaron Smith, then had to find a recognizance in £100 for having delivered to Colledge in the Tower the very papers which were counsel's advice on how to conduct his defence.[64] And apart from the denial of counsel and papers, Colledge complained,

> I have been kept a close prisoner in the Tower ever since I was taken; I was all along unacquainted with what was charged upon me. I knew not what was sworn against me, not the persons that did swear it against me, and therefore I am wholly ignorant of the matter.[65]

Colledge asked for common justice and his right by law, and responded to the doctrine that he was not allowed to have papers by saying, 'God have mercy upon any man that is so accused then: for it is not possible for him to make his defence if he cannot be at liberty to look after it himself, nor any of his friends permitted to do it for him.' 'You can say whether you are not guilty without papers,' retorted North,[66] confirming, perhaps, that without counsel there would often be little more that a defendant could do beyond plead. Not surprisingly, Colledge was found guilty. He was hanged at Oxford Castle on 31 August 1681 where, after hanging for a quarter of an hour, he was cut down by hangman Jack Ketch and quartered under the gallows.

As a consequence, Stephen Colledge was adopted as the first Whig martyr and one modern author described the trial as, 'one of the most unfair in a period abounding in judicial murders'.[67] In the case of William Ireland, who was charged as being in the Popish Plot (1678-81), the defendant made a similar complaint to that of Colledge about his inability to prepare a defence when imprisoned. In his case, he named witnesses who could prove he was in Staffordshire at the time of his alleged offences. Calling for one of them to appear in the courtroom he said, 'It is a hundred to one if he be here, for I have not been permitted so much as to send a scrap of paper'[68] asking him to be present. In those circumstances his witnesses did not appear and Ireland too was convicted and executed.

CONCLUSION

For centuries the criminal law suffered from the survival of medieval legal rules, some of which had originated in the period when there was little criminal law and no lawyers. When lawyers did come on the scene, the judges refused to allow them to represent prisoners except on points of law on the ground that they should not be permitted to give evidence against the monarch. They further restricted the rights of their witnesses in giving evidence by not allowing them to testify on oath as was the practice with prosecutors' witnesses. This, it has been suggested, was because jury trial was seen to be as much a judgment of the Almighty as trial by ordeal and to have opposing sides each swearing to God was not to be permitted.[69]

Yet, even as time passed the most eminent jurists of early modern England, such as Coke and Hawkins, endeavoured to justify the grave disadvantages under which defendants suffered. At the same time, the Crown could engage counsel to prosecute and was free, if it chose, to take advantage of the law forbidding defence witnesses altogether in state and political trials. Prosecutors could also instruct counsel in felony trials but here they, and judges, were often thwarted by jury nullification when the jury acquitted a prisoner who was technically guilty on the basis of conscience or because they thought the penalty of death too severe for the crime.[70] Indeed, 'approximately 40 per cent of all defendants arraigned at Home Circuit assizes between 1558 and 1625 were acquitted by the trial jury.'[71]

Nevertheless, in state trials the situation was exploited by the Crown in the reigns of the later Stuarts and this brought to the fore the opposition of the Whig leaders who helped bring about the Glorious Revolution and the Treason Trials Act of 1696 which permitted counsel to act for prisoners accused of treason. This then was the position before the eighteenth century when, without legislative interference except for the 1696 statute, the legal landscape was transformed, with counsel allowed a limited appearance for prisoners. This was to give rise to the birth of adversary trial and a recognition that prisoners had rights. In doing so it also enhanced the concept of due process of law.

ENDNOTES for *Chapter 2*

[1] Year Books 30 and 31. Edw. I. (Rolls Series) pp. 529-30.
[2] G. Fisher. (1997) 'The Jury's Rise as Lie Detector.' New Haven. *Yale Law Journal.* p. 602.
[3] 8 *State Trials.* cols. 550-746.
[4] E.J. Hobsbawm. (1962) *The Age of Revolution: Europe 1789-1848.* London, Weidenfeld & Nicolson.
[5] Pollock & Maitland. (1898) *The History of English Law.* Cambridge, Cambridge University Press. vol. i. p. 211.
[6] A. Harding. (1973) *The Law Courts of Medieval England.* London, George Allen & Unwin Ltd. p. 78.
[7] Year Books 30 and 31. Op. cit. pp. 529-30.
[8] For the exception on points of law cf. S.C.F. Milsom. (1981) *Historical Foundations of the Common Law.* 2nd edn. London, Butterworths. p. 413.
[9] Year Books 30 and 31. Op. cit. pp. 529-30.
[10] D. J. A. Cairns. (1998) *Advocacy and the Making of the Adversarial Criminal Trial.* Oxford, The Clarendon Press. p. 27.
[11] 13 *State Trials.* col. 222.
[12] J. H. Langbein. (2003) *The Origins of Adversary Criminal Trial.* Oxford, Oxford University Press. pp. 10-11.
[13] *R. v. Boothe.* [1602] British Library *Add. MSS.* 25203, f. 569v. Cited by J.H. Baker. (1979) *An Introduction to Legal History.* London, Butterworths. p. 417.
[14] A. H Shapiro. (1993) 'Political Theory and the Growth of Defensive Safeguards in Criminal Procedure: The Origins of the Treason Trials Act of 1696.' Illinois. 11(2) *Law and History Review.* American Society of Law and History. p. 223.
[15] 10 Howell's *State Trials.* p. 267.
[16] J.H. Langbein. *The Origins of Adversary Criminal Trial.* Op. cit. p. 2.
[17] Ibid.
[18] J.M. Beattie. (1986) *Crime and Courts in England 1660-1800.* Oxford, Clarendon Press. pp. 288-309.
[19] Sir W. Holdsworth. (1938) *A History of English Law.* London, Methuen & Co. Ltd. Sweet & Maxwell. vol. 11. p. 559.
[20] Sir E. Coke. (1797) 3 *Institute.* London. E. & R. Brooke. p. 137.
[21] 7 *State Trials.* col. 1.
[22] J.H. Baker. (1973) 'Criminal Justice at Newgate 1616-1627: Some Manuscript Reports in the Harvard Law School.' *Irish Jurist.* Dublin, Periodical Publications. pp. 307 and 311.
[23] 6 *State Trials.* cols. 516-17.
[24] Ibid. col. 534.
[25] W. Blackstone. (1830) *Commentaries on the Law of England.* vol. iv, London, Thomas Tegg. p. 349.
[26] J.M. Beattie. (1991) 'Scales of Justice: Defence Counsel and the English Criminal Trial in the Eighteenth and Nineteenth Centuries.' 9(2) *Law and History Review.* Illinois, University of Illinois Press. p. 223.
[27] 13 *State Trials.* cols. 1187 and 1190.

28 J. F. Stephen. (1883) *A History of the Criminal Law of England*. London, Routledge/Thoemmes Press. vol. 1. p. 422.

29 OBS Online. (www.oldbaileyonline.org, 17 March 2005) 18 April 1787 Trial of William Priddle, Robert Holloway and Stephen Stephens. Ref: t17870418-118.

30 24 Edw. III, c. 75.

31 *Mounson v. West*. [1588] 74 *English Reports*. p. 123.

32 L. Stephen. (1991 edn) *Hours in a Library*. London, The Folio Society. vol. iii. pp. 291-2.

33 A.H. Manchester. (1980) *A Modern Legal History of England and Wales 1750-1950*. London, Butterworth & Co. Ltd. p. 92.

34 [1714] Canto 111, lines 19-20. In *Five Cantos Written by Mr. Pope*. London, Bernard Lintot. p. 20.

35 45 *Edinburgh Review*. (1827) p. 82.

36 Serjeant W. Hawkins. (1716) *Treatise of the Pleas of the Crown*. London, J. Walthoe. vol. ii. p. 400.

37 Ibid.

38 J. H. Langbein. (1978) 'The Criminal Trial before the Lawyers.' Chicago. 45 *The University of Chicago Law Review*. p. 311.

39 J.M. Beattie. *Crime and the Courts in England 1660-1800*. Op. cit. pp. 350-1.

40 Cro. Car. 291.

41 4 James I. c. 1, s. 6. (1606)

42 Coke. 3 *Institute*. Op. cit. p. 39.

43 Sir M. Hale. (1736) *The History of the Pleas of the Crown*. London, E. and R. Nutt and R. Gosling. vol. ii. p. 283.

44 J.H. Langbein. *The Origins of Adversary Criminal Trial*. Op. cit. p. 51.

45 G. Fisher. 'The Jury's Rise as Lie Detector.' Op. cit. p. 587.

46 1 Howell's *State Trials* (1818) cols. 809-902.

47 Ibid.

48 Ibid. cols. 1271-81.

49 J. H. Langbein. *The Origins of Adversary Criminal Trial*. Op. cit. pp. 54-5.

50 M. Dalton. (1619) *The Countrey Justice, Containing the Practice of the Justices of the Peace out of their Sessions*. London, The Company of Stationers. p.412.

51 G. Fisher. 'The Jury's Rise as Lie Detector. Op. cit. p. 587.

52 1 *State Tryals*. (1719) London, T. Goodwin and others. pp. 580-640.

53 Ibid. p. 628.

54 Ibid. p. 636.

55 Ibid. p. 637.

56 7 H. 4. 36a.

57 J. Hostettler. (1992) *The Politics of Criminal Law: Reform in the Nineteenth Century*. Chichester, Barry Rose Law Publishers. p. 49.

58 R. v. Edward Arnold. [1724] 16 *State Trials*. p. 695.

59 Old Bailey Proceedings.Online. (www.oldbaileyonline.org, 18 October 2004) 4 December 1771, trial of William Davis. Ref: t17711204-26.

60 8 *State Trials*. cols. 550-746.

61 Ibid. col. 587.

62 R. North. (1742) *The Life of the Lord Keeper Guilford*. London, J. Whiston. pp. 66-7.

63 8 Howell's *State Trials*. cols. 563 and 571.

64 Ibid. col. 585.

65 Ibid. cols. 549 and 569.

66 Ibid. col. 571.

67 D. Ogg. (1967) *England in the Reign of Charles II*. Oxford, Oxford University Press. pp. 627-8.

68 J. F. Stephen. *A History of the Criminal Law of England*. Op. cit. vol. i. p. 388 and *R. v. William Ireland*. 7 *State Trials*. pp. 79 and 121.

69 Fisher. 'The Jury's Rise as Lie Detector.' Op. cit.

70 J. Hostettler. (2004) *The Criminal Jury Old and New: Jury Power from Early Times to the Present Day*. Winchester, Waterside Press. p. 30.

71 J.S. Cockburn. (1985) *Introduction to Calendar of Assize Records: Home Circuit Indictments Elizabeth 1 and James I*. London, HMSO. pp. 113-4.

CHAPTER 3

Treason Trials Act: the Birth of Adversary Trial

INTRODUCTION

This chapter will look at the serious judicial misconduct in the trumped-up trials of prominent Whig leaders following the Popish Plot (1678-81) and the Rye House Plot (1683). The outrage which resulted from the hounding to death and execution of such notables as Lords Shaftesbury and Algernon Sidney was a prime factor leading not only to the Glorious Revolution but also to the introduction of the Treason Trials Act[1] which, from 25 of March 1696, allowed defendants accused of treason to be fully represented by counsel. To the provisions of this Act can be traced the beginnings of adversary trial, although the statute was only one of several factors influencing the creation and rise of adversariality. Another aspect was the growing contemporary emphasis on, and understanding of, prisoners' rights. The effect of the subsequent growth of advocacy and the impact of aggressive cross-examination in terms of the rights of the individual citizen will also be examined.

No legislation followed the Treason Trials Act that would permit counsel to appear for the defence in trials of felony, despite the fact that the growth of professional prosecutions was weighing such trials more heavily in favour of the prosecution. According to Langbein, the consequent unequal contest resulted in the judges gradually permitting counsel to appear for defendants and examine and cross-examine witnesses,[2] although still not address the jury. This ignores, however, the wider social transformation which, with other influences such as the use of the courts for political campaigns and the development of exclusionary rules of evidence, eventually resulted in the capture of the courtroom by the lawyers—a sequel unlikely to have been foreseen, or approved, by the judges. In this process, and the growth of criminal advocacy, Sir William Garrow was outstanding at the Old Bailey in the period from 1783 to 1812. Some of his cases will be examined in detail in this and later chapters in order to assess his full impact on the expansion of adversariality and criminal procedure.

PARTISAN JUDGES

In late seventeenth century England, judges held office at the King's pleasure and 'by the end of 1683, after no less than eleven judges had been arbitrarily removed [by the King] in the course of eight years, Charles II had a judiciary just about to his liking.'[3] In order '[t]o gain compliance in Westminster Hall,' his successor, James II, 'removed 12 more judges in less than four years, and appointed in their place men who would serve his purposes. Politics under James II did, in fact, determine law'[4] and the judges of the time 'were subject to a steadily-increasing pressure from James and Jeffreys to execute the royal commands. Those who failed to be sufficiently compliant were abruptly dismissed.'[5]

The Treason Act of 1352[6] had provided, *inter alia,* that it was treason to compass or imagine the King's death and was still in force. It had also declared that it could be amended only by statute and Matthew Hale, commenting on a statute of 1540 that had made certain riots treasonable, had remarked that it showed, 'how careful they were in this time not to be over-hasty in introducing constructive treasons.'[7] Notwithstanding Hale's view, the late seventeenth century also saw a number of treason trials in which the concept of constructive treason[8] was widely used, and extended, by the judges.

The courts had begun to extend the scope of the 1352 Act so that a full defence became difficult and the 'security of men's lives is wholly overthrown by this artifice of construction of the treason statute.'[9] In state trials the judges had inquisitorial powers and were not only biased against defendants, on behalf of their royal masters, but also revealed their prejudices openly in court, as we have seen in the trial of Stephen Colledge in 1678.[10] Lord Justices Scroggs and Jeffreys were particularly prominent in the trials arising from the Popish Plot[11] and the Rye House Plot[12] following both of which Catholics and prominent Whig leaders suffered, often with their lives.

The 'Popish Plot', manufactured by Titus Oates, a depraved cleric who had earlier been found guilty of indecency and perjury, had alleged a Jesuit plan to murder the King, put the Catholic Duke of York on the throne and bring a French army into England. The resultant public panic enabled the judicial enemies of the Whigs to impeach, execute or send to the Tower a number of their leaders in the course of widespread judicial murder. Hearing that warrants were out for his arrest, Lord Shaftesbury, as the leading figure in organizing the Whig party and promoting a theoretical groundwork for its cause,[13] fled to Holland, where he died on 21 January 1683.[14]

As far as the Rye House Plot is concerned, the plan was to seize the King's person on a narrow road near Newmarket but he left the races early and the plot was frustrated. Two leading Whigs, William Lord Russell and Algernon Sidney, were promptly brought to trial on charges of high treason. They were found guilty on slight evidence, and executed for what many believed was merely dissent.[15] As Sir John Rawles, afterwards Solicitor-General in the reign of William III, remarked of the judges in the case, 'the summing up of the evidence against Sidney was barbarous, being invectives and no consequences.'[16] But, of course, the judges—even Jeffreys—were carrying out the policy of the King and this led, as Alexander Shapiro has put it, to critics being 'disturbed that in a trial system already heavily weighted in favour of the prosecution, the government was abusing its advantage.'[17]

Jeffreys' haranguing of witnesses at the 'Bloody Assizes' in the South-west of England, following the Monmouth Rebellion, and his conduct in the trial of Dame Alice Lisle, both in 1685, are well documented.[18] However, in the less remarked, but perhaps more significant, trial of the well-known Rev. Richard Baxter in May of the same year on a charge of sedition for criticizing bishops, Jeffreys openly revelled in his power and prejudice. First he browbeat two counsel for the defence into silence (their fees had been paid by Baxter's friend Sir Henry Ashhurst). Then he described Baxter, who had been a royal chaplain, as a 'sniveling Presbyterian' and when Baxter tried to speak he shouted, 'Richard, Richard, dost thou think we will hear you poison the court? Thou art an old fellow, an old knave; thou hast written books enough to load a cart; every one is as full of sedition (I might say treason) as an egg is full of meat.'[19]

After declaring that Baxter should have been whipped out of the writing trade 40 years before, Jeffreys continued his vituperation. 'Thou pretendest,' he cried, 'to be a preacher of the gospel of peace, and thou has one foot in the grave … but by the grace of God I'll look after thee.' Claiming that he saw friends of the accused in court he vowed he would crush them all.[20] Finally, he told the jury to find Baxter guilty of seditious libel, which they did.

No wonder Leslie Stephen, the usually mildly spoken 'past master in the craft of biography',[21] described Jeffreys as a 'kind of demoniacal baboon placed on the Bench in robes and wig, in hideous caricature of justice.'[22] As seen by Lord Campbell, (the future Lord Chancellor) the Bench 'was cursed by a succession of ruffians in ermine who, for the sake of court favour, violated the principles of law, the precepts of religion, and the dictates of humanity.'[23]

Then three years later, in 1688, there came a change with the celebrated *Seven Bishops Case*.[24] This was not a trial for treason but a charge against the Archbishop of Canterbury and six other Anglican bishops for not only refusing to read from their pulpits the declaration of indulgence towards Catholics issued by James II but also sending him a petition which disputed his power to dispense with legislation. They were charged with seditious libel which, as a misdemeanour, meant they could instruct members of the Bar to appear on their behalf. Counsel acted with such effectiveness for the defence that the judges were divided and the Lord Chief Justice allowed the jury to decide whether the petition was or was not a seditious libel. The jury acquitted the prisoners and that evening the famous letter was sent to William of Orange which invited him to come over and secure the Protestant religion in England.

THE TREASON TRIALS ACT 1696

In the event the actions of Jeffreys and Scroggs, who defiled the name of justice by closely associating the judiciary with royal despotism, proved counter-productive. Together with the success of the defence counsel in the *Seven Bishops Case*, they strengthened the Whigs who, smarting at their cruel treatment by the later Stuarts and their judges, secured both the independence of the judiciary with the Act of Settlement in 1701,[25] and the enactment of the Treason Trials Act of 1696.[26] This radical statute, which transformed the defendant accused of treason from, 'an essentially passive prisoner into an active participant in the trial,'[27] was a direct Parliamentary response to the misconduct of judges in state trials. According to the House of Commons report, 'their design was, to prevent those abuses in trials for treason ... by means of which, during the violence of late reigns, they had observed divers had lost their lives.'[28] It is also true that the dominance of the judiciary by the later Stuarts had diminished the authority and prestige of the judges and their partial disempowerment was by no means unacceptable to the Whig hierarchy.

The statute allowed prisoners in treason trials to have counsel act for them in all respects. Accepting that a defendant might be innocent, the preamble to the Act declared, 'Nothing is more just and reasonable, than that Persons prosecuted for High Treason ... should not be debarred of all just and equal means for the defence of their Innocencies in such cases.'[29]

By section 1, the Act also gave the treason defendant the right to have the indictment against him or her at least five days before the trial, to have the assistance of counsel before the trial and to have counsel act in 'full defence', including address the jury during the trial. For the first time the statute also provided, by section 7, that prisoners should be allowed to subpoena witnesses to appear for them and give evidence on oath.

On 23 March 1696, two days before the Act came into force, the Lord Chief Justice, Sir John Holt, in effect adopted section 7 in the trial for high treason of Sir John Freind.[30] The prisoner asked for a witness he required to call to be brought from the Gatehouse prison where he was incarcerated. Holt granted the request and issued a warrant of *habeas corpus*. He would not, however, allow Freind to instruct counsel to appear for him and when he was asked by the prisoner to act as counsel for him, Holt merely replied that he was 'obliged to be indifferent between him and the King.'

The first case in which counsel appeared for a defendant after the Act came into force was the trial of Charles Cranburne on a charge of high treason on 21 April 1696.[31] After Holt had ordered the removal of the irons in which the prisoner was tightly held, Sir Bartholomew Shower and a Mr Phipps rose to defend him. They questioned what they said were four defects in the Indictment and entered into lengthy legal arguments with the Attorney-General which would undoubtedly have been beyond the competence of the accused. They failed to secure their points, however, but then proceeded with cross-examination of prosecution witnesses throughout the trial, questioning the credibility of witnesses and, on occasion, arguing with the judges. Nonetheless, the case against the accused was a strong one and he was found guilty. What is important is that defence counsel had created a precedent by vigorously defending an alleged traitor and had set an example which was to be followed by other members of the Bar.

To establish a case of treason the prosecution had, from the first Treason Act of 1352, to produce two witnesses and prove an overt act (although these requirements were sometimes circumvented) and as they were not required for felonies it may explain, in part, why the Act dealt with treason alone.[32] Moreover, the Whig leaders were incensed by the treatment of their colleagues in trials for treason, not felony. And, whilst counsel rarely appeared to prosecute alleged felons, the Crown always engaged counsel to prosecute in treason trials. The fact that defendants in felony trials were also burdened, as we have seen, with other grave disadvantages was considered to be of no account.

Hence, these overdue provisions of the Act were not considered at the time to be necessary for defendants in cases of felony where, unlike treason, and apart from the reasons given above, the interests of the Crown were comparatively slight. As Mr Justice Foster was to put it a century later, 'as state prosecutions ... are carried on by the weight of the Crown and too often in the spirit of party ... it is extremely reasonable to allow the prisoner the assistance of counsel, to the full extent of the Act.'[33] From which it is clear that he believed it was not so reasonable in cases of felony. And, even in 1791, Garrow was of the opinion that although prisoners charged with felony should be able to engage counsel that did not include a full defence. He said,

> Every man who is indicted [for felony] is entitled, God knows not to make an ample defence by counsel, but to the assistance of counsel; therefore, though the duty of a profession every now and then imposes a painful task on an individual, every body must feel that it is the duty of that individual to discharge that task manfully, and to the best of his power for the life of the man committed to his care.[34]

However, as this was said in court before a judge it is impossible to know if the statement represented Garrow's true feelings. And, as late as 1824, Mr Justice Park said that if the prisoner on a felony charge saw the depositions of prosecution witnesses he, 'would know everything which was to be produced in evidence against him' and this was not to be permitted.[35]

Fitzjames Stephen considered that the Act was a piece of class legislation to protect prominent men from abuse of the law of treason. Its safeguards, he wrote, were:

> So great a favour that they were to be reserved for people accused of crime for which legislators themselves or their friends and connections were likely to be prosecuted. It was a matter of direct personal interest to many members of Parliament that trials for political offence should not be grossly unfair, but they were comparatively indifferent as to the fate of people accused of sheep-stealing, or burglary or murder ... there must have been ... scores or hundreds of obscure people suffered for common burglaries and robberies of which they were quite as innocent as Stafford was of the high treason for which he was convicted.[36]

Langbein disagrees, however, and argues that, whether or not they were mistaken, the framers of the statute acted from principle.[37] They believed that treason cases presented distinctive problems that required special procedures. In the eyes of contemporaries, he says, four aspects of treason trials differentiated them from felony trials. These were:

- the prosecutorial imbalance;
- the subservience of the bench;
- the complexity of the offence of treason; and
- the rarity of treason cases.[38]

However, the first two and last aspects might well have applied to some cases of felony, including murders. Also, it ignores the fact that the Whig grandees had been badly bruised by the judges' subservience to the later Stuarts and were determined to prevent a recurrence by giving the judges security of tenure.

GROWTH OF ADVOCACY

Little concerned with prisoners in felony trials, Members of Parliament produced no legislation to enable counsel to appear for them. Instead, as we have seen, the importance of lawyers in the criminal courts had commenced in the 1730s when the rule forbidding counsel to the accused started to weaken as counsel began 'to do everything for prisoners accused of felony except addressing the jury for them.'[39] The significance of this was that, in effect, it meant that they could seek to enforce rules of evidence as well as examine and cross-examine witnesses. Adversariality meant direct dispute between the parties with a consequent clear division and conflict within the trial of counsel for the prosecution and counsel for the defence.

In a murder case in 1741 prosecuting counsel, a Mr Vernon, confirmed the exercise of judicial discretion in sometimes allowing counsel to the defence and was upheld by the recorder when he objected to the growing new attitude of judges:

> This I apprehend is a matter purely in the discretion of the Court, and what can neither in this or any other court of criminal justice be demanded as a right. The judges, I apprehend, act as they see fit on these occasions, and few of them walk by one and the same rule in this particular: some have gone so far, as to give leave for counsel to examine and cross-examine witnesses; others have bid the counsel propose their questions to the Court; and others again have directed that the prisoner should put his own questions: the method of practice in this point, is very variable and uncertain; but this we certainly know, that by the settled rule of law the prisoner is allowed no other counsel but the Court in matters of fact, and ought either to ask his own questions of the witnesses, or else propose them himself to the Court.[40]

Plainly there was no agreement between the judges to allow counsel to prisoners and, as Vernon indicated, the judges varied in how they proceeded. The statement is a clear indication that the change proceeded in a piecemeal manner. On the other hand, a fine example of what the new indulgence meant can be found in the trial of John Barbot for murder only 12 years later in 1753 in the reign of George II.[41] The prisoner moved to be allowed counsel for his defence, not only on matters of law but also on matters of fact. Speaking to the request, the Solicitor-General, John Baker, declared:

> It is certain that the practice in England, till a very few years ago, was, that a person indicted for a capital offence was never allowed counsel on a plea of Not Guilty, unless to matter of law only ...
>
> It is very true, that, by the more modern practice, the rigour of this rule hath been something relaxed; but then it is proper to see how far it has been so: and I can venture to affirm, that it has gone no farther than to permit counsel to examine and cross-examine witnesses; and never to the giving them leave to make observations on the evidence; or to draw arguments or inferences from it to the point in issue; or to do any thing else in the way of a formal or full defence.
>
> And this, though at first a pure indulgence, yet now seems to be so far grown into a right, that I believe it would be thought hard to deny it to the prisoner in the present case.[42]

The court decided that counsel should be allowed to the prisoner to speak to points of law to be decided by himself (another indulgence), as well as to examine his own witness, and cross-examine those appearing for the Crown , but no further.[43] It marked a decisive shift.

The importance of the change to adversariality is brought out by Peter King when he writes that, '[c]ross-examination in particular developed as the century wore on into a means of commenting on the evidence, refuting or discrediting the prosecution case, and aggressively, even cruelly, battling for the accused.'[44] In contrast with Langbein's view the change was also described by John Wigmore as, 'beyond any doubt the greatest legal engine ever invented for the discovery of truth.'[45] And, for the purposes of this book, as Beattie says, 'Garrow was the leading exemplar of aggressive advocacy in the 1780s and extended it 'by his willingness to do bruising battle with recalcitrant witnesses, to quarrel with judges, and by his sheer skill as an advocate.'[46] Bringing into the light of day false evidence and malicious prosecutions did much to reveal the truth that Langbein says adversary trial hides.[47]

An example of vigorous cross-examination by Garrow is found in the trial of *R. v. William Stevenson* who was charged with murder on 15 September 1784.[48] The case followed a disturbance in Clerkenwell Prison in the evening of 1 August 1784.[49] A number of women prisoners who had had their beer allowance taken away broke open a gate, threw missiles and threatened to set the prison and the Governor's house on fire. The prosecution alleged that some soldiers who happened to be in the prison were ordered to fire upon a number of the women.

When they refused to fire the accused, who was a watchman, snatched a blunderbuss from one of the soldiers, levelled it at a pregnant prisoner named Sarah Scott and shot her dead.

One prosecution witness was. Thomas Jones who described the scene and said he saw Stevenson fire the fatal shot. Garrow, defending Stevenson, cross-examined him:

> **Garrow:** Mr Jones, pray of what profession are you?
> **Jones:** I am a watch-maker by trade.
> **Garrow:** That is when you are out of gaol?
> **Jones:** No, Sir.
> **Garrow:** How then?
> **Jones:** I get my livelihood as honestly as I can.
> **Garrow:** That is exactly what I thought; honestly if you can, but if not?
> **Jones:** Dishonestly you may suppose, but I do not say that.
> **Garrow:** You was in for no harm?
> **Jones:** No.
> **Garrow:** What unrighteous set of men was it that sent you there for no harm?
> **Jones:** My wife.
> **Garrow:** Is it not the first unrighteous woman that has sent her husband there; by whose help did she send you there?
> **Jones:** I cannot tell you, you must ask her that; I was sent from Hick's Hall, they would not let me speak there; here I am before an honourable Court, she could produce no marks.
> **Garrow:** You half murdered her, and they convicted you?
> **Jones:** The sentence was one month's imprisonment and two bail in ten pounds each, and myself in 20 pounds for my good behaviour for 12 months; I laid there eight weeks, I was in three prisons in three weeks time.
> **Garrow:** Now I recommend to you to take care you do not get into Newgate?
> **Jones:** I have escaped that.
> **Garrow:** You have, have you, why that is a pretty strong prison too?
> **Jones:** I am an honest man.
> **Garrow:** I believe in the third prison you was so bad a fellow, that the keeper himself got some of his own people to bail you, to get rid of you, and in order that you might not corrupt the whole gaol?
> **Jones:** Right, Sir! Very right, Sir! Very right, Sir!

In the event, the judges, Mr Justice Gould and the recorder of the City of London, told the jury that in law force might be used by a gaoler to prevent a riot in a prison and on that direction they found the accused not guilty. Nothing was said about Stevenson not being a gaoler, whether or not there was a riot and, if force was to be used, how much force was reasonable in the circumstances.

Garrow's practice, declares Beattie, illustrated 'a more committed advocacy of cases in the courtroom and a new emphasis on [prisoners'] rights.'[50] The significance of the last point cannot be over-stated in its application to the modern doctrine of human rights. Equal justice was being sought and according to a contemporary, 'in the eye of reason and in the contemplation of English law, the life and liberty of his Majesty's subjects, are of as great value and estimation, as those of the most exalted.[51] Beattie goes on to say of Garrow that, 'in his aggressive behavior, in his insistent and pressing and revealing cross-examinations of prosecution witnesses, in his challenges to the rulings of the bench, he represented a new phenomenon. Even his critics acknowledged his abilities and his pre-eminence at the Bar.'[52]

On the other hand, Cairns disagrees with Beattie, and believes the importance of cross-examination has been exaggerated. The attention, in many cases admiration, he says, which Beattie and Landsman 'bestow on simple interrogations or forensic swagger confirms the warnings of experienced advocates of the deceptiveness of cross-examination. A cross-examination can dazzle the audience, or the reader, and not move the jury; in cross-examination not all that glisters is gold.'[53] Increased aggression in counsel, he urges, was not indicative of an improvement in advocacy, it was rather a sign of poor advocacy.

Undoubtedly, he has a point, but can he be correct when, as we shall see with Garrow's trials, the jury was often convinced when it had little to rely upon in support of the prisoner except the cross-examination? And, in any event, Cairns believes that adversary trial cannot be traced to the eighteenth century at all.[54]

In fact, however, cross-examination fuelled the growth of adversary trial. Garrow was brilliant in securing verdicts for his clients in difficult cases but he could also occasionally be destructive and even annoy juries at times. Nevertheless, as Langbein says, counsel gave more structure to criminal trials, as the 'rambling altercation' between the accused and witnesses was replaced by distinct prosecution and defence 'cases', 'between examination in chief and cross examination and between evidence and argument.'[55] In turn it encouraged evidential objections and the recognition of burdens of proof.[56] Counsel also transformed a non-adversarial system into an adversarial one. From the spotlight being on the prisoner, who had to deal with the charges against him or her, it was turned by defence counsel to probing and seeking to expose the weaknesses of the prosecution case.

Moreover, defendants themselves were encouraged to say less and rely upon their counsel to deal with everything for them. In one case at the Old Bailey, when a prisoner in reply to a question said, 'I leave it to my counsel,' Garrow responded, 'You understand we cannot say anything to the Court or Jury in your defence, we can only examine witnesses.' But, when the prisoner then asked a witness a question the judge, Mr Baron Hotham supporting Garrow, told him, 'God forbid that you should be hindered from saying anything in your defence, but if you have only questions to ask, I would advise you to leave them to your counsel.'[57]

Whereas in earlier cases the prisoner, the judge and members of the jury had all been able to join in the proceedings with questions and comments, now the dynamic of the jury trial was altered. Counsel began to silence the client, at least until the prosecution evidence had been fully disclosed.[58] And, as will be seen in his Old Bailey cases, Garrow frequently stopped his clients from speaking at all to avoid them interfering with his own arguments and approach to the jury. In a trial in 1784 Garrow's client, the prisoner, spoke up during Garrow's cross-examination of the accused, saying, 'I wish to put another question to [the prosecuting victim].' Garrow interrupted to say, 'Send the question to me in writing.'[59]

This was part of the process whereby counsel radically changed the criminal trial and broke down the judge's mastery of the proceedings. 'Over the course of the eighteenth century,' says Langbein, 'our criminal procedure underwent its epochal transformation from a predominantly non-adversarial system to an identifiably adversarial one.'[60]

In addition, defence counsel exploited cross-examination and legal arguments to challenge suspect evidence that might unduly influence jurors, such as hearsay,[61] confessions, and the evidence, often relied upon by the authorities at this time, of 'thief-takers prosecuting for rewards and accomplices testifying under promises of non-prosecution.'[62] It is interesting, though, that in earlier times prosecution witnesses had always been allowed to introduce hearsay evidence—an indulgence not usually permitted to the defence. 'How very partial they had been in giving, and permitting evidence to be given by hearsay … which they would not permit in his defence,' said Sir John Hawles, later Solicitor-General.[63]

As we shall see, Garrow was a pioneer in using cross-examination as a means to comment on the evidence, refute or discredit the prosecution case and aggressively battle for the accused.[64] Such tactics were characterized by Stephen as the 'most remarkable change' in the character of criminal trials, although he admitted that he could not trace their origins.[65]

The Treason Trials Act 1696, by allowing counsel in treason trials, set the scene, and the judges had reluctantly followed its logic for felony trials. But there were other reasons for the change[66] and the judges began to perceive that the balance in the courtroom between defendant and prosecutor was unfair and detrimental to the defendant.[67] Hence, in the 1730s it was not Parliament but the judges themselves who gradually relaxed the long-standing ban on defence counsel, although not to the extent of the Treason Trials Act's 'full defence'. And, by the second half of the eighteenth century more defendants at the Old Bailey were engaging counsel than prosecutors were.[68] An unintended result was that the 'judge and accused—who a century earlier were playing the main forensic roles in the criminal trial—were yielding the centre stage in the courtroom to the lawyers for prosecution and defence.'[69] By the end of the eighteenth century,

> Counsel had had an immense impact on the conduct of criminal trials. They had ushered into criminal procedure the divisions between examination-in-chief and cross-examination and between evidence and argument, nourished the growth of the law of evidence, changed the nature of the judicial involvement in the trial and supplemented the haphazard efforts of prisoners to defend themselves with professional advocacy.[70]

It was a transformation to adversary trial the judges were powerless to reverse even had they wanted to, which is unlikely.

ADVOCACY INDISPENSABLE

According to Landsman the 1780s were the years when a huge leap in counsel participation seemed to occur.[71] The scale of the upheaval is also shown by King who found that whereas between the 1730s and the early 1780s defence counsel were involved in a minimum of around ten per cent of London cases, after 1780 between a quarter and a third of prisoners had counsel while in provincial practice a similar change was occurring. Furthermore, he continues, 'all these figures are considerable underestimates since the presence of counsel was only noted if they made decisive interventions.'[72] Not surprisingly, by 1836 Henry Brougham was able to claim that it was an 'unquestionable proposition that advocacy is indispensably necessary to the administration of justice.'[73]

In the mid-eighteenth century trials began with the reading out of the charge against the defendant, followed by the opening statement of the prosecution counsel, if present.[74] Speeches of defence counsel were often omitted from the record of the proceedings,[75] but according to Beattie, on the information available, by the year 1786,

> close to two hundred men and women on trial for felonies at the Old Bailey had the help of lawyers. And although that was still only a fifth of those tried that year, it represented a remarkable and sudden increase in the number of cases defended by counsel.[76]

Whilst the percentage of cases where defence counsel appeared stood at 0.5 per cent in 1740, it had risen to 36.6 per cent by 1795.[77] At the same time the lawyers themselves were becoming more pro-active in their determination to cross-examine more effectively, to impress the jury and to discredit the prosecutor.[78] Beattie found that in quarter sessions and assizes in Surrey and Sussex, counties adjoining London, trial juries found prisoners not guilty in 35 per cent of property offences in the latter part of the eighteenth century.[79]

Successful criminal counsel, like Garrow and Erskine, had intruded into the criminal trial and had begun to forge a link with juries that had a large impact upon them, often to the discomfort of the judges, and it certainly increased the number of acquittals. The change is described by Landsman in the following words:

> [t]he parties, or more accurately, highly skilled advocates on their behalf assumed ever greater responsibility for interrogation, while the judges retreated from inquisitorial activism and accepted a far more neutral and passive role. Rules of evidence and procedure multiplied and a contentious mechanism arose. Directed by the litigants, emphasizing bi-party examination and regulated by a strict set of forensic prescriptions, the structure clearly conformed to an adversarial pattern.[80]

Hence, he continues, in the eighteenth century, '[r]ather than undertaking an exercise in finding the truth for the case as a whole, English criminal procedure developed the dialectic method of cross-examination to establish whether a case could be proved against a specific defendant.[81] But such cross-examination of itself was more likely to extract the truth than the earlier 'no counsel' system where prosecution evidence frequently went unchallenged.

COUNSEL'S AGGRESSION

A case which illustrates Garrow's aggressive style was heard on 29 June 1785 when Catherine Molley was charged with simple grand larceny in stealing property from John Thorne.[82] Thorne gave evidence that the prisoner had been his servant and had stolen a number of articles from his home. Garrow cross-examined him.

> **Garrow**: I fancy I shall make an end of this business, by a word or two with this old gentleman; you thought it was a good thing to get her bailed, then you had her?
>
> **Thorne**: I had nothing but honour and honesty in me.
>
> **Garrow**: That is certain, my old buck!
>
> **Thorne**: She had left my service about a year and a quarter.
>
> **Garrow**: How many of your apprentices boarded and lodged with her by your desire?
>
> **Thorne**: There was one, and I gave a bond that he should be at liberty in five years.
>
> **Garrow**: That is, in defiance of law, did this young man live with her?
>
> **Thorne**: He did live with her, he cohabited with her.
>
> **Garrow**: Is she not a married woman?
>
> **Thorne**: I do not know that.
>
> **Garrow**: What do you believe?
>
> **Thorpe**: He lay out of my house, and lay with her.
>
> **Garrow**: So that a year and a half after you took her up for stealing these things.

This was clearly a curious, as well as aggressive, cross-examination but it probably influenced the jury who found Molley not guilty.

Another example occurred on 14 September 1785 when William Bear and William Davis were indicted for feloniously stealing from a barge on the Thames 31 deal boards valued at £4.[83] One of the witnesses who gave evidence for the prosecution was John Hyser. Immediately after he was sworn and before his examination commenced Garrow interposed saying, 'Stand up, little honesty.' No objection was raised by either the prosecuting counsel or the court. Hyser testified that he helped Bear and Davis take the boards from the barge. At the end of his evidence prosecuting counsel, William Fielding (the son of Henry Fielding, the novelist and magistrate) asked, 'Now, young man, upon your oath, is it all true that you have told the Court?' and received the reply, 'Nothing but the truth.'

Immediately on his feet, Garrow asked, 'What is it my friend is afraid of, that you will not tell the truth, why you are an honest lad and came to speak the truth?'

'Yes,' replied Hyser. Questioning him further Garrow ascertained that the witness had come to court from prison and the following exchange then took place:

Garrow: Oh! In custody! That was what made my friend so fearful, why what are you in custody for my man? Speak out, don't be bashful.

Hyser: Yes.

Garrow: Is it upon account of this affair?

Hyser: I suppose so Sir.

Garrow: What, somebody was wicked enough to suppose you stole them? (No answer)

Garrow: Why you could speak fast enough just now, now you are as mute as a mackerel, now I am come to speak to you, why don't you speak out, did not somebody take you up about these deals?

Hyser: Yes Sir.

Garrow: Now I ask you upon your oath, (God knows you don't mind that) did not your master turn you away?

Hyser: I went away, they did not take me up, and he wanted to persuade me from going to sea.

Garrow: As the only way of preventing you from being hanged: now whose stitch of bacon was it you stole?

Hyser: I never stole any bacon.

Garrow: Can you state the name of any human being, that you have done one honest day's work for these six months?

Fielding to Hyser: Why do you not answer my friend by asking him the same question?

Garrow to Fielding: I have held many briefs of yours during that time.

Despite the closeness to *Alice in Wonderland* scenarios in some of these exchanges, the judge, Mr Baron Hotham, made no attempt to intervene and at the end of the trial Bear, against whom the evidence was clear, was found guilty and Davis was acquitted.

Nevertheless, the aggressive style could sometimes upset witnesses (as, indeed, it was no doubt intended to) as was shown in the case of John Elliott, an apothecary charged on 11 July 1787 with shooting a Mary Boydell.[84] Garrow prosecuted the case against Elliott who pleaded insanity when he did the shooting. A witness for the defence was Elliott's former partner, another apothecary, named John O'Donnell:

Garrow: He gave directions for bleeding and blistering and taking proper care of his patients?

O'Donnell: In that respect I saw no insanity, but in particular points the man was always insane.

Garrow: How many of them might he have poisoned in the course of that six months?

O'Donnell: I do not know that he poisoned any.

Garrow: Then during the six months he was visiting?

O'Donnell: He was getting into his own back parlour standing and swearing, and d—n-g like a madman, and he had every appearance of a madman; in short he was a madman.

Garrow: But during this time he was a mad apothecary, attending his patients in partnership with you, and taking care of his patients?

O'Donnell: Men are partially insane.

Garrow: And that does not make them worse apothecaries perhaps?

O'Donnell: Perhaps not.

Garrow: Then I am sure I will not ask you another question.

Court: I am a little at a loss to understand from you.

O'Donnell: I have been so bullied; witnesses should be examined with candour, and not put out of temper, and out of their senses, so as not to be able to understand what they say.

Then, on 12 December 1787 Thomas Duxton was charged with theft and the prosecutor, William Wheeler, had the misfortune to be faced with Garrow for the defence.[85] A witness, Francis Fleming, was a pawnbroker who took in a waistcoat that was one of the stolen items. When questioned by Garrow he said that he did not like the business and was thinking of finding another and getting married. 'It is very unlucky', retorted counsel, 'for the family you meant to honour with your alliance; you are the same Mr Fleming that has been a receiver of stolen goods for six months.' Later he said, 'Now my honest, worthy friend, Mr Fleming,' you kept a secret for six months and only disclosed it to avoid the danger of the gallows. When another witness was giving evidence, Garrow asked him, 'How many scores of pounds may you have turned in stolen goods during the time you have been in business?' to which the judge told the witness he need not answer. Garrow persisted with a similar question only to be rebuked again. In the end, however, the jury acquitted the prisoner.

This was followed, in 1792, by the case of Edward Cox who was charged at the Old Bailey on 13 January 1792 with theft. Early in the trial, when Garrow was questioning a 13-year-old, a juror interrupted to say, 'We consider it only as the evidence of a child, Mr Garrow, and you should not try to draw things from him'. Garrow predictably responded that they were doing him a great injustice.[86]

What counsel's aggression meant in practice by the commencement of the nineteenth century was illustrated in the trial of John Taylor in 1800.[87] In this case, heard not at the Old Bailey but at the Chelmsford assizes in Essex, Garrow challenged every witness, prevented prosecution witnesses from answering key questions by introducing points of law, and arrogantly told the court that 'where the law of England does bear me out, I am not afraid of giving offence to any judge.' He also argued that defence counsel's right to cross-examine opened up an opportunity to address the court on all matters. 'I had a right if I could,' he maintained, 'indirectly to convey observations to the fact; and whatever other people may say, I shall certainly take the liberty of doing it; for what the law of

England will not permit me to do directly, I will do indirectly, where I can.'[88] A clear example of how far counsel had gone in predominating in the courtroom.

Garrow was, 'not always popular—the jury in the Taylor trial harangued him for wasting their time—but his aggressive advocacy, his knowledge of complex evidential rulings and his systematic scrutiny of the prosecution case could be very influential.'[89] And, indeed, his overall success was such that at this time his fee for defending Joshua Palmer for receiving stolen goods valued at £200,000 was rumoured to be the enormous sum of 200 guineas.[90]

Thomas Hague, who was hostile to Garrow, described him as pert, vulgar and garrulous, saying that the 'brutal insolence' and 'wanton scurrility' he employed in cross-examining witnesses 'wounded private feelings, insulted the dignity of the court and violated public decorum; more important, it tended to upset the ends of justice.'[91] Such sentiments and cases do, of course, confirm that Garrow could be both too aggressive and too insensitive but other counsel followed his example and it was a small price to pay for his contribution to establishing adversary trial.

CONCLUSION

After the Glorious Revolution, the Whigs provided a new appreciation of the place of the individual in society and sought with the *Bill of Rights* to give them protection against arbitrary rule by the Crown. Then the Treason Trials Act 1696, by allowing prisoners in treason trials to have counsel act for them fully, opened the way to adversary trial. Although similar rights to defence counsel were not extended to those on trial for felony the impediments under which defendants suffered, amounting to injustice, together with the social transformation referred to earlier, led to the growth of defence counsel appearing in such trials.

Early in the eighteenth century counsel began to act on behalf of prisoners, apart from addressing the jury, and, by exerting themselves in examination and aggressive cross-examination, they gradually captured the courtroom and relegated the judge to the role of umpire above the fray and the jury to passive adjudicators. This outcome was undoubtedly not anticipated by the judges, some of whom were content to accept defence counsel in court in a piecemeal manner over years because they believed that prisoners were at a disadvantage when the prosecution had counsel and thief-takers were prepared to perjure themselves for the financial rewards on offer.

By 1822, when there were still a number of developments in adversariality to follow, including a provision for counsel to address the jury, the French observer, Charles Cottu, visited England to study the country's criminal procedure. Viewing the scene in the criminal courts he concluded that the English judge, 'remains almost a stranger to what is going on' and that the accused did so little for his own defence that, 'his hat stuck on a pole might without inconvenience be his substitute at the trial.'[92] This was a consequence of the adroitness of Thomas

Erskine, William Garrow and other members of the Bar who cultivated a virtuosity with juries in state trials and at assizes that was remarkably successful. And it was at the Old Bailey in London that Garrow established himself and helped transform the face of English legal procedure.

ENDNOTES for *Chapter 3*

1 7 & 8 Wm III, c. 3.
2 J.H. Langbein. (2003) *The Origins of Adversary Criminal Trial*. Oxford, Oxford University Press.
3 A. F. Havighurst. (1950) 'The Judiciary and Politics in the Reign of Charles II.' 66 *The Law Quarterly Review*. London, Stevens & Sons. pp. 247.
4 Havighurst. (1953) 'James II and the Twelve Men in Scarlet.' 69 *The Law Quarterly Review*. Op. cit. p. 522.
5 G.W. Keeton. (1965) *Lord Chancellor Jeffreys and the Stuart Cause*. London, Macdonald. p. 112.
6 25 Edw. III, st. 25, c. 2.
7 Sir M. Hale. (1736) *The History of the Pleas of the Crown*. London, E. and R. Nutt and R. Gosling. vol. i. p. 293.
8 The judicial doctrine that a conspiracy to do some act in regard to the King which might endanger his life was itself treason, although not defined as such by statute until the Treason Act, 1795.
9 Sir R. Atkyns. (1689) *A Defence of the Late Lord Russel's Innocency*. London, Timothy Goodwin. p. 10.
10 8 *State Trials*. cols. 550-746.
11 See D. Ogg. (1967) *England in the Reign of Charles II*. Oxford, Oxford University Press. pp. 557-619.
12 Ibid. 646-50.
13 A.H. Shapiro. (1993) 'Political Theory and the Growth of Defensive Safeguards in Criminal Procedure: The Origins of the Treason Trials Act of 1696.' Illinois, 11(2) *Law and History Review*. American Society of Law and History. p. 219.
14 D. Ogg. *England in the Reign of Charles II*. Op. cit. p. 647.
15 9 *State Trials*. cols. 666-935.
16 Ibid. col. 1004.
17 A. H. Shapiro. 'Political Theory and the Growth of Defensive Safeguards in Criminal Procedure: The Origins of the Treason Trials Act of 1696.' Op. cit. p. 222.
18 For example, see D. Ogg. (1969) *England in the Reigns of James II and William III*. Oxford, Oxford University Press. pp. 150-54.
19 11 *State Trials*. col. 494.
20 Ibid.
21 Sir C. Ilbert. (1895) 11 *The Law Quarterly Review*. London, Stevens & Sons Ltd. p. 383.
22 L. Stephen. (1991) *Hours in a Library*. London, The Folio Society. vol. iii. p. 302.
23 Lord J. Campbell. (1868) *Lives of the Lord Chancellors*. London, John Murray. vol. iv. p. 416.
24 12 *State Trials*. p. 183.
25 12 & 13 Wm. III. c. 2.
26 7 & 8 Wm. III. c. 3.
27 A.H. Shapiro. 'Political theory and the Growth of Defensive Safeguards In Criminal Procedure:' Op. cit. p. 216.
28 5 Cobbett's *Parliamentary History*. p. 693.
29 Preamble to the 1696 Act.
30 13 *State Trials*. col. 1.
31 Ibid. col. 222.
32 Shapiro. 'Political Theory and the Growth of Defensive Safeguards in Criminal Procedure.' Op. cit. p. 226.
33 Sir M. Foster. (1792) *A Report of Some Proceedings on the Commission of Oyez and Terminer and Gaol Delivery for the Trial of the Rebels in the Year 1746 etc*. London, M. Dodson. p. 231.

34 Old Bailey Proceedings Online. (www.oldbaileyonline.org, 6 November 2004) 14 September 1791 Trial of George Dingler for Murder. Ref: t17910914-1.

35 Cited in *The Edinburgh Review*. (1884) Edinburgh, Longman Ross and Ors. vol. clix. p. 332.

36 J. F. Stephen. *History of the Criminal Law of England*. London, Macmillan. vol. i. pp. 226, 415.

37 J.H. Langbein. *The Origins of Adversary Criminal Trial*. Op. cit. p. 98.

38 Ibid.

39 J. F. Stephen. *A History of the Criminal Law of England*. Op. cit. vol. i. p. 424.

40 Trial of Captain Goodere and M. Mahony for the Murder of Sir John Goodere. 17 *State Trials*. p. 1022.

41 18 *State Trials*. p. 1231-2.

42 Ibid.

43 Ibid.

44 P. King. (2000) *Crime, Justice, and Discretion in England, 1740-1820*. Oxford, Oxford University Press. p 228.

45 J. H. Wigmore. (1974 edn.) *Evidence in Trials at Common Law*. Chadbourn. vol. 5. p. 32.

46 J. M. Beattie. 'Scales of Justice: Defence Counsel and the English Criminal Trial in the Eighteenth and Nineteenth centuries.' Op. cit. p. 239.

47 J.H. Langbein. *The Origins of Adversary Criminal Trial*. Op. cit. p. 332.

48 OBP Online. (www.oldbaileyonline.org, 1 November 2004) 15 September 1784. Trial of William Stevenson. Ref: t17840915-66.

49 Another example of the speed with which prisoners were brought to trial.

50 J.N. Beattie. 'Scales of Justice.' Op. cit. p. 238.

51 R.W. Bridgeman, (1804) *Reflections on the Study of the Law*. Cited by D. Lemmings. (2000) *Professors of the Law: Barristers and English Legal Culture in the Eighteenth Century*. Oxford, Oxford University Press. p. 225.

52 J.M. Beattie. 'Scales of Justice.' Op. cit. p. 247.

53 D. J.A. Cairns. (1998) *Advocacy and the Making of the Adversarial Criminal Trial 1800 – 1865*. Oxford, The Clarendon Press. p. 34.

54 Ibid. p. 177.

55 Ibid. p. 3.

56 J.H. Langbein. (1983) 'Shaping the Eighteenth Century Criminal Trial: A View from the Ryder Sources.' Chicago, 50 *University of Chicago Law Review*. pp. 130-2.

57 OBP Online. (www.oldbaileyonline.org, 15 October 2004) 10 December 1783. Trial of Jacob Thompson for Theft. Ref: t17831210-148.

58 D.J.A. Cairns. *Advocacy and the Making of the Adversarial Criminal Trial 1800-1865*. Op. cit. p. 30.

59 OBP Online. (www.oldbaileyonline.org, 7 January 2005) 21 April 1784. Trial of Humphry Moore for Theft from a Dwellinghouse. Ref: t17840421-92.

60 J.H. Langbein. (1983) 'Shaping the Eighteenth Century Criminal Trial: A View from the Ryder Sources.' Op. cit. p. 123.

61 S. Landsman. (1990) 'The Rise of the Contentious Spirit: Adversary Procedure in Eighteenth Century England.' Op. cit. pp. 564-72.

62 D.J.A. Cairns. 'Advocacy and the Making of the Adversarial Criminal Trial 1800-1865.' Op. cit. p. 30 and see Beattie. 'Scales of Justice.' Op. cit. pp. 233-34.

63 Sir J. Hawles. (1689) *A Reply to a Sheet of Paper, entitled, The Magistry and Government of England Vindicated*. London, p. 13. Cited by Shapiro. Op. cit. p. 223.

64 P. King. *Crime, Justice and Discretion in England 1740-1820*. Op. cit. p. 228.

65 J. F. Stephen. *A History of the Criminal Law of England*. Op. cit. vol. i. p. 424.

66 See *Chapter 1*.

67 J.M. Beattie. 'Scales of Justice.' Op. cit. p. 224.

68 S. Landsman. (1990) 'The Rise of the Contentious Spirit: Adversary Procedure in Eighteenth Century England.' Op. cit. p. 607.

69 J.H. Langbein. 'The Criminal Trial before Lawyers.' Op. cit. p. 307.

70 D.J.A. Cairns. *Advocacy and the Making of the Adversarial Criminal Trial*. Op. cit. p. 3.

71 S. Landsman. 'The Rise of the Contentious Spirit. Adversary Procedure in Eighteenth Century England.' Op. cit. p. 524. note. 126.

72 P. King. *Crime, Justice and Discretion in England 1740-1820*. Op. cit. p. 228.

73 H. Brougham. (1836) Review of *A Popular and Practical Introduction to Law Studies* by Samuel Warren. 64 *Edinburgh Review*. Edinburgh, Longman, Ross & Ors. p. 163.

74 www.oldbaileyonline.org/proceedings/value.html

75 Ibid.

76 J.M. Beattie. (1991) 'Garrow for the Defence'. *History Today*. London, History Today Ltd. p. 50.

77 Beattie. (1991) 'Scales of Justice: Defence Counsel and the English Criminal Trial in the Eighteenth and Nineteenth Centuries'. *Law and History Review*, American Society for Legal History, University of Illinois Press. vol. 9 (2). p. 227. Original data from Old Bailey Sessions Proceedings.

78 Ibid.

79 J.M. Beattie. *Crime and the Courts*. Op. cit. p. 411.

80 S. Landsman. (1990) 'From Gilbert to Bentham: The Reconceptualization of Evidence Theory.' In 36 *The Wayne Law Review*. University of Oregon School of Law. p. 1150.

81 D. Dwyer. (2003) Review of Langbein's *The Origins of Adversary Criminal Trial*. 66 *The Modern Law Review*. Oxford, Blackwell Publishing. p. 943.

82 OBP Online. (www.oldbaileyonline.org, 7 January 2005) 29 June 1785. Trial of Catherine Molley. Ref: t17850629-13.

83 OBP Online. (www.oldbaileyonline.org, 12 January 2005) Trial of William Bear and William Davis. Ref: t17850014-80.

84 OBP Online. (www.oldbaileyonline.org, 17 October 2004) 11 July 1787. Trial of John Elliott. Ref: t17870711-41.

85 OBP Online. (www.oldbaileyonline.org, 18 March 2005) 12 December 1787 Trial of Thomas Duxton. Ref: t17871212-78.

86 OBP Online.(www.oldbaileyonline.org, 17 October 2004) 13 January 1792 Trial of Edward Cox. Ref:t17920113-22.

87 P. King. *Crime, Justice and Discretion in England*. Op. cit. p. 229.

88 Ibid.

89 Ibid.

90 *The Times*. 23 January 1800.

91 T. Hague. (1812?) *A Letter to William Garrow, Esquire, in which the Conduct of Counsel [especially W. Garrow] in the Cross-examination of Witnesses, and Commenting on their Testimony, is Fully Discussed and the Licentiousness of the Bar Exposed*. London, J. Parsons. pp. 3, 6.

92 C. Cottu. (1822) *On the Administration of Criminal Justice in England; and the Spirit of the English Government*. London, Richard Stevens, Charles Reader. pp. 88 and 105.

CHAPTER 4

Rights of the Individual

INTRODUCTION

This chapter will consider in more detail the legal, political and cultural background against which lawyers came to act for defendants and cross-examine the testimony of prosecution witnesses in felony trials in the early eighteenth century.

Statutory payments to thief-takers had been introduced by government and, because they frequently led to perjury and false prosecutions, they played a significant part in the decision of judges gradually to allow bounty hunters to be cross-examined by counsel. A number of other factors which also influenced the judges arose from social and political movements of the time.

England was changing rapidly and, in a sense, the political events that gave rise to the Glorious Revolution in opposition to royal and aristocratic power acted as a midwife in bringing into the world a new philosophy stressing the importance of the individual in society. Moreover people themselves demanded the right to a fair trial and a presumption of innocence.[1] But there were other fundamental and far-reaching adjustments also taking place that would alter the cultural face of society worldwide. In particular, the Industrial Revolution and the growth of the market, the Enlightenment and the American and French Revolutions, with their *Declarations of Rights*, each evoked powerful responses in bringing to light the importance of individual human rights. In such circumstances adversariality, alongside the criminal jury, became a crucial component of the judicial system, a safeguard against abuse of power or maladministration by the state.

It was in this situation that lawyers in England (and some from Scotland), consciously or unconsciously, acted in a manner that developed adversary trial and its accompanying rights for prisoners. Indeed, such a form of trial extended process rights to all prisoners and 'the proposition that the Crown in a criminal prosecution was an adversary on equal terms with the humblest subject was startling and far-reaching in its application. The same lawyers who achieved this practical transformation from deference to debate, went on to elevate the doctrine to a full-blown political ideology in the revolutionary creeds of the late eighteenth century.'[2]

ENTRY OF DEFENCE LAWYERS IN CRIMINAL TRIALS

Apart from the example given by the enactment of the Treason Trials Act 1696 arising from the provocative political prosecutions of the later Stuarts, three factors are generally put forward to explain the entry of defence lawyers in criminal trials. The first is the creation of a rewards culture for bounty hunters. This commenced with a statute in 1692[3] which provided for a bounty of as much as £40 a head for thief-takers[4] and was aimed at the capture and conviction of highwaymen.[5] In other words, as Beattie says, the government was paying the costs of prosecuting not only those who directly threatened its existence, but also a wide range of felons indulging in violence and depredations that seemed to threaten public order.[6]

The Act was followed by others, including two in 1752[7] and 1754,[8] which gave the courts power to award expenses to poor prosecutors and witnesses in felony cases which resulted in a conviction. The reason for these statutes is suggested by Beattie:

> The accession of George I, the Elector of Hanover, brought a regime to power that was — or certainly thought itself — challenged by a range of domestic enemies, particularly the Jacobite supporters of the exiled Stuarts ... It responded to the threats to the security of the regime and to *evidence of social disorder* in a variety of ways, some of which had important consequences for the administration of the law ... by taking a much more active part than governments normally had done in encouraging prosecutions and even paying for them.[9] [Italics added.]

These three Acts were followed by another statute in 1778[10] which extended expenses to all prosecutors and witnesses whether there was a conviction or not and a final Act in 1818[11] that gave the courts power to reward an allowance for time and trouble to all prosecutors and witnesses in felony cases.[12]

In addition to the government giving bounty payments to thief-catchers, there was a perceived increase in criminal activity which gave rise across the country to numerous Associations for the Prosecution of Felons which not only paid the expenses of criminal investigation and prosecution for victim members but also offered rewards for information.[13] Such rewards by these associations and the government, whereby the conviction of a highway robber could be worth £140 to a thief-taker, rising in multiples where there were co-accused,[14] were a free-market 'solution' to rising crime and proved to be a potent inducement to perjury and false prosecutions. For example, in 1732 a John Waller,

> was convicted at the Old Bailey of a misdemeanour in attempting to prosecute a person falsely for a highway robbery in order to collect the reward. Evidence was adduced that Waller had succeeded in bringing such prosecutions in other counties. He was convicted and sentenced to be pilloried. When he was exposed in the pillory

at the Seven Dials [today's Cambridge Circus in London], Edward Dalton, the brother of one of his victims set upon him and beat him to death.[15]

Indeed, solicitors, who often managed the prosecution associations, arranged not only the investigations of crimes but also controlled the prosecutions themselves and sometimes attempted to bribe jurors.[16]

Moreover, prosecution counsel 'began to appear in a small number of cases, especially murder trials, in the second and third decades of the eighteenth century, followed by a more substantial increase in numbers' in later years.[17] Langbein, supported by David Lemmings,[18] has concluded that together the use of prosecution counsel at trial, the reward system and the Crown witness system of using accomplice evidence, all prompted the judges to allow counsel to assist the felony defendant.[19] But this view is not accepted by other academics and should not obscure the vital function played by the lawyers in the change to adversary trial.

As for the role of the defendant, as Vogler has put it,

> In such a market-orientated system of prosecution, hiring a lawyer to manage the prosecution in court, represented merely a prudent means of protecting an investment. The natural response to a procedure which was thus becoming increasingly lop-sided, was the licensing of counsel for a limited role in defence.[20]

The second factor, put forward by Landsman, as leading to the introduction of defence lawyers in trials for felony[21] is the conduct of campaigns through the criminal courts by political reform movements such as those of John Wilkes in the mid-eighteenth century and the anti-slavery campaigners at the end of that century. The people involved in these movements were keen to engage defence counsel,[22] and the latter were sometimes happy to act for political reasons.

Beattie, for example, suggests that Garrow's defence of prisoners in the 1780s 'betokens a political stance,' with the Old Bailey as an arena for expressing political views about the American war and the policy of the administration 'to overturn liberty at home as it had in America.' After all, 'the defence of the constitution could be carried on in the criminal courts as well as in Parliament.'[23] This, he suggests, may explain not only Garrow's career but the striking movement of lawyers into the Old Bailey and other criminal courts in the last quarter of the eighteenth century.[24] It is also likely, however, that the income and fame were at least contributing factors. For Garrow, for example, although criminal work was not generally as well paid as civil work his practice, and no doubt his income from it, were extraordinary. One has only to look a the fee of 200 guineas he was believed to have received for one case in 1800[25] when fees were generally two or three guineas for a brief.[26]

Garrow was certainly a Whig in the early years of his career (he joined the Whig Club on 26 June 1784). However, Beattie may be overstating the case since Parliamentary reports of the time when Garrow was an MP show no signs of his being concerned about liberty. Indeed, as far as criminal law is concerned it was otherwise. In the House of Commons, he opposed Romilly's proposed reforms of the outdated and severe criminal law in strong terms. He believed that discretion in punishment was sufficient and safe with the jury, the judiciary and the Crown and claimed that in 30 years' experience of the criminal law he had not met with six instances in which he would have differed from the jury's verdict.[27] He also declared that, '[t]he severity of the law was not too much for some cases; for the utmost rigour was sometimes called for out of mercy to society.'[28] It is significant that when offered a position as a law officer he changed his political allegiance and on behalf of Pitt's government prosecuted constitutional and law reformers for sedition. Prior to that, however, his concern, not only for his fees, but also for his clients' rights and liberty were at the forefront in his professional career at the Bar.

The third reason put forward for the entry of defence lawyers into criminal trials is the creation of rules of evidence. However, since it was the presence of lawyers in trials that enabled them to advance rules of evidence, that is putting the cart before the horse. Prior to the early 1700s, the general difficulties prisoners facing trial had to contend with were:

- being kept in custody until trial and unable to prepare their defence;
- having no knowledge of the evidence against them;
- not being allowed to call sworn witnesses on their own behalf or give evidence on oath themselves;
- confessions of accomplices being treated as specially cogent evidence; and
- no rules of evidence: often witnesses did not confront the accused and originals of documents were not required.[29]

However, after the birth of adversariality the 'best evidence' rule, the rule against hearsay and other rules of evidence grew at the insistence of Garrow and other defence counsel so that by the middle of the seventeenth century books dealing with exclusionary and adversary rules existed in some numbers.[30]

Beattie considers the evidential rules to be a consequence of the rise of defence lawyers. As we have noticed, he says,

> It seems certain that it was the insistent questioning by defence counsel that raised as matters of immediate urgency many of the issues whose resolutions by the judges in their post-circuit meetings at Serjeants' Inn, helped to form what amounted to a law of evidence in criminal trials.[31]

More significantly Landsman sees the growth of rules of evidence as being used as a tool by Old Bailey lawyers in their efforts to control the litigation process and take over the criminal courts.[32] This is contrary to Langbein's view that the judges created the law of criminal evidence without being prompted, although even he accepts that, despite his considering that it was a judicial creation, 'it played into the hands of the lawyers, by opening to oversight and demand of counsel matters of trial conduct that had previously been the preserve of judge and jury.'[33]

A CHANGING WORLD

These three practical explanations for the entry of defence lawyers into criminal trials may or may not be convincing, says Vogler. There has been, he says, 'a strong tendency in the recent academic literature to see the whole creation of adversariality as merely an *ad hoc* development'.[34] But, he continues, 'whilst the practical reasons may have been important and may go some way to explain the chronology of change, it is not unreasonable to link the birth of adversariality' with wider movements in Britain and the world.[35] After all, it was a period of breathtaking commercial expansion and demands for political and economic freedoms and individual liberty. And, 'by directing political attention to individuals and their rights ... the Whig political theory shifted attention from the prosecutor to the defendant,' who had a right and duty to resist arbitrary and illegitimate authority.[36] This theory, based on the authority of the philosopher, John Locke, 'greatly enhanced the trial reformer's appreciation of the defendant's predicament and the vulnerability of the innocent.'[37]

Moreover, says Vogler,

It is not unreasonable to link the birth of adversariality with the more profound shifts in contemporary understanding of the world and the political economy which followed from the Glorious Revolution of 1688.'[38]

He argues that during the period prior to 1688 the bloody judicial retribution of judges such as Jeffreys and Scroggs brought the rights of criminal defendants to the heart of the Whig political agenda. As a consequence, the Whig ascendancy of Hanovarian England was content with the disempowerment and growing neutrality of the trial judge. But even more important:

Whereas these explanations may give us some insight into the timing and logistics of change, it is impossible, bearing in mind the subsequent spread of adversariality around the globe, to escape the conclusion that it bore some deeper relationship to the social and industrial changes then underway in England. It seems too much of a coincidence that the first industrial nation should also be the first to develop this mode of trial process and at the very same time. As has already been pointed out, the 'lawyerization' of the trial was in many respects an opening of the feudal court hierarchy to the market and in that sense, just as much a 'commercialization'. Moreover, the constitution of the defendant as a rights-bearing actor in the process cannot be unconnected with changes in the status of the individual in the new employment market.[39]

That was a consequence of the Industrial Revolution and the explosive nature of the European Enlightenment in the century of revolutions.

LAWYERS OF THE ENLIGHTENMENT

Amongst the Scots who were an integral part of the intellectual movement known as the Enlightenment were David Hume and his friend Adam Smith, both of whom lived for some years in France. Hume, who was an historian, an economist and a sceptic, was on friendly terms with the French Encyclopaedists. Smith was sympathetic to the Physiocrats and Voltaire in France and he was exposed to both the English and French political-economic systems of the day.[40] He laid the intellectual framework that explained the free market. The Enlightenment meant, among other things, the progress of human knowledge and civilization and it is significant that it occurred against a background of the awe-inspiring 'galaxy of revolutions', by which Phyllis Deane described the Industrial Revolutions.[41] Largely unremarked at the time, they were to make Britain the workshop of the world for decades to come.

The Scottish Enlightenment included not only Smith and Hume but also the leading lawyers attracted to London's Inns of Court, namely, Henry Brougham, Thomas Erskine and John Campbell who were part of the age of Western thought that ignored the boundaries between disciplines.

Brougham, for example, enrolled in the University of Edinburgh in 1791 at the age of 13 and chose to read humanity and philosophy which included mathematics, natural philosophy, ancient languages, political economy, rhetoric, logic, astronomy and natural philosophy.[42] Before long, he helped to launch, and write extensively for, the influential *Edinburgh Review*.[43] By the time he was 25 years of age he was active in the campaign against slavery about which he wrote, *An Inquiry into the Colonial Policy of the European Powers*. He framed the Felony Act 1811 which restricted the slave trade in the British Empire and 'must be accounted one of the most effective pieces of legislation in history.'[44] He was always a whole-hearted supporter of the causes of education, law reform, anti-slavery, Catholic emancipation, Parliamentary reform and a free press.[45]

Sir John Campbell also campaigned against slavery and for Parliamentary reform and was responsible for ending imprisonment as a punishment for most types of debt. He actively supported the campaign for the Prisoners Counsel Act 1836 arguing, as Attorney-General, that change was, 'absolutely necessary to vindicate the law of England from a deep and disgraceful stain.'[46] He also secured enactment of the Fatal Accidents Act 1846 with the intention of helping dependants of men killed in accidents through the act or default of another.

Erskine used his talents successfully in a long series of state trials in which he championed English liberty, including the trials of Tom Paine, for publishing his *Rights of Man*, in 1792 and Thomas Hardy and others in 1794 when freedom hung in the balance.[47] Although they did not form a group with a political agenda, each of these three great lawyer advocates seems to have been steeped in the spirit of the Enlightenment. And each in his own way followed in the footsteps of one of its giants, Cesare Beccaria, whose book *Of Crimes and Punishments* became the inspiration for a new philosophical movement for people's rights in law and the reduction of all punishments which quickly swept across continental Europe in the mid-1700s.[48] Although initially largely opposed in England, it came shortly after adversariality had taken root and contributed to the modern notion of human rights. But, although all three lawyers were contemporaries and attended Lincoln's Inn, I cannot trace any evidence that they campaigned together or even met socially.

On the other hand, when some of Erskine's speeches to juries were published in two volumes, Brougham reviewed each volume in the *Edinburgh Review* with glowing praise.[49] Erskine, with Garrow, was a precursor in the growth of adversary trial, often appearing before juries for defendants in cases at the Old Bailey as well as state trials and it is to be hoped that the extracts from Garrow's cases that follow later in the book will add to our knowledge of defendants as 'rights-bearing actors' entitled to a full defence in a court of due process as a human right.

In regard to Erskine's defence of Captain Baillie in 1779, Brougham wrote of his 'dauntless love of liberty' and his 'matured genius with a power that carried everything before it, and bore down the utmost efforts of the court against the independence of the British press.'[50] Brougham explained his interest in Erskine by saying,

> Had he not been the first in this path—had his powers been exerted in obsequiousness to the government, or in time-serving or timid submission to the court of justice, *we*, at least, should not have stepped aside to attempt the task of praising his eloquence.[51]

Garrow did not have the intellectual power of the Scottish trio but was an exemplar of the new commercial lawyers, rather than someone with a clear political agenda. Notwithstanding this, he played a more significant part than the others in the birth of adversary trial. He was crucial to what Landsman has said as to how such procedure fell into place in society:

> Tendencies towards adversarial procedure were further sharpened by the lawyers and judges who controlled the legal system. Members of the bench and Bar ... knew their society and shared the social and economic values it was coming to adopt. Undoubtedly, in their legal activity they attempted to respond to the needs they perceived. Further, the adversarial process was in the interest of lawyers as a group. It created more work for attorneys because increased numbers of potential litigants availed themselves of legal advice. For all the above reasons, adversary procedure was the right procedure for the times; it did not pose a threat of radical change, but could, in a credible manner, accommodate the demands of the forces of change at work in English and American society.[52]

CONCLUSION

Vogler refers to 'The Strange Birth of the Adversarial Principle' and this change happened without its significance being appreciated at the time or, indeed, until recently. Clearly there were the practical causes for its origin as outlined above and they each played a significant part in its birth. But the period of the rise of adversary trial was one of a profound transformation in society which was undermining the earlier trial procedure and helped determine the direction which the new procedure took.

The effects on Britain and the rest of the Western world of the Industrial Revolution, the Enlightenment and the American and French Revolutions were both awe-inspiring and enduring. They involved new forces and new ideas coming to the fore in society and to them originally must be ascribed the modern conception of individual and collective human rights of which the adversarial principle is an integral part. This principle was not part of a thought-out plan by governments, judges or lawyers but arose largely under the impact of developments in society and the impetus of advocates for the defence like Garrow who played what amounted to a substantial role in what became a revolutionary change in criminal procedure. It could not have arisen earlier when counsel were unable to appear for prisoners or before the onset of the spirit of the individual and a recognition of prisoners' rights.

ENDNOTES for *Chapter 4*

[1] A.H. Shapiro. (1993) 'Political Theory and the Growth of Defensive Safeguards in Criminal Procedure. The Origin of the Treason Trials Act of 1696.' Illinois, 11(2) *Law and History Review*. American Society of Legal History.

[2] R. Vogler. (2005) *A World View of Criminal Justice*. Aldershot, Ashgate Publishing. p. 131.

[3] 4 & 5 W. & M. c.8. s. 2.

[4] J.H. Langbein. (2003) *The Origins of Adversary Criminal Trial*. Oxford, Oxford University Press. p. 148.

[5] L. Radzinowicz.(1956) *A History of the Criminal Law. The Enforcement of the Law*. London, Stevens & Sons Ltd. p. 57.

[6] J. N. Beattie. (1991) 'Scales of Justice: Defense Counsel and the English Criminal Trial in the Eighteenth and Nineteenth Centuries.' Illinois, *University of Illinois Press*. p. 225.

[7] 25 Geo. II, c. 36, s. 11.

[8] 27 Geo. II, c. 3, s. 3.

[9] J.N. Beattie. 'Scales of Justice: Defense Counsel and the English Criminal Trial in the Eighteenth and Nineteenth Centuries.' Op. cit. p. 225.

[10] 18 Geo. III, c. 19, ss. 7-9.

[11] 58 Geo. III. c. 70.

[12] L. Radzinowicz. (1956) *A History of English Criminal Law and its Administration from 1750*. London, Stevens & Sons Ltd. vol. ii. p. 76.

[13] J.H. Langbein. *The Origins of Adversary Criminal Trial*. Op. cit. p. 133.

[14] J. N. Beattie. (1986) *Crime and Courts in England 1660-1800*. Oxford, The Clarendon Press. pp. 50-9.

[15] J. H. Langbein. *The Origins of Adversary Criminal Trial*. Op. cit. p. 152.

[16] Ibid. pp. 136-40.

[17] D. J.A. Cairns. (1998) *Advocacy and the Making of the Adversarial Criminal Trial 1800-1865*. Oxford, The Clarendon Press. p. 29.

18 D. Lemmings. (April 2005) 'Criminal Trial Procedure in Eighteenth-Century England: The Impact of Lawyers.' 26(1) *The Journal of Legal History*. London, Routledge. pp. 65-9.

19 J.H. Langbein. *The Origins of Adversary Criminal Trial*. Op. cit. p. 4.

20 R. Vogler. *A World View of Criminal Justice*. Op. cit. pp. 140-41.

21 S. Landsman. (1990) 'The Rise of the Contentious Spirit: Adversary Procedure in Eighteenth Century England.' New York, 75 *Cornell Law Review*. p. 583.

22 Ibid. p. 581.

23 J.M. Beattie. 'Scales of Justice: Defense Counsel and the English Criminal Trial in the Eighteenth and Nineteenth Centuries.' Op. cit. p. 238.

24 Ibid.

25 Ante. p. 46.

26 A.N May. (2003) *The Bar and the Old Bailey 1750-1850*. Chapel Hill, University of North Carolina Press. p. 84.

27 Hansard. [24] cols. 567-72.

28 *Parliamentary Debates*. [24] (February 1813) cols. 571.

29 J. F. Stephen. (1883) *A History of the Criminal Law of England*. London, Macmillan. vol. i, p. 350.

30 See post chapter 8.

31 J.M. Beattie. Scales of Justice.' Op. cit. p. 233.

32 S. Landsman. (1990) 'The Rise of the Contentious Spirit: Adversary Procedure in Eighteenth Century England.' Op. cit. p. 564.

33 J.H. Langbein. *The Origins of Adversary Criminal Trial*. Op. cit. p. 5.

34 R.Vogler. *A World View of Criminal Justice*. Op. cit. p. 142.

35 Ibid. pp. 142-3.

36 A. H. Shapiro. (1993) 'Political Theory and the Growth of Defensive Safeguards in Criminal Procedure: The Origins of the Treason Trials Act of 1696.' 11 (2) *Law and History Review*. Illinois, American Society of Legal History. pp. 228, 233.

37 Ibid. p. 236.

38 R. Vogler. *A World View of Criminal Justice*. Op. cit p. 142.

39 Ibid.

40 J. S. Watson. (1960) *The Reign of George III: 1760-1815*. Oxford, The Clarendon Press. p. 329.

41 P. Deane. (1979) *The First Industrial Revolution*. Cambridge New York, Cambridge University Press. p. 84.

42 R. Stewart. (1986) *Henry Brougham 1778-1868: His Public Career*. London, The Bodley Head. p. 8-10.

43 Ibid. pp. 19-20.

44 P. Johnson. (1991) *The Birth of the Modern: World Society 1815-1830*. London, Weidenfeld and Nicolson. pp. 325-6.

45 R. Stewart. *Henry Brougham 1778-1868*. Op. cit.

46 *Hansard* .[31] (17 February 1836) col. 500.

47 J. Hostettler. (1996) *Thomas Erskine and Trial by Jury*. Chichester, Barry Rose Law Publishers. pp. 89-96 and 109-123.

48 Count C. Beccaria. (1764) *Of Crimes and Punishments*. In R. Bellamy (ed) (1995) *Of Crimes and Punishments and other Writings*. Cambridge, Cambridge University Press.

49 See notes 50 and 51.

50 H. Brougham. (April 1810) 'Speeches of Thomas Erskine when at the Bar, on Subjects connected with the Liberty of the Press, and against Constructive Treasons.' *Edinburgh Review*. Edinburgh, Longman Ross and Ors. vol. 16. p. 103.

51 Brougham. (February 1812) 'Speeches of Lord Erskine when at the Bar, on Miscellaneous Subjects'. *Edinburgh Review*. Edinburgh, Longman Ross and Ors. vol. 19. p. 363.

52 S. Landsman. (1989) 'A Brief Survey of the Development of the Adversary System.' 44(1) *Ohio State Law Journal*. p. 738.

CHAPTER 5

Sir William Garrow

INTRODUCTION

In an age when the rights of individuals were growing in importance, the focus of the criminal trial became 'the defence of the individual against the power of the state, rather than the state finding the offender on behalf of the victim'.[1] As Beattie puts it in regard to Garrow, who exemplified the change, he placed a new emphasis on defendants' rights, indulged in aggressive behaviour, was insistent and pressing in cross-examining prosecution witnesses, challenged the rulings of the Bench, and his presence dominated in the courtroom'[2] His importance lies in the fact that he was the first to develop such techniques and skills and in doing so change the nature of the trial.

It is also interesting that, although Garrow was famous for his skills in reducing hostile witnesses to incoherence with annihilating cross-examination, Brougham believed his greater skill was shown in examination in chief. He wrote,

> Mr Garrow's real forte was in truth his examination in chief, which was unrivalled, and which is, indeed, a far more important and not less difficult attribute than the cross-examination which so captivates the ignorant.[3]

But Brougham would not have been aware of the role of cross-examination in helping produce adversary trial or of Garrow's pivotal part in developing it.

This chapter will contain a brief biography of Garrow, including his call to the Bar at Lincoln's Inn and an indication of his powers as an advocate. However, as a Member of Parliament and law officer he never really succeeded in Parliament. Ironically, although a brilliant advocate who helped innumerable prisoners secure their freedom, he opposed criminal law reform and incurred the wrath of Sir Samuel Romilly. He was also an undistinguished judge when elevated to the Bench as Baron of the Exchequer. He is remembered, however, for his career at the Old Bailey which was unrivalled in his day and which made an outstanding contribution to changing the face of procedure in criminal law in England and across the globe. As Landsman puts it,

> Garrow's rise to the top of his profession was the clearest demonstration that adversarial attitudes and methods had come to dominate the courtroom. Garrow was the archetype of the contentious advocate, zealous on his client's behalf and merciless to his opponents. That such a man had reached so lofty a position is powerful proof that the contentious spirit had triumphed.[4]

CALL TO THE BAR

Garrow's career as counsel was distinguished and he was the first man to establish a public reputation as a criminal barrister.[5] He was the dominant figure at the Old Bailey during his ten years there from 1783 to 1793 and he left an indelible mark on the style of adversary trial that lives on today. Little is known about his personal life, his marriage or his interests and there is no biography of him—he seems to have been subsumed in the law.

He was born in Middlesex on 13 April 1760, the third son of the Reverend David Garrow, who kept a school at Hadley in the county, and it was at his father's school that he was educated.[6] At the age of 15 he was articled to Thomas Southouse, an attorney in Milk Street, Cheapside, but, showing great ability in the law, he was encouraged to study for the Bar. He was admitted by Lincoln's Inn on 27 November 1778 and was called to the Bar on the same date five year later. By then he was twenty-three years of age, and had married his wife Sarah three years earlier. A contemporary, Thomas Hague, alleged that Sarah was an 'Irish lady of high birth' whom Garrow had seduced[7] but Hague disliked Garrow and there is no confirmatory evidence of this except that Farington confided to his diary that his marriage was 'somewhat irregular.'[8]

As a pupil of Richard Crompton, Garrow copiously notated a book on the law of pleading which he subsequently presented to Lincoln's Inn Library, saying:

> All the written notes are written by me; they were copied whilst I was a pupil with Mr Crompton from his books, which I understood were formed by Mr Justice Yates and augmented by Mr Justice Ashhurst and Mr Justice Buller, to the latter [of whom] Mr Crompton was a pupil.

His efforts won high praise from Chief Justice Willes.[9]

Determined to succeed, Garrow trained himself in 'the cut and thrust of argument and in public speaking' at the meetings of debating societies then flourishing in taverns and public rooms in London.[10] It was not easy at first, however, as is shown by a reprint in *The Times* of 7 November 1840 of a memoir of Garrow in the monthly *Law Magazine*. This claimed that as a young man he 'knew the English language well; had a moderate acquaintance with the Latin, and, as an accomplishment, added a considerable proficiency in French.' But it added that when he went with friends to the Coachmaker's Hall in Cheapside in order to learn the art of oratory his timidity was such that they had to force him from his seat and hold him while he delivered his maiden speech. Although to those who knew him in later life this was incredible, it was, in fact, 'perfectly in keeping with his reserved and retiring disposition.'

Battling to overcome his shyness, he soon acquired a formidable reputation in the taverns as a speaker and was referred to in the press as 'Counsellor Garrow, the famous orator of Coachmakers' Hall' which was where one of the largest of the debating clubs met.[11] According to Edward Foss, he was a powerful debater, 'and his speeches were so admired for their eloquence and ingenuity, that his presence was always welcomed.'[12]

The *Law Magazine* memoir continued with praise of Garrow's career at the Bar and as a judge. Others also referred to Garrow as being in his profession, 'as impudent as any of his brethren [but] in private is modest and reserved' and as having a 'peculiarly reserved and retiring disposition.'[13] His shyness out of court was contrasted with his boldness in it, but after the death of his wife in 1808 he was credited with more self-assurance in society.[14]

LEGAL EAGLE

With the rule against barristers appearing for prisoners having been partially breached by the time of his call to the bar, Garrow commenced appearing at the Old Bailey in 1783. He first made his name there when, on 14 January 1784, a few weeks after his call, he successfully prosecuted John Henry Aikles for feloniously stealing a bill of exchange.[15] He had prepared himself well for the role of counsel having, he claimed, attended the Old Bailey for eight years prior to his call to the bar.[16] Nevertheless, in the Aikles case, which is considered more fully later, he had already set himself apart from other counsel with his aggression and irony at the prisoner's expense.

He joined the home circuit, of which Thomas Erskine[17] was the leader, and in a short time established a great reputation in *nisi prius*[18] and criminal cases. Acquiring a substantial practice he was sometimes engaged either as junior counsel to Erskine or opposing him.[19] In one case where Erskine was acting for the defence,[20] Garrow joined other prosecuting counsel in an endeavour to diminish the impact on the jury of Erskine's eloquence. This involved objections at every possible stage with strong warnings to the jury and statements such as:

> you will admire his talents; you will say, pity so much ingenuity should be exerted in behalf of men so undeserving; pity it is that his great abilities are not employed on the other side, to bring these men to justice; if they had, he would have made us all shudder at their iniquity; and we should have sat down, lamenting, that such men ever existed, and that the Court had it not in their power to inflict a more exemplary punishment on such atrocious offenders.[21]

Although, in other cases, Erskine could have used a similar tactic against Garrow there is no evidence that he did so and they were clearly men of different character.

Garrow was a consummate advocate, soon unrivalled in the art of cross-examination, and such was his power at the Bar that he was appointed King's Counsel in the Hilary term of 1793 and ceased to practise at the Old Bailey. All his successes there and his lasting achievements had been won in the short period of ten years. An example of his reputation was seen when a man being accused of forgery was advised by his attorney to go before a Bow Street magistrate. Instead, his companion said, 'No, we will not go into the lion's mouth, we will go first and consult Mr Garrow.'[22] His contemporary Thomas Hague wrote that Garrow's name was 'stuck up ... on the felons' side of Newgate: an hand-post, on the high road, to direct highwaymen to an able advocate.'[23]

Despite apparently being a shy man in private life Garrow was entirely extrovert and fearless when appearing in court.[24] As will be seen, he toyed with and bullied witnesses with a 'verbal net which tightened until it became a noose'.[25]

It is also reasonable to assume that Garrow would have agreed with Erskine on the importance of not pre-judging a case and declining to act for prisoners he may have thought might be guilty. In his defence of Tom Paine in 1792 on a charge of seditious libel, Erskine set out what became known as the 'cab rank rule' when he stoutly declared that,

> If the advocate refuses to defend from what he may think of the charge or of the defence, he assumes the character of the judge—nay, he assumes it before the hour of judgment—and, in proportion to his rank and his reputation, puts the heavy influence of perhaps a mistaken opinion into the scale against the accused, in whose favour the benevolent principle of the English law makes all presumptions.[26]

There were cases in which Garrow appeared for prisoners in which it is likely that he was not over-confident of his clients' innocence, but, if so, he never allowed his feelings to show in either his words or his manner.

Although Garrow was able to take silk because of his formidable success as a barrister, it was widely believed that his political views were crucial to the appointment and that he, and others, were engaged to defend the government against the radical challenges to the unreformed Parliamentary franchise. Certainly, his leadership in the Crown side of the King's Bench in the 1790s was seen as reflecting the Tory party's reputation.[27] It was the time of such organizations as the London Corresponding Society which, although peaceful, were inspired to seek political reform by the French Revolution[28] and caused panic in the government. As a consequence, Garrow had turned from Whig to Tory, his allegiance from Fox to Pitt, and newspapers claimed he was given silk to help defend the constitution in the courts against the radicals.[29] Indeed, he did become an important government prosecutor in state trials in the early 1790s[30] having previously acted mainly for defendants at the Old Bailey.[31]

MEMBER OF PARLIAMENT

In April 1805 Garrow was elected Member of Parliament for the borough of Gatton in Surrey, although, like Erskine, his skills as an advocate were not successfully translated into a gift for debate in Parliament. He was provided with a safe seat and Gatton was almost as notorious as Old Sarum as a rotten borough having, before the Great Reform Act 1832, only six houses and one resident elector.[32] Garrow was returned by Sir Mark Wood 'to defend ... Lord Melville; without one sixpence of expense' and was not called upon to speak or canvass but, having been returned at Pitt's instigation, was listed in Parliamentary records in July 1805 as his supporter.[33] In 1806 he became MP for Callington in Cornwall.

In the Hilary term a year later, by Erskine's influence, he became Attorney-General to the Prince of Wales and, in June 1812, was made Solicitor-General in Lord Liverpool's administration. Within a month he was knighted on 17 July 1812.[34]

The idea of Garrow as an MP did not appeal to *The Times*. 'Some of the papers,' it had said in 1789,

> have been recommending Mr *Garrow* as a proper person to sit in the House of Commons; God forbid, says the writer of this, that any such an event should ever take place. There are too many lawyers there already, — too many speakers whose bread depends upon letting out their voice to any purchaser, and ... to either and so both sides of the question, arguing, that *black was white* one day, and that the very same white was black the next day. We want men of independence, of honour, and not of oratory and loquaciousness in the House of Commons.[35]

But that speaks more of opposition to Garrow as a lawyer than as a man and implies that he was neither independent nor honourable. More personal were the remarks of William Hazlitt, primarily a literary critic, who wrote with gusto when he said of Garrow's performance in the House of Commons:

> We have heard him stringing contradictions there with the fluency of water, every third sentence giving the lie to the two former; gabbling folly as if it were the last opportunity he might ever have, and as regularly put down as he rose up — not for false statements, nor for false reasoning, nor for common-place absurdities or vulgar prejudices, (there is enough of these to be found there without going to the Bar), but for such things as nobody but a lawyer could utter and as nobody (not even a lawyer) could believe ... No one there but a lawyer fancies himself holding a brief in his hand as a *carte blanche* for vanity and impertinence — no one else thinks he has got an *ad libitum* right to express any absurd or nonsensical opinions he pleases, because he is not supposed to hold the opinions he expresses.[36]

It is indisputable that Garrow did not shine as a Member of Parliament. Although there have been many successful barristers in Parliament, for some the skills of oratory required there are different from those that are successful before a jury in a court of law. Lawyers like Pitt were politicians first and generally gave up work at the Bar, and a barrister used to weighing arguments in detail and treating all causes with equal gravity could easily bore the Commons or treat its members as if they were an undiscerning jury.[37]

Indeed, Garrow appears to have paid little active attention to his role an as MP, at least until he became a law officer. Although elected to the House of Commons in April 1805 he did not venture on his maiden speech until a year later, on 22 April 1806. The debate which he then favoured was on a charge against Marquis Wellesley for alleged dereliction of duty in India where he was said to have squandered the property of the East India Company. Objecting to a proposed adjournment of the debate Garrow said he had not intended to speak, having made a 'sort of league and covenant with himself to remain silent.' Nevertheless, he felt he must oppose the impeachment of Wellesley as the charge had been brought forward without evidence to support it:

> It was for the sake of precedent that he opposed it; it was because he thought the House should not suffer the valuable privilege of impeachment to be in any case, or even for a short time, the instrument of calumny.[38]

His remarks appeared to raise no interest and certainly no comment.

He then spoke again in a debate on the affairs of India on 18 June 1806 not out of interest in the sub-continent but on a legal technicality. Lord Teignmouth was being questioned about treaties entered into with native princes when he was Governor-General in India. Garrow showed himself to be out of touch with the nature of proceedings in the Commons when he intervened to say that the opinion of the noble lord should not be sought. 'In any other place' he said, 'the rules of evidence would not permit an inquiry as to the opinion of the witness.'[39] In response, another Member (Dr Laurence) pointed out that, in proceedings before the House, strict legal evidence was not required, 'as nothing could be more different than the situation of the House of Commons in search of information and that of a court of law'. Garrow immediately withdrew remarking that, 'it seemed he had strayed from the courts below to this Place, where he found that legal knowledge was totally useless in the examination of witnesses.'[40]

Ironically thanking the doctor for his lecture, he continued that

> it seemed from his report, that this House had resolved most magnificently to depart from the rules of evidence which had been established by the wisdom of ages for the protection of our lives and liberties. He was decidedly of the opinion that no hearsay evidence could be received in any British court of justice to advance the conviction of any man, for a conspiracy or otherwise.[41]

However, he could not have been unaware that the rule against hearsay evidence, far from being established by the wisdom of ages, was in the process of being established in criminal courts by the efforts of defence barristers among whom he was in the forefront. Thereafter he did not intervene in any debate for over six years, until 12 February 1813 when he was a law officer and, speaking in a debate on delays in justice, opposed the transfer of common law judges to relieve the courts of equity.[42]

SOLICITOR-GENERAL

In June 1812 Garrow became Solicitor-General in the ministry of Lord Liverpool and at the following General Election he was returned for Eye, in the interest of the Marquess of Cornwallis, as a friend of the Tory government. The appointment aroused some rancour. James Scarlett, (later Lord Abinger) described him as,

> An eloquent scolder with a fine voice and most distinct articulation, a great flow of words, considerable quickness in catching the meaning of a witness, and great abilities in addressing juries in ordinary cases, [who] without education, without taste and without law, acquired and maintained a high reputation with the public, but none in the profession. He was not much known in private life ... but I believe he was kindhearted, generous and humane.[43]

Such remarks may stem from a distaste for Garrow's lowly background but they are too common to ignore. Furthermore, they give credit for the very attributes that not only made him such a powerful defence lawyer but also had an ineradicable effect on the establishment of adversary trial.

Garrow was opposed to both political and law reform and clashed more than once with the reforming zeal of Romilly who led the nineteenth century movement to mitigate the rigours of the penal law, which may well account for Romilly's attacks upon him. On 5 April 1813 Romilly's Bill on attainder of treason and felony was before the Commons. Its purpose was to take away in cases of treason and felony the feudal doctrine of 'corruption of the blood' by which a person found guilty could not hold or inherit land or, more importantly since the penalty for these offences was frequently death, transmit a title by descent. As Solicitor-General, Garrow declared that the Bill would remove one of the safeguards of the constitution.[44] When the question was debated again a few days later he repeated the remark and drew from Mr Ponsonby the response that he was astonished at the assertion that the mode of execution for high treason was one of the safeguards of the constitution.[45]

According to Sir Leon Radzinowicz, Garrow maintained that he would never have voted for the old law if it were then to be enacted, but since it had the sanction of centuries, he was against changing it.[46] There can be no doubt that despite his revolutionary approach to advocacy, Garrow remained at heart a traditionalist. When the Bill was defeated Romilly wrote in his *Memoirs* that,

> the Ministers have the glory of having preserved the British law, by which it is ordained that the heart and the bowels of a man convicted of treason shall be torn out of his body while he is yet alive.[47]

This 'safeguard of the constitution' was not abolished until the Forfeiture Act 1870[48] — over half a century later.

ATTORNEY-GENERAL

With Liverpool still in the early years of his long premiership, Garrow became Attorney-General on 4 May 1813, succeeding Sir Thomas Plumer. A little-known MP, Joseph Jekyll, suggested that, 'Garrow's vanity on his new office is the joke of the Bar. As a vulgar man he wonders to find himself at Ministers' dinners and talks of nothing else.'[49] But again one questions how reliable such remarks are with the condescending reference to a 'vulgar man'.

ATTACKS BY ROMILLY

In 1814 Garrow was appointed Chief Justice of Chester.[50] This led to a protest in the House of Commons by Romilly, who opposed his taking the judgeship on the ground that the offices of judge and Attorney-General were incompatible. He considered that the appointment as Chief Justice was 'objectionable in its nature' as the Attorney-General was proposing to hold the two offices together. He declared,

> To appoint a gentleman, holding a lucrative office at the sole pleasure of the Crown (and removable from that office the very moment that he might give dissatisfaction to the Crown) to a high judicial situation, was extremely inconsistent with that independence of the judicial character which it was so important to preserve inviolate.[51]

In some cases persons would be tried by an individual who had advised and directed their prosecution. Could, he asked, such a person be considered as an independent judge?[52]

To a large extent however, Romilly undermined his position by indicating, without giving any reason, that he did not propose to make a motion on the matter, and Garrow was left free to proceed in both posts. Apparently, Garrow had absented himself when the attack was made and next day wrote to thank Romilly for his compliments![53]

In his *Memoirs*, Romilly also complained that Garrow, as Attorney-General, had dealt with a matter about which, Romilly claimed, he knew little. He objected that,

> He appeared at the Bar of the House of Lords with a written argument, the whole of which he very deliberately read, without venturing to add a single observation or expression of his own. In the Stafford peerage, which stood for the same day, he did exactly the same thing. He merely read an argument which somebody had composed for him.

And, he continued:

Two days afterwards, in the Court of Chancery ... I said that it would be difficult for a counsel to do his duty in that court by writing arguments and sending them to some person to read them for him. The Lord Chancellor interrupted me by saying, 'In this court or in any other?' And after the Court rose, he said to me, 'You knew, I suppose, what I alluded to? It was Garrow's written argument in the House of Lords.' So little respect has his Lordship for an Attorney-General, whom he himself appointed because he was agreeable to the Prince.[54]

Few of Garrow's cases whilst Attorney-General have been reported but one was *Dixon v. Bell*[55] in April 1816. Here the defendant had left a loaded gun at his lodgings and sent his servant, a young girl aged about 13, to collect it, asking the landlord to remove the priming and give it to her. Later, the girl injured the plaintiff's small son when she drew the trigger. The jury found for the plaintiff (the landlord) on the ground that the defendant had negligently entrusted the young girl with the gun. As Attorney-General, Garrow moved for a new trial but his motion was dismissed by Lord Ellenborough and Mr Justice Bayley who said it was incumbent on the defendant to render the gun safe and innocuous.

In September 1816 Garrow, as Attorney-General, prosecuted two senior police officers, George Vaughan, and his agent, John Dannelly. Although both men were charged with burglary, they were found guilty only of stealing in a dwellinghouse and Dannelly's conviction was overturned on a technicality. The case, and other similar cases, had, however, aroused serious public disquiet and Garrow had shown no hesitation in bringing the prosecutions.

Whilst Attorney-General Garrow, chastened by his earlier experiences in debates, generally spoke only briefly in the Commons on legal questions although he intervened on a number of occasions in the summer of 1816. First, he defended Lord Ellenborough from attack on 30 April 1816[56]. He then made a defence of an illiberal aliens Bill on 10 May[57] and he also moved, on 10 June, a Bill to impose speed limits on, and prevent inconsiderate driving of, stage coaches. In doing so he referred to enormous abuses of stage coach drivers which put at risk lives and limbs of passengers and others, and proposed that magistrates should have the power to imprison for three months in atrocious cases.[58]

In one of these more frequent interventions in the House of Commons, he told Members on 30 April 1816 that, as he had himself done, counsel should not fear to point out to a judge, even in a trial of the meanest individual, that the judge had erred in law. He should do so, 'treating the noble and learned judge with all the respect due to his high character and situation, without fear of his displeasure, or without thinking of courting his approbation by a different line of conduct.'[59] An example of his having done so is to be found in Garrow's altercation with Mr Justice Heath in the trial of William Bartlett at the Old Bailey on 11 January 1786, which is cited later.[60]

On 8 May in the same year Brougham had introduced in the Commons a Bill entitled, 'For securing the Liberty of the Press'. In introducing the Bill he stated that in all cases of criminal libel prosecuted by information *ex officio* the Crown 'never went to trial without a special jury.' He added that,

> all other crimes and misdemeanours, felony, and even the highest crime known to the law, high treason, were always tried before a common jury. He saw no reason for giving to the Crown, in the instance of libel, a right of selection which it did not possess in any other case.[61]

Garrow opposed Brougham and argued that, in trials of libel prosecuted by the Crown, it was the defendant who could choose to be tried by a special jury.[62] This seems an odd claim, however, since, apart from Brougham's claim that in libel cases the Crown always had a special jury, such a jury, made up of men of higher social standing than those on a petty jury, was not generally favoured by prisoners.

According to Garrow a special jury was formed by the sheriff attending the master of the Crown office, with an agent for each party to the case, and selecting 48 names of prospective jurors. Each party was then allowed to strike out the names of 12 of them so that it was impossible for any man to say which 12 out of the remaining 24 would form the jury on the trial.[63] The resulting jury became known as a 'struck jury.' Although, to an extent, this allowed the parties to pick the jury there can be little doubt that special handpicking went on, a court official collaborating with the Crown solicitor for the purpose.[64]

ANIMAL RIGHTS

In the early 1800s appalling cruelty to many kinds of animals was widespread. William Hogarth had earlier drawn studies revealing four stages of cruelty in order to show that brutality to animals leads to brutality to humans. Jeremy Bentham, for his part, insisted that cruelty to animals should be made a crime punishable by law.[65] But, in general, the public remained unmoved. Then, in 1809, Erskine introduced into the House of Lords a Bill for the prevention of 'malicious and wanton cruelty' to animals. 'Extending humanity to them', he exclaimed, 'would have a most powerful effect on men's moral sense and upon their feelings and sympathies for each other.'[66] His speech was published as a pamphlet and the Lords found no difficulty in accepting the Bill. In the Commons, however, William Windham sneered that for Erskine to be the first who stood up as the champion of the rights of brutes was, indeed, a marked distinction, and the Bill was defeated.[67]

As we have seen, in 1816, Garrow, when he was Attorney-General, was to introduce his own Bill, known as the 'Stage Coach Bill.' This sought to increase the penalties for overriding horses, which often ended in their death, but it too had been defeated. Here Garrow was siding with Bentham and the Utilitarians and in respect of cruelty to animals, both lawyers were in advance of their time. However, a few years later they must have felt vindicated when, in 1820, another

Bill drafted by Erskine was introduced into the Commons where, with Windham no longer present, it was accepted and, after passing through the lOrds, was enacted.[68]

CONFLICT WITH BROUGHAM

On 31 January 1817 Garrow was again attacked in the House of Commons for misconceiving the duties of an MP.[69] Petitions calling for reform of Parliamentary representation from various parts of the country had been presented to the House by MPs and, as the Speaker of the House pointed out, the right to present petitions had existed for centuries. Nevertheless, Garrow, as Attorney-General, attempted to modify the right, saying it was not the absolute duty of a Member to present whatever petitions were offered to him. Indeed, he added, he had that very day objected to a petition and refused it because he had no knowledge of the facts it contained.

No doubt some petitions could be tiresome to MPs, and were not always presented by them, but Garrow's approach brought a response from Brougham who complained that the Attorney-General was going too far. It was no longer enough, he declared, that a Member must ascertain whether the language of the petition was unobjectionable; he must also see whether the subject itself was fit to be laid before Parliament. His honourable and learned friend, he continued, 'had totally and entirely misconceived the duty of a Member of Parliament (which was, indeed, often painful and disagreeable), upon the subject of presenting petitions. He had often felt the evil, but it was a necessary one.' It was, he concluded, 'most irregular to obstruct the subject's right of petitioning by the interposition of their own private judgment.' Garrow lamely replied that he had only sent back the petition that it might be revised.[70]

PARODY

As Attorney-General, in April 1817 Garrow filed three informations against William Hone, charging him with publishing prints calculated to injure public morals and bring the prayer book into contempt. The prints were in fact political squibs of a type quite familiar at the time. However Hone was held in prison, in poor health, from May until December because he was unable to find £1,000 bail. He was tried at the Guildhall in three separate trials before special juries, chosen for their wealth and general inclination towards the government, on 18, 19 and 20 December. The trials were really political and Hone defended himself with great skill and determination. Despite the judge Lord Ellenborough telling the jury that the prints were impious and profane libels they acquitted him in each case. In addressing the jury Hone complained bitterly that Lord Ellenborough had treated him with great injustice but went out of his way to add that Garrow had not attempted to produce an unfavourable impression of him in the public mind. It is said that, after the verdicts, the unlamented Ellenborough retired to his sick-room never to return to court. Thereafter, all such parodies and squibs were immune from prosecution.[71]

GARROW AS A JUDGE

On 6 May 1817, Garrow was promoted to be a Baron of the Exchequer in which office he remained until he retired in 1832. When he was appointed, William Pole MP commented,

> It will be a great relief to government to get him out of the House of Commons. He did not succeed there. I believe he had good taste enough to detest it. He was not thought equal to the Chief Baron's place, which is given to Richards of whom the law authorities speak well.[72]

On 22 February Garrow was sworn in a Privy Councillor at a levee of William IV—four years before the enactment of the Prisoners' Counsel Act. He was generally considered to be an undistinguished judge, mainly, it was said, because his knowledge of the finer points of law was rather weak.[73] Indeed, Campbell, whose views on lawyers were not always reliable, claimed that, 'he had never read anything except a brief and a newspaper.'[74] And, the more dependable Brougham expressed a similar attitude when he wrote,

> With so slender a provision of law, his ignorance of all beside, of all that constitutes a science or learning, or indeed general information, nay even ordinary information, was perfect.[75]

But this weak knowledge of the law may well have worked to Garrow's advantage in the development of criminal advocacy.

On the other hand, it may have resulted in his being strict as a judge. When he sat with Sir Vicary Gibbs at the Lincolnshire Lent Assizes on Saturday, 7 March 1818 they heard 22 cases and sentenced ten prisoners to death, although it is not clear how many were actually executed. Possibly none, because in this connection it is interesting that in that year there were some 1,170 capital convictions in England and Wales with 103 prisoners executed; i.e. 90 per cent were reprieved, most being transported to Australia.[76]

In general, few of the cases Garrow heard outside the Old Bailey have been reported but there was a case of some interest that he heard at Stafford Assizes on 23 July 1817. Two solders, John Hall, aged 22, and Patrick Morrison, aged 25, were charged, on the evidence of a thief-taker, with assault in a drunken brawl at a public house. The man assaulted was Jack Read, an unemployed vagabond in his early fifties, from whom it was alleged the solders stole a shilling and a bad penny. Writing a history of his family from 1742 to 1998, Nicholas Mander outlines the trial and states that Garrow was 'a hanging judge ... and the soldiers were allowed no counsel,'[77] which, if correct, reveals a different Garrow from the robust defence counsel of the Old Bailey.

Hall and Morrison were found guilty of robbery and sentenced to be hanged. However, they were generally considered to be innocent and public outcry secured a reprieve from the Home Secretary, Viscount Sidmouth, and a subsequent free pardon which was supported by Garrow.[78]

In 1824 Baron Garrow dealt with a case in which death was caused by collision with a cart driven at an unusually rapid pace. He ruled that it was the 'duty of every man who drives any carriage, to drive it with such care and caution as to prevent, as far as in his power, any accident or injury that may occur.'[79] For some reason, in medical cases he accepted a lower standard of care. In the case of *R. v. Long*,[80] he set a subjective standard of care as the same for the presidents of the College of Physicians as for the 'humblest bone-setter of the village', namely, to 'perform as well as he can.' He distinguished cases of driving by saying, 'Why is it that we convict in cases of death by driving carriages?' 'Because', he replied, 'the parties are bound to have skill, care and caution' — qualities he did not require of medical men.

At the Old Bailey Garrow sat as a judge in scores of trials from May 1817 to April 1831. In some of them his close attention was shown by his asking questions of witnesses but questions of law do not appear to have been raised and, unfortunately, his summings-up to the jury are not recorded so that it is impossible to assess his attitude to the offences and offenders before him. The cases were remarkably similar to those in which he had earlier appeared as counsel and the sentences were frequently death or transportation with prosecution or jury recommendations for mercy, usually on the grounds of the prisoners' youth or distress.

LINCOLN'S INN

In later life Garrow was elected a Bencher of Lincoln's Inn. The published records of the Inn, commonly known as the Black Books, have a few references to him which show that he was an active member of the Inn's governing body. He held all five major offices of the Inn culminating in 1801 as Treasurer.[81] The other great offices he held were Master of the Walks, 1799; Keeper of the Black Books, 1800; Master of the Library, 1802 and Dean of the Chapel, 1803.

In 1798 he proposed a motion (which was passed) that the Inn should donate £1,000 to the Bank of England as a voluntary contribution 'towards the exigencies of the country.'[82] This was no doubt meant to assist the prosecution of the war against Napoleon and 1798 was the year in which Pitt introduced income tax. He also served on the committee that was set up in 1814 to deal with the building of a new court within the Inn.[83] He left the Honourable Society of Lincoln's Inn on becoming a Serjeant-at-law in May 1817 when his arms were ordered to be painted in the Hall and he was given by the Inn £10.10s (and £1.8s. for a silver net purse).[84] The Inn has an oil painting of Garrow by George Henry Harlow which was presented by an anonymous donor in 1904.[85] There is no biography of Garrow, and the birth of criminal advocacy raised no interest in 1904, so it is difficult to imagine why someone would donate the oil painting unless it was because the donor too had been an active member of the Inn and was versed in its proud history.

DEATH

Whilst practising at the Old Bailey Garrow lived at 25 Bedford Row, just west of Gray's Inn,[86] but he died at Pegwell Cottage near Ramsgate in Kent on 24 September 1840, aged 80. He was survived by a daughter, his wife and son having pre-deceased him. His wife, Sarah, had died on 30 June 1808 aged 56 and was buried in the churchyard at Darenth in Kent.[87] His son, D. David Garrow, died Rector of East Barnet[88] and his daughter, Eliza, had married Samuel Fothergill Lettsom, a colliery owner in South Wales whom it was said Garrow had backed financially until he visited Lettsom's mine at Cwmavon after which he withdrew his support, although the reason is not known.[89]

On 20 October 1840 an advertisement appeared in *The Times* newspaper asking for debtors and creditors of Garrow's estate to come forward and on 1 June 1841 his house at Ramsgate was sold by auction on the instructions of trustees under a settlement Garrow had made. It appears that Garrow had invested his income wisely. Whether the auctioneers, Daniel Smith & Son of London, were 'puffing' the property or not they described Pegwell Cottage as a 'singularly beautiful marine villa, unrivalled on the coast.' It no longer exists but at the time it also included a pavilion, salt and fresh water baths, adjacent ornamental cottages, good stabling, walled gardens and a full south aspect of Ramsgate Bay. Clearly its name was a misnomer. In any event, for whatever reason the person who purchased the estate put it up for re-sale only five years later in March 1846. In July of that year the same auctioneers, Daniel Smith & Son, also sold freehold properties owned by Garrow in Barnet in North London.

Some nine years after Garrow's death the following advice to young barristers appeared in *The Times*:

> During the trial of a prisoner for burglary last week, before Mr Baron Alderson, Mr Harrison of Staleybridge, was counsel for the prosecution (it being the first brief he had held); and in consequence of the mode in which the learned gentleman examined the witnesses his Lordship observed, that he wished all his young friends would follow the advice that was given to him by the late Sir William Garrow. When he (Mr Baron Alderson) first appeared at the Bar, 'he told me' said his Lordship, 'that no one ought ever to examine his witnesses and look at his brief at the same time. A counsel ought to know from his brief what a witness will say, and then look at the witness as

he examines him, and arrange in his own mind, as the examination proceeds, the whole of the facts, so as to form a complete and connected narrative.'

That learned judge, his Lordship continued, was the most exquisite examiner-in-chief that ever appeared at the Bar, and it was infinitely more useful to be a good examiner-in-chief than a good cross-examiner; the one is useful every day of the week, the other only occasionally.

Mr Overend, who appeared for the prisoner, said, 'I don't think it would be useful to examine now, my Lord;' to which his Lordship replied, 'He defends a prisoner best who asks the fewest questions.[90]

CONCLUSION

Garrow wore more than one hat but not all of them sat well on his head. He was certainly not successful as an MP and was not particularly suited to being a law officer. He was uneasy in the House of Commons, he opposed the reforming measures of Romilly, and appears to have been promoted for political, as well as legal, reasons. Equally, he was not really successful as a judge although this is difficult to assess because of the lack of reports of the cases over which he presided. His great success was as a barrister and, given both his background and his achievements, that was success indeed. Moreover, although an opponent of both political and penal reform it is paradoxical that he helped to produce a revolution in criminal trial procedure that has had global repercussions for the human rights of prisoners.

But it is significant that at the time of his death in 1840, three-quarters of a century after his great successes at the Old Bailey and after the enactment of the Prisoners' Counsel Act, no mention was made in the law journals or *The Times* of his, or any other lawyer's, contribution to the establishment of adversarial trial. The same applied four years later when *The Law Review* wrote in a belated obituary that Garrow had, 'reached the lead of the Old Bailey practice and domineered without a competitor at the bar.' [91] Not a word about adversarial trial – the real significance of Garrow's advocacy being hidden then and for a long time to come. As is so often the case, contemporaries are blind to what is happening and even an upheaval as overwhelming as the Industrial Revolution was not seen for what it was for many years.

As indeed was the case with adversary trial for Garrow himself. He could not have been at all conscious that he was one of the prime architects of the adversary system of trial in the criminal courts. No mention of such a system passed his lips or those of any contemporary lawyers. Equally, it is clear from his remarks in court that he would have been only dimly aware that with his advocacy he also played a prominent part in securing the rules of evidence for criminal trials.

In the event, adversariality and the rules of evidence soon travelled to, and became rooted in, many parts of the globe which suggests that society was ready for them. Indeed, the process is still continuing in Russia, China and elsewhere.

As a contributing factor in the establishment of a culture of human rights, adversariality has had a large and lasting impact on world-wide jurisprudence. For the crucial part played in the drama of the birth of criminal advocacy by this intrepid lawyer from a humble background, his name shines forth like a beacon.

ENDNOTES for *Chapter 5*

[1] D. Dwyer. (2003) Review of Langbein's *The Origins of Adversary Criminal Trial*. 66 *The Modern Law Review*. p. 943.

[2] J.M. Beattie. (1991) 'Scales of Justice: Defense Counsel and the English Criminal Trial in the Eighteenth and Nineteenth Centuries'. *Law and History Review*. University of Illinois Press. pp. 238 and 247.

[3] Lord Brougham. (1845) 'Memoir of Mr Baron Garrow.' 1 *Law Review*. pp. 318-28.

[4] S. Landsman. (1990) 'The Rise of the Contentious Spirit: Adversary Procedure in Eighteenth Century England. 75 *Cornell Law Review*. p. 564.

[5] D. Lemmings. (2000) *Professors of the Law: Barristers and English Legal Culture in the Eighteenth Century*. Oxford University Press. p. 211.

[6] Some of the details here are to be found in G.F.R. Barker. (1975) *The Dictionary of National Biography*. Oxford, Oxford University Press.

[7] R.G. Thorne (ed.) (1986) *The History of Parliament: The House of Commons 1790-1820*. London, Secker & Warburg. vol. iv. p. 7. note 1.

[8] J. Farington. (1796) *Diary*. (ed. K. Cave 1982). New Haven, Yale University Press. vol. 11 p. 4017.

[9] Sir W. Holdsworth. (1966) *A History of English Law*. London, Methuen & Co. Ltd. Sweet & Maxwell. vol. 5. p. 387.

[10] J.M. Beattie. 'Scales of Justice'. Op. cit. p. 237.

[11] Ibid. note 45.

[12] E. Foss. (1864) *The Judges of England; with Sketches of their Lives and Miscellaneous Notices Connected with the Courts at Westminster from the time of the Conquest*. London, John Murray. vol. 9. p. 87.

[13] J. Farington, *Diary* (ed. K. Cave, 1982) Op. cit. vol. ii. p. 614. and Adolphus. Cited in May Op. cit. p. 42. note 43.

[14] R.G. Thorne. (ed.) *The History of Parliament*. Op. cit. p. 6.

[15] Old Bailey Proceedings Online. (www.oldbaileyonline.org, 24 October 2004) 14 January 1784. Trial of John Henry Aikles. Ref: tr17840114-80.

[16] OBP Online. (www.oldbaileyonline.org .28 October 2004) 12 January 1785. Trial of George Norris, Thomas Freeman and William Johnson for Housebreaking and Theft. Ref: t17850112-12.

[17] See J. Hostettler. (1996) *Thomas Erskine and Trial by Jury*. London, Barry Rose Law Publishers.

[18] Trial by jury before a single judge.

[19] A. N. May. (2003) *The Bar and the Old Bailey, 1750-1850*. Chapel Hill, The University of North Carolina Press. p. 40.

[20] Old Bailey Proceedings Online. (www.oldbaileyonline.org, 27 October 2004) 18 April 1787 Trial of William Priddle and Others for Perverting Justice. Ref: t17870418-118.

[21] Ibid.

[22] *The Times*. 6 May 1786.

[23] T. Hague. (c. 1810) *A Letter to William Garrow Esq., in which the Conduct of Counsel (especially of William Garrow) in the Crossexamination of Witnesses, and Commenting on their Testimony, is fully Discussed and the Licentiousness of the Bar Exposed*. London, J. Parsons. p. 47.

[24] A. N. May. *The Bar and the Old Bailey*. Op. cit. p. 42.

[25] Lord Brougham. 'Memoir of Mr Baron Garrow.' Op. cit. p. 320.

[26] J. Ridgway (ed) (1810) *Speeches of the Right Hon. Lord Erskine When at the Bar, with a Preparatory Memoir by the Right Hon. Lord Brougham*. London, vol. i. pp. 90-91.

[27] D. Lemmings. *Professors of the Law: Barristers and English Legal Culture in the Eighteenth Century*. Op. cit. p. 168.

[28] L. Werkmeister. (1967) *A Newspaper History of England: 1792-3.'* Lincoln, University of Nebraska Press. p. 207.

[29] J.M. Beattie. *Scales of Justice*. Op. cit. p. 237.

30 E. Foss. (1864) *The Judges of England:* Op. cit. vol. 9. p. 88.
31 OBP Online. (www.oldbaileyonline.org)
32 G.D.H. Cole and R. Postgate. (1938) *The Common People 1746-1938.* London, Methuen & Co. Ltd. p. 87.
33 R.G. Thorne. (ed) *The History of Parliament.* Op. cit. p. 5.
34 G.F.R. Barker. (1975) *TheDictionary of National Biography.* Oxford, Oxford University Press.
35 *The Times.* 28 December 1789.
36 W. Hazlitt. (1998) 'Illustrations of *The Times* Newspaper: On Modern Lawyers and Poets.' In *Selected Writings.* (ed. Duncan Wu). London, Pickering and Chatto. vol. iv. pp. 130-31.
37 R. Stewart. (1986) *Henry Brougham 1778-1868: His Public Career.* London, The Bodley Head. p. 63.
38 *Hansard.* [6] (April 22 1806) cols. 865-66.
39 Ibid.[7] (18 June 1806) cols. 748-9.
40 Ibid.
41 Ibid. cols. 749-50.
42 *Hansard.* [24] (12 February 1813).
43 Ibid. p. 6.
44 *Hansard.* [25]. col. 584.
45 Ibid. col. 764.
46 Sir L. Radzinowicz. (1948) *A History of English Criminal Law and its Administration from 1750: The Movement for Reform.* London, Stevens & Sons Ltd. vol. 1. p. 519.
47 Sir S. Romilly. (1840) *Memoirs of the Life of Samuel Romilly, Written by Himself.* London, John Murray. vol. iii. p. 100.
48 33 & 34 Vict. c. 23.
49 R.G. Thorne. (ed.) *The History of Parliament.* Op. cit. p. 6.
50 17 *Parliamentary Debates.* (1810) col. 1207.
51 *Hansard.* (1 March 1814) vol. xxvii col. 330.
52 Ibid. cols.331-2.
53 R.G. Thorne. (ed.) *The History of Parliament.* Op. cit. p. 6.
54 Romilly. *Memoirs of the Life of Samuel Romilly, Written by Himself.* Op. cit. vol. iii. pp. 127-8.
55 5 M. & S. p. 198.
56 *Hansard.* (April-July 1816) [34] First series cols. 121-7.
57 Ibid .col. 463.
58 Ibid. cols. 1040-1.
59 Ibid. col. 126.
60 Post. p. 91-2.
61 *Hansard.* [34] (April-July 1816). First series. col. 393.
62 Ibid. col. 394.
63 Ibid. col. 395.
64 W.R. Cornish. (1968) *The Jury.* London, Allen Lane The Penguin Press. p. 131.
65 Internet. www.rspca-act.org.au/default.asp?dsx=history
66 14 *Parliamentary Debates.* (1809) col. 553.
67 17 *Parliamentary Debates.* (1810) col. 1207.
68 3 Geo. IV. c. 71.
69 *Hansard.* [35] (January-April 1817) cols. 147-152.
70 Ibid. cols. 150-51.
71 See E.P. Thompson. (1968) *The Making of the English Working Class.* London, Pelican Books. p. 793.
72 R.G. Thorne (ed.) *The History of Parliament.* Op. cit. p. 7.
73 Lord Brougham. *Memoir of Mr Baron Garrow.* Op. cit. pp. 319 and 327.
74 M.S. Hardcastle. (ed) *Life of John, Lord Campbell.* Op. cit. vol. i. p.198.
75 Brougham. *Memoir of Mr Baron Garrow.* Op. cit. p. 319.
76 Internet. http://wuff.me.uk/assizes/P5.html
77 N. Mander. (1998) *Varnished Leaves: a Biography of the Mander family of Wolverhampton, 1742-1998.* Internet.http://www.localhistory.scit.wlv.ac.uk/geneology/Mander/The%20Book/Charles Mander.
78 Ibid.
79 *R. v. Walker.* [1824] 1 Carrington & Payne Reports, 320, 171 English Reports, 1213.
80 [1834] C & P 398. 175 ER 756.
81 *Black Books of Lincoln's Inn.* vol. iv. p. 90.

82 Ibid. p. 73.

83 Ibid . *w*pp. 134-6.

84 Ibid. p. 147.

85 Information about Garrow at Lincoln's Inn supplied by Mrs. F. Bellis, Assistant Librarian.

86 A.N. May. *The Bar and the Old Bailey, 1750-1850*. Op. cit. p. 264.

87 Internet. www.kentarchaeology.org.uk/Research/Libr/MisMIsDarenth/MisDarenth.htm

88 E. Foss. *The Judges of England*. Op. cit. p. 90.

89 Port Talbot Historical Society.

90 *The Times* 28 March 1849. p. 7.

91 1 *Law Review*. Op. cit. p. 318.

CHAPTER 6

Garrow at the Old Bailey (1)

INTRODUCTION

By the last quarter of the eighteenth century defence counsel had become an established and growing feature of trials at the Old Bailey and other assize courts. They had two main functions. The first was to establish facts by means of cross-examination of prosecutors and their witnesses. Secondly, to secure acquittals by exposing prosecution testimony where it involved misunderstandings or mistaken identity, or, often, lies and perjury. Their efforts were directed at influencing the jury whom they were still not permitted to address directly. As a consequence, as Fitzjames Stephen wrote, 'The cross-examination tended to become a speech thrown into the form of questions, and it has ever since retained this character to a greater or less extent.'[1]

This approach appears to have been similar in assizes across the country and this is borne out by research by Beattie[2] in Surrey and Sussex and King[3] in Essex and the home counties. The most extensive records available, however, are those of the Old Bailey. In all, Garrow appeared in more than 961 cases there, and in some three-quarters of them he was defence counsel. In the year 1786 alone he acted in 117 of the 182 trials in which counsel were named in the reports, which is a remarkable record.[4] And by his aggressive advocacy in so many trials he was foremost in causing adversarial changes in criminal procedure, as will become apparent.

As Vogler has put it,

> There can be absolutely no doubt that what is being recorded in the OBSP [Old Bailey Sessions Papers] and elsewhere is nothing short of a procedural revolution which was to have huge consequences for the criminal trial. This revolution was accomplished by the lawyers themselves, albeit with judicial acquiescence. Their presence in the trial produced immediate affects, not only in terms of the radical reorganization of the procedure but also in the creation of a network of defence rights. Notwithstanding that they appeared in only a relatively small proportion of cases, their influence had an universal impact and the reformed procedure was soon extended to all trials.[5]

This chapter and the next will deal with some of Garrow's trials that are reported in the Sessions Papers which will make it possible to trace in detail the growth of adversary trial and the part Garrow played in it. His hatred of thief-takers and attacks on them will be shown with extracts from trials as well as examples of his aggressive style of cross-examination and his conflict with the bench. An indication of Garrow's working environment, his dealing with points of law, as well as his attitude to indictments and benefit of clergy will also be considered. This, and the following chapter, will give some indication of Garrow's impact on criminal trial procedure and his dominant role in the development of adversary trial in the late eighteenth century.

LONDON LIFE AND THE CITY'S ASSIZE COURT

Trials at the Old Bailey in the eighteenth century give a flavour of life in the small city of London (albeit the largest city in Europe) for people who were generally poor and who committed crimes to obtain money or goods of which they felt themselves to be – or were—deprived. Despite the wealth concentrated in the West End, the poor lived in insalubrious and crime-ridden areas. There were 'criminal districts in the metropolis, hot beds of particular crimes … a school for coiners, another for burglars, another for shoplifting, another for horse stealing.'[6] As the felons pass before us in these trials, we can feel their poverty and helplessness whether they were charged with minor misdeeds or capital offences such as murder and robbery.

Details of some of the offences tried at the Old Bailey are set out in *Glossary 2* at the end of the book and for them the most frequent sentences were the gallows or transportation. At that time many goods which are mass produced and cheap today were made by hand and were expensive to buy. These included handkerchiefs, clothing, pots and pans, goods made of wood or cast iron, rope, spoons and forks, all of which were frequently stolen and easily sold. Despite the severity of the sentences for felony, including even fairly trivial theft, large numbers of people were charged at assize courts with offences which today would be dealt with in the magistrates' courts.

However, although the gallows faced almost everyone convicted of felony, including many types of theft, the law was not so severe in practice as would appear from a perusal of the statute book. Against the severity of sentences must be set the exercise of discretion that was available during criminal proceedings.[7] The Grand Jury might reject a bill of indictment by endorsing it with the words 'no bill', and the trial jury would often deliver a partial verdict by reducing the value of goods stolen to make the offence non-capital. For those found guilty, they might claim benefit of clergy for a first offence and be branded with a hot iron instead of being executed, or receive a royal pardon which would set them free or substitute a lesser punishment of transportation. These means of mitigating harsh punishments were quite widespread and, indeed, had to be so since otherwise the numbers hanged, 'would have been such as to create public revulsion and to destroy any legitimacy the law possessed.'[8]

The Old Bailey was the assize court for London and, in addition to high court judges, leading officials of the city sat there following the grant to the city by Henry I of a degree of control over criminal jurisdiction within its boundaries. The court dealt with felonies committed in both the county of Middlesex and the city of London and, unlike assizes elsewhere, it held *oyer and terminer* sessions eight times a year at first and, after it officially became the Central Criminal Court in 1834, as many as 12 times a year.[9] The cases in the Sessions Papers reveal a great deal about the murky and criminal life of the time when a great deal of petty crime was dealt with at assizes and the Old Bailey in addition to serious felonies such as highway robbery, rape and homicide. The significance of the papers cannot be over-estimated since the type of cases dealt with, and the style of advocacy practised there, and at other assize courts, determined the modern development of English trial procedure.

Beattie found that in the late seventeenth century two 12-man juries were called to the Old Bailey from both London and Middlesex, and that in each county the same 12 men would serve through the entire session which lasted several days. When some eight or ten trials were completed for Middlesex the jury would retire to deliberate on them all together and the London jury would then hear their cases.[10] In the period under review trials were much shorter than today. A single session lasted several days and processed between 50 and 100 cases of felony.

The situation was different at county assizes where an alternative jury from the same county had to sit when the first jury retired, and indeed a succession of juries was usually impanelled. This often caused practical difficulties in finding enough jurors, with the result that in the second half of the seventeenth century juries in the counties began to deliberate in open court on each case as it concluded and announce their verdict without retiring. This practice was not adopted at the Old Bailey until 1738.[11] When it was, the Lord Mayor of London announced that the jurors' seats at the Old Bailey would be re-arranged so that the jurors, who previously had sat divided on both sides of the courtroom, could sit together and 'consult one another and give in their verdict immediately.'[12]

GARROW'S EARLY SUCCESS

Contemporaries such as Brougham thought that Garrow was not much interested in the law as such. On the other hand, it is evident from his cases and approach to prisoners that, to put it colloquially, he had the common touch. Unlike Erskine, who was also born in relatively poor circumstances but from the start was concerned with corruption and tyranny by authority,[13] Garrow was more at home in the cut and thrust of the courtroom or, more strictly, the criminal courtroom as he and others began to establish it as a working environment for defence lawyers.

Other barristers at the Old Bailey in the eighteenth century included John Silvester, an important figure both before and, for a while, during Garrow's time. He was, however, not as effective as Garrow and increasingly he appeared for the prosecution. According to May he, 'was a Tory more concerned with the maintenance of law and order than with the rights of prisoners.'[14] He was raised to the Bench at the Old Bailey as common serjeant from 1790 to 1803 and served as recorder of London from 1803 to 1822.[15]

Others included Richard Peatt, James Agar and William Fielding—the son of Henry Fielding, the novelist and Bow Street magistrate. In 1785 the *Morning Chronicle* claimed that, 'Mr Fielding and Mr Garrow may be said to have all the Old Bailey business in their own hands. At the late sessions it was clearly obvious, that the other gentlemen of the tie attended had very little opportunity of opening their mouths, except at dinner.'[16] It was not long, however, before Fielding and all the others were eclipsed by the rising Garrow. Farington thought that Garrow owed much to Fielding who, he said, was lazy and turned work over to him thus damaging his own career.[17]

Despite the fact that defence counsel were not frequently engaged before Garrow came upon the scene, nevertheless there had been some 40 years of advocacy experience before him and, in his own words, he had sat in on cases at the Old Bailey for eight years before being called to the Bar. This shows a keen and deep interest in criminal trials and it is reasonable to conjecture that he must have taken something from the style and techniques of his predecessors even though he projected a new combative style from the outset of his career. Moreover, whereas before the eighteenth century the judge dominated the court, by the end of the century Garrow had led the lawyers in capturing the courtroom and turning the judge into an umpire who was no longer a participant in the fray. His cross-examinations were usually lengthy and directed towards the jury. Judges seldom interrupted as Garrow gradually adopted a more sophisticated approach, developed his technique and, although not allowed to address the jurors directly, often managed to speak to them obliquely through his cross-examination of prosecution witnesses.

In his defence of Queen Caroline in 1820 Brougham was to say that the first quality of an advocate was 'to reckon everything subordinate to the interests of his client.'[18] He was rebuked by the Lord Chief Justice, Sir Alexander Cockburn, who said that the 'arms which counsel wields' were to be 'the arms of the warrior and not of the assassin.' He ought, he said, to know how to reconcile the interests of his client with the eternal interests of truth and justice.[19] Nevertheless, Cockburn was not as great and successful an advocate as Brougham having, the *Law Times* said, 'the passion for advocacy' that had 'carried him into the arena, with the pamphlet as his weapon.'[20]

Garrow was a perfect example of counsel following Brougham's dictum by doing everything possible in his power for his client and often this would have helped secure truth and justice. All these attributes will be illustrated in the extracts from trials cited in this and the next chapter. It is interesting that not only Brougham, but Garrow also, are featured in the large-scale oil painting entitled, 'The House of Lords 1820—The Trial of Queen Caroline' by Sir George Hayter which hangs in the National Portrait Gallery in London.[21]

Garrow's rise to become the star barrister at the Old Bailey in his time was clearly presaged in one of his earliest cases at the Old Bailey. It was the trial that first brought him to the attention of the public when he prosecuted John Henry

Aikles, who was charged with obtaining by false pretences a bill of exchange on 14 January 1784.[22] It was alleged that Aikles had feloniously stolen the bill valued at £100 from a Samuel Edwards the previous 31 December by promising to get it discounted but instead he had converted it to his own use. Clearly, trials were brought on far more quickly in the eighteenth century than in the Old Bailey today and, interestingly, as Aikles claimed to be a Hessian (a citizen of Hesse in Germany), a jury was sworn with one-half its members Hessians. Such a jury was called a *jury de mediate linguae* (of half-tongue) and was not unusual at the time.[23] As its existence suggested that, without such a device, the English legal system was prejudiced it was eventually abolished, but not until 1870.

In opening the case for the prosecution, Garrow immediately spoke with heavy irony to the jury of Aikles as 'one of those virtuous and benevolent men, who have discovered the secret of acquiring large fortunes, and of supporting elegant houses and superb equipages by acts of patent philanthropy, and the most enlarged benevolence.'[24] In order to please the judges in this early stage of his career, he went on to say that he would state the facts and the '[j]udges eminent for their learning and integrity' would determine the law resulting from them. Then, at the end of his opening speech, Garrow concluded by saying to the jury,

> I assure myself, that having heard those facts, if the directions of the Court shall warrant you to say, that under the law of the case the prisoner may be guilty of the crime imputed to him by the indictment, you will feel great pleasure that it has become your duty to diminish, by one at least, a nest of vermin, who have but too long infested this metropolis, to the utter ruin of some of the first families in the kingdom.

Clearly, there were no strict rules of etiquette at the Bar to restrain counsel at this time and even so early in his career Garrow had started, in attacking a party in the case, in a manner in which he intended to continue over the succeeding years and which brought him in a great deal of work, fame and wealth.[25] On that basis, on the facts of the case and, no doubt influenced by Garrow's unprovoked attack on the reputation of the prisoner, the jury found him guilty and he was sentenced to death.

In addressing the jury during the course of this trial Garrow set out the generally accepted relationship between the judge and the jury in criminal trials:

> Gentlemen, I shall now proceed to state the facts which I shall submit to you in evidence, which I shall do with some particularity, as it will be necessary for the Court to attend to them, and to determine on the law resulting from those facts. And, Gentlemen, I am very much relieved in stating to you my imperfect notions of the law of the case, by feeling that I do it in the hearing of Judges eminent for their learning and integrity, under whose correction it is impossible that I should lead you into error.[26]

For someone promoting the role of the unfettered advocate Garrow was being quite servile and this contrasts vividly with the more urbane Erskine who, in the celebrated case of the *Dean of St Asaph* who was charged with seditious libel, asserted that the jury should preserve their independence by judging the *intention* which was the essence of every crime. A man's motives he told the jury, 'only an English jury shall judge. It is therefore impossible, in most criminal cases, to separate law from fact; and consequently whether a writing be or be not a libel, *never can be an abstract legal question for judges.'*[27] [Italics added].

It is interesting that the conception of different roles for counsel was fluid at the period and, in another contrast with Erskine, Garrow first came to public attention in this case (Aikles) in which he was prosecuting. But he showed a clear understanding of the law of larceny, he was forthright in his assault on the character of the accused and he carefully drew in the jury. Whilst defence counsel were not allowed to address the jury, prosecuting counsel were, although usually only in opening their case. In this trial, however, Garrow went further and, after the evidence, said, 'my Lord, I should leave this case with the utmost pleasure to the Court, but that all arguments of this sort are addressed to the Jury, and are intended to have their operation there, it therefore becomes my duty to trouble your Lordship with a few words by way of reply.' It was a new and effective oblique approach to the jury which he was to continue to use throughout his career as an advocate.

A curious incident occurred some six years later when Garrow was addressing the jury in a case of alleged highway robbery. For some reason, although he was appearing for the prosecution, he explained the extent of defence counsel's role when he said, 'By the wisdom of the law it is denied to the [defence] advocate, on the part of his client, to make any address in his defence. All that is permitted to us who stand as counsel for prisoners is to endeavour, by such questions as may occur to us, to impress on the minds of the Jury observations tending to excite distrust of the evidence.[28]

INFANCY CASES

A century or so earlier, as reported by Sir Matthew Hale (1609-76), it was sometimes known for children as young as eight and ten to be executed if they were found guilty of felony.[29] In Garrow's time he could be found acting for a young boy named William Horton who, although only eleven years of age, was charged with simple grand larceny and faced transportation if found guilty.[30] It was alleged he had been a 'look-out' for two men who had stolen goods from a dwellinghouse but managed to escape from the watchman, leaving William to be caught. He was taken to Isaac Barney, a peace officer, who, Garrow alleged, frightened the boy. In court Garrow then questioned Barney about bounty:

Garrow: Do you know what reward there is for the conviction of this poor infant?
Barney: Upon my oath I do not know.
Garrow: Do you mean to say that you, a patrol, do not know?
Barney: I am sure it is a thing I never had.
Garrow: You shall not slip through my fingers so.
Barney: Upon my word and honour I do not know.
Garrow: Did you never hear there was a reward of 40 pounds upon the conviction of
    that child?
Barney: I never knew such thing.
Garrow: Come, come Sir, it is a fair question, and the Jury see you and hear you.
Barney: Your honour, I cannot say.
Garrow: But you shall say before you leave that place.
Barney: I have heard other people talking about such things.
Garrow: So I thought; and with that answer so given I leave your testimony with the
    Jury.

The judge raised no point about the alleged bounty but told the jury that the
law fixed no particular time for the age of discretion and told them that even eight-
year-olds had been found guilty of capital offences. Otherwise, he said, people of
full years would employ children to commit crimes of almost every description. If
they thought the child knew he was breaking the law they would find him guilty,
otherwise they would acquit him. Undoubtedly, Garrow's shameless, although
legitimate, cross-examination of Isaac Barney about a bounty that was not payable
for the alleged offence, would have influenced the jury and they found the boy not
guilty.[31]

In a trial in 1789 Peter Miller, a boy aged nine, was indicted for pick-pocketing
ten shillings in cash—a capital crime.[32] The victim was a poor man living in a
workhouse and the evidence against the boy was strong but Garrow persisted, in
front of the jury, in asking the victim if he had not been told that if the boy was
convicted he would lose his life. He also drew out from the victim that he had heard
there was a reward of £40 if the boy was convicted. Finally, Garrow asked the
victim if his memory was affected by his poverty and if his head was affected. To
the latter he replied, 'It is a good deal.' In face of the evidence the jury could hardly
acquit the accused but they did find him guilty of stealing only ten pence for which
he was ordered to be whipped.

At what age a child could be a witness was a matter for the court. In a capital
trial in April 1787 one witness, aged nine, was not allowed to give evidence whilst
her sister, aged eleven, was. The reason was not age but the first girl told Garrow
that she did not know the consequences of swearing falsely whereas her sister said
that she knew that if she did not tell the truth she would go to hell.[33]

POINTS OF LAW

Garrow was criticized by some of his fellow-lawyers, including Campbell and
Brougham, for having only slight knowledge of the finer points of the law (and,

indeed, of learning generally). Campbell said that Garrow was wholly uneducated and Brougham, for his part wrote of Garrow that, 'There have probably been few more ignorant men in the profession than this celebrated leader. To law, or anything like law he made no pretence.'[34] William Cockburn, too, observed to Robert Peel, 'Garrow was never thought a lawyer. He is a quick, sharp clever fellow — but no profound thinker and never read anything of law. I have had occasion to consult him some times but never found his opinion right in my life on the whole.'[35]

According to Foss, Garrow did not pretend otherwise and, 'he made no pretensions, but modestly acknowledged and freely relied on the superiority of his colleagues.' Moreover, Foss added, 'the best technical lawyers are not always the best advocates. '[36] In any event, in some of Garrow's cases he will be seen to argue points of law both forcefully and accurately. Equally important is the fact that he was able to speak to the jury by means of comments to the judge on points of law.[37]

As an example there is the case of William Tatum who on 11 May 1785 was charged with simple grand larceny.[38] The prisoner had shortly before been employed as a clerk by Garrow but was in ill health and when he needed medicines he often pawned some of his landlord's property and redeemed it later. On pawning articles belonging to his landlord on this occasion he was charged with theft.

Garrow told the judge that it was more important to the prisoner that his character should be cleared than that he should be barely acquitted. He referred to an Act of 13 Geo. II, c. 24. which provided a specific penalty for persons who pawned the goods of others without the consent of the proprietor, as had happened in this case. Since the Act provided a penalty of 20 shillings it was clear, he said, that the prisoner's act was not to be considered a felony [for which the penalty was death or transportation] and, in point of law, he could not be convicted on the wording of the indictment that he had feloniously stolen, i.e. with intent to retain the goods.

The judge thought the question a difficult one and that it was almost impossible to reconcile the law. He continued,

> [w]here things are taken with a felonious intention, and afterwards pawned, then the circumstance of pawning does not make the act less penal, it remains a felony … but where there is no offence but that of pawning without the consent of the owner, with an intention of restoring the property

the offence must be within the statute. Therefore, he said, he would leave it to the jury to decide whether the prisoner intended to steal the things and convert them to his own use, in which case it would be a felony. If not, it would not be a felony under the statute since 'all Acts of Parliament inflicting lesser penalties, repeal greater ones.' The jury acquitted the prisoner.[39]

Immediately afterwards Tatum was brought back to the dock on another charge of simple grand larceny.[40] This time it was alleged that he had stolen and pawned 18 books owned by an earlier landlord. In cross-examining witnesses Garrow played on the prisoner's ill health but in this case he was found guilty of stealing. The judge spoke of his previous good conduct and also referred to the sympathy shown to him by the witnesses in the case. He said that in point of justice he should be transported but could not be in his present condition and confinement in prison would be fatal to his health. Therefore, 'I will order you to be burnt in the hand for this offence.' Although 'a certain disease' was mentioned by one witness and another stated that the prisoner had difficulty in walking it was not made clear, at least in the sessions' report, from what the prisoner was suffering[41].

In another case, six weeks later, James Boston, was tried at the Old Bailey on 6 April 1785 for burglary in breaking and entering a dwellinghouse owned by a James Danvers.[42] The facts of the case were curious in that Danvers virtually incited the crime by arranging for his maid to invite the prisoner into the house, whilst he lay watching from a neighbouring dwelling, to see if the prisoner would take a quantity of calico left in a cellar there. After a good deal of evidence, and the judge had accepted that burglary had not been made out as there was no breaking into the house, Garrow addressed the judge as follows:

> My Lord, I have a few observations to offer, by when I trust to convince your Lordship that there has been no felony committed by this prisoner. As to the burglary; your Lordship has delivered me from that, and the crime must be therefore that of larceny. The books lay down this principle, that it must be a fraudulent or felonious taking and carrying away by any person of the goods of another; when they say that there shall be a fraudulent or felonious taking, it is to be observed, that all felony includes a trespass: if the party be guilty of no trespass in taking the goods, he cannot be guilty of a felony in carrying them away. I take the liberty in order to apply the law to this case, shortly to state the law. This man does not against the will of the proprietor break into the premises, he does not commit any trespass whatever; but by the express direction and permission, and by the planning of the prosecutor, he has compleat dominion of the goods.
>
> I am disposed in this part of the case, to admit, without risk, that the Jury must find that he carried away the indigo; but if I have laid down the principle of the law right, the felony cannot have been committed. Has there been a trespass? How has that trespass been committed? This prosecutor planning in this manner with this woman, has acted a very strange part, to say no more of it: they watch him, they do not apprise him, they do not tell him he shall be hanged, but they suffer him to compleat the offence by carrying away the goods.

Garrow then drew the attention of the court to a similar case decided by all the judges, where a man named Salmon had agreed to be robbed by accomplices in order to claim a reward. This he argued should be accepted in effect as a precedent:

Now how in God's name, and the name of common sense [he asked] does this differ from Mr Danvers's case? … Can you say that there was a felonious taking against the will of the proprietor, he not only assenting to it, but ordering the man to be let in?[43]

After considering the submission the judge said he had looked at the case mentioned by Garrow and would leave it to the jury whether upon the evidence they believed the calico was taken by the will of Mr Danvers or not. It did not appear, he said, that Danvers had any distinct knowledge of what was to be committed but waited to see and as to that extent there remained a degree of uncertainty he thought it fit it should go to the jury. He made no mention of Garrow's point about trespass but, in any event, the jury found the prisoner not guilty.[44]

THIEF-TAKERS

Parliamentary rewards, known as bounties, were frequently claimed by persons alleging others had committed crimes[45] among which were robbery, housebreaking, larceny of goods valued at five shillings or more, burglary and coining. Sums ranging from £10 to £40 were payable if the accused were found guilty and the people claiming them were called 'thief-takers' or 'bounty hunters.' As the crimes involved were all capital the rewards were often referred to as 'blood money'.[46] Such people were generally unpopular since they were often considered to be sending innocent people to the gallows out of personal spite or for personal gain. Not surprisingly, Garrow disliked them intensely and his cross-examination, and even baiting, of many of them fuelled the development of his combative style. Of course, although he despised bounty-hunters Garrow was primarily interested in winning cases and earning his fees and not in changing the face of English criminal procedure but in the end that is what he did so much to achieve with this type of trial.

A bounty case in which Garrow was early involved for the defence was the trial of Robert Mitchell for highway robbery in 1784.[47] The prosecutor was a Simon Sheppard from whom in cross-examination Garrow obtained an admission that twice before he had prosecuted for robbery, and had secured a conviction in one of the cases. In this present trial Sheppard claimed Mitchell and two others had attacked him with a knife and stolen money from him. Garrow rose to establish the defence by cross-examination:

Garrow: Here my old friend, a word with you; so they beat you for half an hour?
Sheppard: They beat me like a dog.
Garrow: Was it with a knife that they beat you?
Sheppard: No, with their fists, and kicked me with his foot, he knocked out my teeth with the toe of his shoe; one tooth, Sir.
Garrow: What sort of knife had he?
Sheppard: A long snig-a-snee knife, a spring knife.

Garrow: He took it out deliberately, and opened it before all the people?

Sheppard: Not before all the people, but before the people in the yard.

Garrow: How often have you had the misfortune to be robbed in your life?

Sheppard: Four or five times.

Garrow: So I thought: how often have you been a witness here of robberies on your own person?

Sheppard: Two times.

Garrow: How many of the people you have prosecuted have died in Newgate?

Sheppard: Only one.

Garrow: Upon an average, how many prosecutions had you in the course of the last two years?

Sheppard: One before this.

Garrow: They have been both within the year?

Sheppard: Yes.

Garrow: Did you convict the last man?

Sheppard: Yes.

Garrow: What did you get for it?

Sheppard: I cannot tell, I got nothing at all.

Garrow: Upon your oath, Sir, what did you get, do not you remember what was added to the stock of 60 you had before?

Sheppard: Please you, my Lord, only my expenses.

Garrow: Do you mean to swear you had no more allowed you but your expenses?

Sheppard: Lucas is dead.

Garrow: Then you will not get above 40 if you convict now, my old friend, you will not get 80 this time?

Sheppard: No.

Garrow's withering attacks on the prosecutor achieved what he wanted and the jury speedily found the prisoner not guilty.

In a case on 12 January 1785 Garrow questioned thief-takers who gave evidence about what his clients were alleged to have said when they were arrested. The trial was of three men, George Norris, Thomas Freeman and William Johnson, charged with housebreaking and theft, and a fourth man, William Terry Fenley, charged with receiving stolen goods.[48]

One of the witnesses was Joseph Levy, a barber who claimed that Norris had confessed the crime to him as they went to the magistrate's office for a preliminary examination. Garrow set out to destroy his credibility in the eyes of the jury.

Garrow: You are the man they call the Barber?

Levy: Yes.

Garrow: Your other name is Cockey Barber is not it?

Levy: Yes.

Garrow: I want to know your flash name in short?

Levy: Joe Barber.

Garrow: Had you not said, that if he would not tell the whole story, Norris and Freeman would weigh their weight, they would weigh 80 pounds?

Levy: No.

Garrow: Had you intimated to him, that unless he told the whole story, you would hang him?

Levy: No.

Garrow: Now, Master Levy, otherwise Joe the Barber, how long have you been engaged in this honourable business of thief-taking?

Levy: I cannot rightly tell.

Garrow: Now guess a little, ever since you was convicted and pardoned, ha! Speak man; how long have you been a thief-taker?

Levy: Longer than you have been a Counsellor.

Garrow: I know that, because during the eight years I attended as student, I remember you?

Levy: Very likely; I do not attend any office now.

Garrow: How many trials did you appear upon last Sessions?

Levy: Never a one, only one.

Garrow: What, there was no blood money last Sessions?

Levy: If there were no thieves, how would you get a brief?

A nice exchange, illustrating the commercialization of justice in the eighteenth century. Garrow was attacking such commercialization whilst benefiting from it himself as the witness was quick to point out. As Vogler has said, 'the 'lawyerization' of the trial was in many respects an opening of the feudal court hierarchy to the market and in that sense just as much a 'commercialization'.'[49] As for the verdict, after being addressed by the judge on the law relating to housebreaking, the jury found all four of the accused not guilty.

Another bounty case in which Garrow was involved was the trial of John M'Carty and Thomas Hartman for highway robbery on 12 December 1787[50] when, after the victim denied knowledge of any bounty, Garrow repetitively pressured him with 24 questions on the point. In the event the accused were found guilty of stealing but not violently and were sentenced to be transported for seven years.[51] This was presumably the result Garrow desired as there was evidence that the prisoners took the watch and if the offence had been violent they would have been sentenced to death.

Thomas Gibbs was charged with highway robbery on 10 December 1788.[52] When a prosecution witness, John Morgan, was asked by Garrow what reward he was to have he replied that he had heard nothing about a reward. Garrow persisted, saying a reward of £40 had been mentioned. Morgan said he thought there was a £40 penalty if he did not appear. Garrow would not give up, however, and eventually Morgan admitted that he had heard of the reward and had, of course, lied to Garrow. So strong was the feeling against bounty hunters that, although the case against the prisoner was compelling, the jury found him not guilty.

Although Garrow's forays against thief-takers were clearly a serious matter, *The Times* turned his very success against them into a subject for parody. The following is an extract from the newspaper of 16 March 1790:

A set down. — I say to you once again, *Feller,* (says *Garrow,*) — at the Old Bailey — my honest friend, — are not you a *Thief Taker?* — 'Vell, vat if I am,' said honest *Nob,* nattily enough — 'an't you a Thief's Counsel — so there's *tit* for *tat.'*

Yet, in fact, as is clear from extracts in this book, the humorist has come quite close to the truth as it occurred in some trials. Nonetheless, the point is that, with the desire to secure a conviction and win the bounty, thief-taking, as part of a trade in human beings, encouraged perjury and could result in innocent men and women going to the gallows. As a consequence, more and more prisoners turned to counsel to conduct their defence whilst the judges interfered less and less. It was in tackling this serious problem in the criminal justice system that defence lawyers were instrumental in bedding down the adversary system of trial.

BENEFIT OF CLERGY

A curious case occurred in 1785 when two men and a woman were indicted for feloniously coining a farthing.[53] They were James Scott, Thomas Pickering and Susannah Johnson. The illegal making of coins outside the Royal Mint was, of course, a serious crime. It was a skill in many working class districts of London and had become so simple it required only two people working together behind securely barred doors.[54] In this case, Crown witnesses for the prosecution swore that they entered a locked cellar in the premises of the accused and found them working with a press, a die set, a quantity of blanks and several farthings. Both men, whose hands were dirty from coining, admitted the offence and were found guilty but they insisted that the woman, whose hands were clean, was innocent and she was acquitted by the jury. The prisoner Scott claimed he was entitled to be awarded benefit of clergy and be released.

After sentence, counsel for the prosecution claimed that since the prisoners had once before been convicted for a similar offence and received the benefit of clergy they should be sentenced to death. The judge, the recorder of London, told Scott that by law a person could not claim benefit of clergy twice and the prosecution were claiming that he had been allowed it on a former occasion. 'You have a right,' he said, 'to deny that fact.' At this point Garrow intervened and suggested to Scott, 'I recommend it to you to deny that there is any such record, and that if there is, you are not the person.' The prisoner immediately declared that he was not the man. The jury were recalled and Garrow pointed to deficiencies and omissions in the Indictment. The judge then treated the jury to a lengthy statement on the origins of the benefit of clergy and repeated that it could not be claimed more than once. The jury found against the prisoners and the judge passed sentence of death which, at Garrow's request, he postponed.

Subsequently Garrow raised another point of law in regard to Pickering to the effect that the Indictment was not correct. The judge accepted Garrow's point and told the jury to find in favour of the prisoner, which they did. The judge told him, however, that he had the good fortune to escape the danger, under which his companions still laboured, by which he would have forfeited his life 'with great justice' by a mere mistake in point of law 'which I am bound to allow you.' Despite the jury's verdict he had directed he then sentenced him to be fined one shilling and imprisoned for 12 months in Newgate prison.

CROSS-EXAMINATION

Another example of Garrow's remarkable skill in cross-examination is shown in the trial of George Stevens and James Day in December 1786 charged with burglary.[55] He was questioning prosecution witness Elizabeth Mason, who had turned King's evidence after being held in custody for several days, about receiving stolen goods from the prisoners.

Garrow: You deal wonderfully in alias's, how many names have you besides Mason?
Mason: No more.
Garrow: Have you always told the same story?
Mason: I have.
Garrow: That you swear positively?
Mason: Yes.
Garrow: And that is as true as anything else you have been saying?
Mason: Yes.
Garrow: I believe they were wicked enough, these officers that disturbed you, to take you to the Justice's?
Mason: They took me there; I told the Justice as near as I could.
Garrow: Then you was examined the second time, and you told him the same story?
Mason: Yes.
Garrow: Now upon your oath, the first and second time did not you say that Stevens knew nothing of the matter?
Mason: I said no such thing; I never swore any such thing neither on the first or second examination.
Garrow: You know Mr Lucy?
Mason: Yes.
Lucy: She said, if Stevens did not bring them there, she did not know how they came?
Mason: I did not say that; I did not know Stevens; I said, that the first time that Stevens was in my house, I did not know that he brought the property.
Garrow: They did bring it?
Mason: I told the Justice that at the first examination.
Court: I shall lay every word that she says out of the case.

As Landsman says of this case,

the effectiveness of the examination in serving a variety of goals is apparent. It forcefully attacked the witness's credibility. It also drove her into an ever tighter corner with respect to her prior statements. It used impeaching materials to the most telling effect. Finally, it welded all this together into an interrogation that cried out for the exclusion of her testimony.[56]

Although Stevens was found guilty and sentenced to seven years' transportation, Day was acquitted.

What we miss from the reports, of course, are the rhythms of Garrow's speech and his tone and gestures, but we do get a good impression of his aggressive behaviour. As his obituary in *The Law Review* put it, '[i]n the courtroom he was quick, nimble, bold, skillful; he seemed now and then to destroy, almost to annihilate, an adverse witness ... he could not resist the temptation of making a great impression on the jury and on bystanders.'[57] Clearly, he was something of an actor and Campbell recalled, 'the effect of a most beautiful voice which no one could hear and not listen to irrespective of the sentiments it conveyed.'[58]

DISPUTE WITH THE BENCH

In defence of his clients, and pressing forward the role of counsel for the defence, Garrow was also prepared to do battle with the Bench. In the case of William Bartlett, charged with theft on 11 January 1786, he objected to a prosecution witness, John Rasten, being sworn. He argued that as Rasten was deaf and dumb he could testify only through an interpreter, his wife, to whom Garrow also objected.[59] Mrs Rasten claimed to be a satisfactory interpreter because, she said, she would look up to heaven to show her husband that he should answer seriously. The dispute between counsel and Mr Justice Heath then arose.

Garrow quoted from Sir Matthew Hale that a deaf mute was presumed to be an idiot and could not communicate with the court. The judge said he remembered a deaf and dumb man being sworn in the court of common pleas and he accepted that sign language was sufficient, although Garrow continued to disagree. This led to the following exchange:

Heath: You must not interrupt; your objection is premature.

Garrow: My Lord I was not objecting. I was going on with my Examination and your Lordship did me the honour to interrupt me.

Heath: You will examine your Witness with some degree of decency. Your conduct and behaviour are very improper. What you do here is by permission of the Court in a Criminal Case.

Garrow: My Lord, I object to the Witness being examined and I take the liberty to state my objection to the Court.

Heath: You must examine your Witness.

Garrow: I have a right to my Objection.

Heath: If you do not examine your Witness you shall sit down.

Garrow: My Lord, I shall not sit down.

Heath: Then I shall commit you.

Garrow: So your Lordship may.

Heath: Then I certainly will commit you.

Garrow: There is a point of Law to be argued.
Heath: There is no point of Law and if there was you are to be Assigned to the Court
  but you are to behave with Decency.
Garrow: So I do my Lord. I have not been used to be interrupted. I am here to argue
  points of Law for the prisoner.
Heath: You have no right until you are Assigned.[60]
Garrow: If you tell me so my Lord, I sit down.
Heath: I tell you so.
Garrow: I sit down.

Later, Garrow made a long speech to the judge in the hearing of the jury. He pointed out that even if the witness and the interpreter could converse that did not prove the witness was capable of understanding complex ideas, particularly the principles of the Christian religion that underlay the binding power of the oath. He then added, 'My Lord, I wish I could also address the jury on this trial. I should be glad to ask them whether they should choose to convict a man of felony upon the testimony of a man with whom they could not hold a conversation'. Bearing in mind the presence of the jury, he concluded with an apology for what might have been considered his earlier 'intemperance or indecency', adding that by his zeal on behalf of his client he had intended no disrespect to the 'great and brave and venerable and learned judges of the law of England'. In the event, on the evidence of the witness, Bartlett was convicted and transported for seven years.

So that even at that time the earlier discretion of the court in allowing counsel limited assistance to defendants was recalled by the judge although by now the lawyers had more or less captured the courtroom and the process could not be reversed. In the words of Langbein,

> The judges of the 1730s who turned common law criminal procedure down this path had no way of knowing that defence counsel would overcome the limitations that the judges placed upon him, indeed, that defence counsel would recast the dynamic of the criminal trial so fundamentally that the judges would ultimately cede mastery of the criminal trial to counsel.[61]

Furthermore, not only did defence counsel recast the dynamic of the criminal trial; in doing so they also had a positive impact on the outcome for prisoners.

CONCLUSION

In the eighteenth century the Old Bailey was the assize court for London and Middlesex. Not surprisingly, the court for the metropolitan capital attracted more trials—and sat more often—than other assize courts and it was to a large extent there that the drive towards adversary trial occurred. As we have seen, the number of cases in which prisoners were represented by counsel rose from 0.5 per cent in 1740 to 36.6 per cent in 1795. Although, of course, the procedural changes were taking place in other assize courts as well it is the records of the Old Bailey trials that are so outstanding and so instructive. Some 100,621 cases are recorded and, although the trials are not always fully reported, they remain arguably the most extensive record of criminal trials of the time anywhere in the world.

As cases cited here indicate, Garrow's success at the Old Bailey came early in his career, and from the start, he revealed his self-confident, aggressive, and often ironic, style when dealing with prosecution witnesses. He also showed an understanding of the law, which was often denied by his contemporaries, and a willingness to stand up to the judges when he thought it necessary. Over the years he was a major influence in turning cross-examination into an art form and a vital component in adversary procedure which itself changed the thrust of the criminal trial. Without counsel such as Garrow it is not clear that adversary trial would have come into being although it is likely that, as Langbein suggests, the English would not have turned to the inquisitorial system at the time because of its use of torture.[62] Be that as it may, in the extracts in this chapter from criminal trials at the Old Bailey we can see Garrow exerting his new powers so that defence counsel became the dominant force in the courtroom.

ENDNOTES for *Chapter 6*

[1] J. F. Stephen. (1883) *A History of the Criminal Law of England.* London, Macmillan. vol. ii. p. 431.

[2] J.M. Beattie. (1977) 'Crime and Courts in Surrey 1736-53.' In J.S. Cockburn (ed.) *Crime in England 1550-1800.* London, Methuen & Co. Ltd.

[3] P. King. (2000) *Crime, Justice and Discretion in England 1736-1753.* Oxford, Oxford University Press.

[4] Old Bailey Proceedings Online.

[5] R. Vogler. (2005) *A World View of Criminal Justice.* Aldershot, Ashgate Publishing. p. 137.

[6] L. Pickard. (2005) *Victorian London: The Life of a City 1840-1870.* London, Weidenfeld & Nicolson. p. 61. Citing G. Doré and B. Jerrold, (1872) *Dorés London,* Dover, Charles.

[7] P. King. *Crime, Justice and Discretion in England.* Op. cit.

[8] A.N. May. (2003) *The Bar and the Old Bailey, 1750-1850.* Chapel Hill, *University of North Carolina Press.* p. 14.

[9] Ibid. p. 147.

[10] J.M. Beattie. (1988) 'London Juries in the 1690s'. In Cockburn and Green (eds) *Twelve Good Men and True: The Criminal Trial Jury in England, 1200-1800.* New Jersey, Princeton University Press. p. 218-9.

[11] Ibid. p. 221.

[12] J. H. Langbein. (2003) *The Origins of Adversary Criminal Trial.* Oxford, Oxford University Press. p. 21.

[13] See his first case, *R. v. Baillie* [1778] 21 *State Trials.* p. 1.

[14] A.N. May. *The Bar and the Old Bailey.* Op. cit. p. 39.

[15] Ibid. p. 36.

[16] Ibid. p. 43. note. 55.

[17] J. Farington. (1807) *Diary.* (ed. Kathryn Cave, 1982) New Haven, Yale University Press. vol. 8. p. 2956.

[18] Lord Brougham. (8 November 1864) Speech in Middle Temple Hall. *The Times,* 9 November 1864.

[19] J. Hostettler. (1992) *The Politics of Criminal Law: Reform in the Nineteenth Century.* Chichester, Barry Rose Law Publishers. p. 35.

[20] 70 *Law Times.* (27 November 1880) p. 56-7.

[21] Other paintings including Garrow which are owned by the Gallery are, 'Evidence to Character' by James Gillray and a Group including John Scott 1st Earl of Eldon by Sir George Hayter. There is also a well-known cartoon by Rowlandson entitled, 'Being Nervous and Cross-examined by Mr Garrow.'

22 OBP Online. (www.oldbaileyonline.org, 24 October 2004) 14 January 1784, trial of John Henry Aikles. Ref: t17840114-80.

23 P. Darbyshire and Others. (2001) 'What Can the English Legal System Learn from Jury Research up to 2001?' http//www.kingston.ac.uk/~ku00596.elsres01.pdf

24 OBP Online. (www.oldbaileyonline.org. 11 June 2005) . 14 January 1784. Trial of John Henry Aikles. Ref: t17840114-80.

25 G.F.R. Barker. (1975) *Dictionary of National Biography*. Oxford, Oxford University Press.

26 OBP. 14 January 1784. Trial of John Henry Aikles. Ref: t17840114-80.

27 Lord J. Campbell. (1847) *Lives of the Lord Chancellors*. London, John Murray. vol. vi. p. 430.

28 OBP Online. (www.oldbaileyonline.org, 5 December 2004) 8 December 1790 Trial of George Platt and Philip Roberts for Highway Robbery. Ref: t17901208-35.

29 Sir M. Hale. (1736) *The History of the Pleas of the Crown*. London, E & R Nutt and R. Gosling. vol. i. chap. 2.

30 OBP Online. (www.oldbaileyonline.org, 27 October 2004) 7 July 1784. Trial of William Horton. Ref: t17840707-77.

31 Ibid.

32 OBP Online. (www.oldbaileyonline.org, 15 April 2005) 22 April 1789 Trial of Peter Miller. Ref: t17890422-92.

33 OBP Online. (www.oldbaileyonline.org, 18 March 2005) 18 April 1787 Trial of Hannah Pleasant Jones for Highway Robbery. Ref: t1787318-19.

34 Lord Brougham. 'Memoir of Mr Baron Garrow.' (1844-5) 1 *Law Review*. p. 319.

35 Ibid.

36 E. Foss. (1864) *The Judges of England, with Sketches of their Lives and Miscellaneous Notices connected with the Courts at Westminster from the time of the Conquest*. London, John Murray. vol. 9. p. 87.

37 J.M. Beattie. 'Scales of Justice: Defense Counsel and the English Criminal Trial in the Eighteenth and Nineteenth Centuries.' Op. cit. p. 233.

38 OBP Online. (www.oldbaileyonline.org, 6 December 2004) 11 May 1785 Trial of William Tatum. Ref: t17850511-17

39 Ibid.

40 OBP Online. (www.oldbaileyonline.org, 6 December 2004) 11 May 1785 Second trial of William Tatum. Ref: t17850511-18.

41 Ibid.

42 OBP Online. (www.oldbaileyonline.org, 23October 2004) 6 April 1785 Trial of James Boston. Ref: t17850406-70.

43 Ibid.

44 Ibid.

45 See ante for the relevant statutes. p. 51.

46 L. Radzinowicz. (1956) *A History of English Criminal Law and its Administration from 1750*. London, Stevens & Sons Ltd. vol. ii. p. 57.

47 OBP Online. (www.oldbaileyonline.org. 1 February 2006) 8 December 1784. Trial of Robert Mitchell. Ref: t17841208-181.

48 OBP Online. (www.oldbaileyonline.org, 28 October 2004) 12 January 1785 Trial of George Norris, Thomas Freeman and William Johnson. Ref: t17850112-20.

49 R.Vogler. *A World View of Criminal Justice. Op. cit*. p. 144.

50 OBP Online.(www.oldbaileyonline.org, 28 October 2004) 12 December 1787 Trial of John M'Carty and Thomas Hartman. Ref: t17871212-24.

51 Ibid.

52 OBP Online. (www.oldbaileyonline.org, 30 March 2005) 10 December 1788 Trial of Thomas Gibbs. Ref: t17881210-44.

53 OBP Online. (www.oldbaileyonline.org, 31 January 2005) 19 October 1785. Trial of James Scott, Thomas Pickering and Susannah Johnson. Ref: t17851019-45.

54 D. Thomas. (1999) *The Victorian Underworld*. London, John Murray. p. 56.

55 OBP Online. (www.oldbaileyonline.org, 1 December 2004) 13 December 1786. Trial of George Stevens and James Day. Ref: t17861213-112.

56 S. Landsman. (1990) 'The Rise of the Contentious Spirit: Adversary Procedure in Eighteenth Cenutry England' New York. 75 *Cornell Law Review*. p.552.

57 1 *The Law Review*. (1844) pp. 318-28.

58 M. S. Hardcastle. (1881) *Life of Lord John Campbell, Lord High Chancellor of Great Britain consisting of a Selection from his Autobiography, Diary and Letters.* p. 198. London, Murray.

59 OBP Online. (www.oldbaileyonline.org, 7 December 2004) 11 January 1786 Trial of William Bartlett. Ref: t1786111-30. The exchange between Garrow and the judge is not reported fully in this Old Bailey Proceeding but is quoted by Beattie from the Sessions Papers at Harvard University at pp. 247-8. Beattie. 'Scales of Justice.' Op. cit. pp. 264-5. note 66. Beattie claims that the absence of this material is a reminder of how limited the Old Bailey Papers are as a source for the history of trial. However, there is supplemental material in the Old Bailey Proceedings under ref: 017860111-1 which Beattie does not mention which includes the whole of the altercation between Garrow and the judge as well as Garrow's motion to the judge.

60 Prior to the Prisoners' Counsel Act 1836, defence counsel were not instructed by the prisoner to argue points of law but were assigned by the court, even if not requested by the prisoner. The point of law could be raised by the prisoner, the judge or *any* Barrister present in court. D. J.A. Cairns. (1998) *Advocacy and the Making of the Adversarial Criminal Trial 1800-1865.* Oxford, The Clarendon Press. pp. 46-7.

61 J.H. Langbein. *The Origins of Adversary Criminal Trial.* Op. cit. p. 177.

62 Ibid. p. 339.

CHAPTER 7

Garrow at the Old Bailey (2)

INTRODUCTION

This chapter continues with examples of the new aggressive style Garrow brought to criminal trials at the Old Bailey once defence counsel were permitted to cross-examine prosecution witnesses. It also illustrates the law relating to Indictments and how the continuation of their strict interpretation could be used to advantage by defence counsel even though they were withheld from the defence until the last minute. Garrow's skills in prosecuting are outlined in some of the striking and significant trials in which he appeared for the defence. Jury nullification and 'pious perjury' are examined as is Garrow's compassion in his occasional work without fee. Part of Garrow's success and fearsome reputation lay in the advocacy of his clients' rights and the fact that his devastating cross-examination often exposed prosecutors as liars and perjurers whom juries refused to believe. Occasionally, he might go too far and be admonished by the judge or criticized by the jury but this was rare and his success with juries was phenomenal. He was also prepared to do battle with judges, and the case of William Bartlett in which he faced down Mr Justice Heath even at the risk of being committed for contempt is a classic example.[1]

In addition to his acting for the Crown in sedition trials, from time to time Garrow acted for the prosecution at the Old Bailey and some examples are given in this chapter. Even then, if he thought the prosecution might produce injustice he was prepared to indicate so and his aggressive style of cross-examination rarely extended to defence witnesses. Cairns claims that the late eighteenth century criminal trial in England was not adversarial,[2] but all these trials are clear examples of adversariality in practice and form part of the remarkable welding together of adversary trial and evidential rules at that time.

AGGRESSION

We have seen that Garrow could be rude to witnesses but in the main he was endeavouring to expose those who were intent on lying and, of course, this went beyond thief-takers. In one case, on 26 May 1784, four months after the Aikles case and when he was still new at the Bar, he defended James Wingrove on a charge of theft with violence in the course of highway robbery.[3] In cross-examining the prosecutor, William Grove, with a series of hostile questions Garrow got him to change his story about the two men whom he alleged had apprehended Wingrove. Grove had testified that they too had been robbed but under merciless and lengthy questioning by Garrow he admitted that they were smugglers and had made no claim to having been robbed when taken before the examining justice the morning after the robbery. Here are some examples of Garrow's style:

Garrow: Who were these two men, let us hear a little about them?

Grove: They are not here, they live at Sunbury, one is Humphries and the other Marchant.

Garrow: What business are they, are they not a sort of moonlight men?

Grove: It was not moonlight.

Garrow: Are they not a couple of smugglers?

Grove: They may be as far as I know.

Garrow: So they told you they had been robbed?

Grove: Yes.

Garrow: Did they give any charge against Mr Wingrove?

Grove: I do not know what you mean by charges.

Garrow: I believe you do, you are pretty well used to charges; did these two smugglers of yours give any charge against this prisoner?

Grove: They are no smugglers of mine.

Garrow: They are friends of yours?

Grove: They are no friends of mine.

Garrow: They, these two fellows, did they make any charge against Mr Wingrove for robbing them?

Grove: Yes, they did make a charge.

Garrow: Do not shuffle, Master Grove.

Grove: I do not know what you say.

Garrow: I will make you know directly; upon your oath, did not these two men attend the next day at Mr Taylor's and say that Mr Wingrove was not one of the men who robbed them?

Grove: He is the man that robbed me, I will tell you the truth, he was the man that robbed me, I did not hear them say that he was not the man.

Garrow: That they swore?

Grove: Yes.

Garrow: Was he committed for robbing them?

Grove: No, he was committed for robbing me.

Garrow: Who were the two men that robbed you a little while ago?

Grove: I never was robbed before.

Garrow: No, Mr Grove!

Grove: Yes, I have been robbed, but I do not know who they were, and pilfered and too much robbed.

Garrow: I will put it now most unequivocally to you, and ask you upon your oath, whether you have never said to Mr James Clarke by name, that you had been robbed some time since by two men, whom you have not prosecuted, who lived at Brentford; that they were good friends, and that if you called on them at any time, you could have a guinea of them?

Grove: No, never in my life; no, no, they mistook, they came to me and wanted me not—

At this point Grove was interrupted and in the end he capitulated and admitted that the two men had not made a charge. Eventually, Garrow came to the question of the statutory reward for the conviction of a highwayman, and Groves' identification of Wingrove as the man who had robbed him.

> **Garrow:** You know it is not every day that one gets 40 pounds for hanging a man; had you no conversation at 'The Cock' at Stains about the reward for conviction?
> **Grove:** You ask 100 questions, I will answer you what I know; no, not about no reward, I have been there, and there they have been asking me about it, that is, we drank together, and I said to him, as I might say to you, I do not know anything about it. I did not say any such thing. I never said anything about any reward, that I can say. I have said nothing about no reward.

As Garrow could not address the jury, Wingrove (unusually when counsel was appearing) made his own defence and, more normally, called a number of witnesses to speak of his good character. The jury found him not guilty and Garrow applied to have Grove committed for perjury. He suggested that he would prosecute him at his own expense but Wingrove would not bring such a charge. It appears likely that the Groves (father and son) prosecuted Wingrove to obtain the reward; indeed the judge told them that they had rashly charged a man where there was a reward. Not surprisingly, when thief-takers prosecuted maliciously for this purpose Garrow always cross-examined them at length and with vigour to reveal their true natures to the jury.

In a case in 1788[4] the prosecutor, James Lyons, under repeated questioning by Garrow persisted in denying that he had heard statements made to the judge by Garrow in a previous hearing. On one such denial Garrow exclaimed, 'Oh, mighty good, mighty good. Will you dare to swear you did not hear me state that distinctly to the Recorder of London, who now sits as Judge. Were not you standing here, within three feet of me?' This time the witness could not remember. Eventually Garrow exploded. 'Will you dare deny it?' he shouted twice at the witness who continued to do so. Garrow then threatened him saying, 'Why it is in the memory of every man that hears me now; deny it if you dare, and I will indict you at the next sessions.' Upon an intervention by the judge Lyons made a partial admission and not surprisingly the jury found the accused not guilty.

Garrow is seen in unrelenting form in a case in February 1790 when defending John Jones and Thomas Wix on a charge of highway robbery.[5] The prosecutor was Sarah Sneezby who testified that the prisoners had attacked her on Blackfriars Bridge and stolen her money. In cross-examination Garrow told her that he knew more of her history than she was aware of and on her saying she was unable to answer a question he threatened that if she did not do so she would spend the night in Newgate prison. Suggesting that the prisoners had taken her for a whore he sarcastically attacked her reputation in saying, 'So these people treated you as if you was not the virtuous creature you are, but as a woman of the town?' He also suggested she had been engaged in a pub crawl and was seen drinking with a man not her husband. After this character assassination it is not surprising that the prisoners were both acquitted.

On 24 April 1790 Garrow's aggression led to strong support from the judge in a case of highway robbery.[6] The alleged victim, John Phillips, was giving evidence and Garrow cross-examined him about his knowledge that there was a reward if the prisoners were convicted and whether he had been drunk at the time of the alleged robbery. Asking him about his employment, Garrow said, 'What did you deal in, moon-shine and tobacco?' followed by, 'You was a smuggler?' The witness replied, 'No; I was employed by a man.' 'What trafficking, upon your oath?' demanded Garrow which reduced Phillips to admitting, 'In smuggling, if I must tell you.' Upon this the judge, Mr Justice Hotham, told the jury:

> Gemtlemen, it is one of the great blessings of the constitution of this country, that no man can be put upon a trial for his life, without evidence, and the party being produced who gives that evidence: these men are upon trial for their lives; and one is sorry to hear a man give this sort of evidence on such an occasion: upon my word, I think it affronting to you, and every man, to hear such evidence as this: if you think it proper these men should stand in jeopardy of their lives any longer, I am willing to go on.

Not surprisingly the jury acquitted the prisoners and, once again, Garrow's approach was successful.

INDICTMENTS

If an Indictment contained an error, such as mis-describing a place or a person's name, the case against the prisoner would be thrown out. A clear example of this was shown in the trial of Lewis Henry Scipio Duroure, charged with an assault with a firearm on 8 December 1784.[7] Although it might well have been the prisoner's name that was wrongly spelt it was, in fact, the ownership of the scene of the shooting that was shown to be incorrectly set out. The place was a room in a dwellinghouse in Covent Garden said to be the property of James Brewer and John Sandy. In an interesting pairing, Erskine and Garrow acted jointly for the prisoner and Erskine asked a prosecution witness who worked as a servant in the house who kept it? She replied that it was Mr James Soundy and John Brewer. 'Then there is an end to it', declared Erskine. 'My Lord, I submit here is a fatal variance on the indictment.'

Prosecuting counsel submitted that it was merely what he called a 'surplusage' to which Erskine retorted, 'It is too plain, it is A B C.' Mr Baron Hotham told the jury:

> Gentlemen of the Jury, there can be no doubt at all in this case, they have taken upon themselves to state in the indictment, whose house it is; I do not know that it was necessary for them to have done, but having done it, they are bound in point of law to prove it, and the evidence turns out that it is not the dwelling house of James Brewer and John Sandy but of James Soundy and John Brewer, that is a fatal variance in the

indictment, and where a man is charges on a capital offence, strict law is adhered to, so that you cannot do anything but acquit him.

And this the jury immediately proceeded to do. It is interesting that neither the prisoner nor the victim had any connection with the house except that the alleged assault was said to have occurred there. As the judge said, it is a puzzle why the Indictment should give its ownership at all, but it did so with fatal consequences.

As we have seen, Garrow defended John Henry Aikles on 14 January 1784 Eighteen months or so later, on 29 June 1785, Aikles was again before the court, this time for having illegally returned from transportation.[8] The sentence for returning from transportation was hanging and Garrow pleaded that 'this poor devil' should be acquitted as the indictment was defective in not setting forth the original sentence, and he was found not guilty and remanded until the next sessions.

Aikles was further charged with feloniously returning from transportation on 14 September 1785, this time on a fresh indictment and before three judges.[9] The prosecution alleged that the prisoner was discharged from custody on 9 March 1785 on condition that he would transport himself within 14 days but was found at large near The Angel public house at Islington on 26 May. On this occasion Garrow argued that the onus was on the prosecution to prove the date of discharge with direct evidence which they were failing to do as their witness was reading the date from a book and had no direct knowledge of the date. This was not best evidence. He also argued that by the common law every man was entitled to full and uninterrupted enjoyment of personal freedom which could only be forfeit by the commission of a crime. Aikles, he declared, had not committed any crime at common law and, quoting various statutes relating to transportation, claimed he had breached no statutory requirement either. The judges were not inclined to agree but such was the force of Garrow's plea that they thought the issue might be reserved for consideration of all the judges.

Leaving aside the question of law, Garrow then produced witnesses who said they had met Aikles after his original release from Newgate prison following his conditional pardon and found that his health was seriously impaired and he was without resources. His legs, they testified, were swollen from the prison irons and he was suffering from an 'ugly malignant fever'. This and his want of money, they agreed with Garrow, prevented his getting abroad. As a consequence, the court told the jury that 'all laws must be considered with liberality, and a sort of equity, in order to put a due construction on the meaning of them.' If they believed the prisoner was really ill and this prevented him from going abroad when he meant to do so they should acquit him. If, however, they thought the claim was an artifice not founded on reality they would find him guilty. No medical evidence was offered to assist the jury but, in any event, they found him not guilty.

Similarly, a Samuel Higby brought to trial on 22 February 1786 for unlawfully returning from transportation was found not guilty after Garrow had insisted that the prosecution had not proved that the prisoner was the same person who was convicted of the specific offence mentioned in the Indictment.[10]

Stephen thought the technicalities surrounding indictments made the administration of justice a solemn farce but he also saw another side to the coin. 'Such scandals,' he wrote, 'do not seem, however, to have been unpopular. Indeed I have some doubt whether they were not popular, as they did mitigate, though in an irrational, capricious manner, the excessive severity of the old criminal law.'[11]

A PERSONAL TOUCH

At the Old Bailey on 9 December 1789 a D'Arcy Wentworth was charged with assault and theft as a highwayman on the King's highway at Finchley in London the previous July.[12] The victim, a John Pemberton Heywood, gave evidence that he recognized Wentworth whom he had seen in York many years earlier. Garrow, appearing for the defence, cross-examined Heywood on the changes in Wentworth's appearance since he had met him in York and continued thus:

> **Garrow:** Now, Mr Heywood, I must ask you a question, which we frequently ask witnesses, to discredit their testimony; you will do me the justice to believe that I do not ask it you with that intention; soon after the robbery did you meet nobody on the [Finchley] common that you might have communicated this to? [that he had seen the prisoner before in York].
> **Heywood:** I had the pleasure to meet you, Sir, on the common soon after.
> **Garrow:** And very kindly let me go on to be robbed, I believe?
> **Heywood:** I had no idea that you would be robbed.
> **Garrow:** I had the good fortune to escape your kind wishes.
> **Heywood:** I dare say you had; I do not think you was in any danger of being robbed.

On that intervention, and with Garrow advising the prisoner to stay silent, the jury found him not guilty.[13]

Garrow's humanity was shown in proceedings for punishment at the Old Bailey in 1789.[14] A number of women convicted of felony were brought up before the judge to be granted a royal pardon, on condition of being transported for life. All agreed except a Sarah Cowden who said she would accept the death penalty unless the sentence of death on Sarah Storer, who was innocent, was mitigated. After clearing the court the judge told her she had forfeited her life and the King was being merciful in granting her a royal pardon. She replied that Storer was as innocent as a child unborn having merely entered the place where a robbery was committed to borrow a pair of bellows. She, Cowden, was willing to die with her although she was only a young girl of 21. The judge thereupon ordered her execution for the following Thursday.

At this point Garrow asked permission to speak to Cowden and the judge raised no objection. Cowden maintained her position, however, and the judge declared that she was trifling with the court. Nevertheless, Garrow asked to be allowed to see her again but this time the judge said no application could be heard from one who treated the mercy of the King with contempt. Garrow asked that the order of execution should not be treated as irrevocable but the judge remained adamant. Garrow, appears to have seen the prisoner again, however, and persuaded her to save her life. He now made one last appeal in court pleading with the judge, 'My Lord, I do not attend your Lordship, nor address myself to the Court, in the character of a Counsel, but as a very humble supplicant, for a very miserable wretch, who desires now, having seen the folly of her behaviour, humbly to intreat, that she may be permitted to accept that pardon of his Majesty, which she has dared contumaciously to refuse.'

The judge responded to what he called a 'very humane intercession' and had Cowden brought up again when she agreed to accept transportation for life, to which the judge then sentenced her.

GARROW AS PROSECUTOR

Altogether Garrow acted for the defence far more often than for the prosecution. In the early 1790s, however, he drew close to the Pitt government and began a career as a prosecutor of sedition[15] including the Treason Trials of 1794. He had already prosecuted before this, although nowhere near as frequently as he defended. Apart from what is revealed in other cases mentioned elsewhere in this book, his style in the role of prosecutor is clearly revealed in a trial on 14 September 1785. On this date William Cook was charged with stealing cash and articles valued at over £200 from a Charles Lockwood and certainly faced the gallows if found guilty.[16] Garrow was the prosecuting counsel at the trial. The only witness to give evidence against the prisoner was an Ann Rose who said she saw him at the Coach and Horses in Bishopsgate Street where he asked her to have a drink with him and pulled from his pocket four or five guineas saying it was 'old Charles's money.' Two witnesses claimed to know Ann Rose, one of whom said he did not know if she should be believed 'but she may' and the other said he considered her evidence should not be believed.

Garrow told the judge, Mr Baron Hotham, '[t]hen my Lord, I do not ask the Jury to convict a man upon the testimony of such a witness'. Thereupon, the judge told the jury, '[t]hat is very handsomely given up; you will acquit the prisoner' whom they then found not guilty. Later, on 9 September 1789, William Power was charged with murder in a trial in which Garrow prosecuted.[17] In this case he acted more in character as prosecutor but at the start told the jury that, under direction from the judge, they would have to consider whether the crime was murder or some lesser offence. It was not questioned that the prisoner had stabbed to death a John Wilkinson. Power did not know Wilkinson, said Garrow, and bore no malice towards him but in a self-induced frenzy in a public house had violently struck out with a knife at three people, one of whom was the hapless Wilkinson. Witnesses were called to confirm what counsel had said and that the prisoner had acted with deliberation. A peace keeper had been called and he, with two other men, had detained Power but only after the affray was over and without a warrant from a magistrate.

Mr. Justice Gould, with the concurrence of Judges Wilson and Grose who were also sitting on the Bench, told the jury that they must put aside indignation and apply the law which said that in the circumstances the prisoner had been illegally assaulted and arrested. Because of that the prisoner could be guilty only of manslaughter and so the jury found. Power was then branded in the hand with a red hot iron in open court and sentenced to a year's imprisonment in Newgate gaol.

On the same date, in the trial of Richard Pitham for animal theft, Garrow showed that he could also be aggressive when prosecuting.[18] After verbally abusing a witness named John Lowin, Garrow threatened him saying, 'I will make you answer it, or else you will drive no more chases, except in Newgate.' Perhaps on this occasion Garrow went too far in the eyes of the jury who acquitted the prisoner he was prosecuting.

Garrow was on his most persuasive form with the jury in the case of Jordan Waine on 7 December 1791.[19] Waine was charged with fraud in obtaining money from the wife of a convicted felon by false pretences. The husband of Mary Yostus had been sentenced to 14 years transportation for receiving six bushels of coal valued at five shillings. Although no fees were payable on applying for a royal pardon the prisoner promised Mary Yostus that he could obtain a pardon if she gave him several guineas to pay the appropriate fees. Mrs Yostus sold her bed and sold and pawned everything she could to raise the money which she paid to the prisoner. No pardon was obtained, however, and her husband was duly shipped to Botany Bay.

Garrow told the jury that although he was frequently in the Old Bailey he had never been called upon 'to lend my poor assistance to a prosecution in which I have contributed my aid with so much satisfaction as on the present occasion.' He continued, 'One would hardly believe that depraved human nature would furnish a man with pretences to strip a miserable widow, deprived of her husband, and to strip five miserable orphan children, of every rag they had to cover them, to support himself in his vices.' Waine questioned the widow at length and declared that he had done his best to obtain a pardon and had taken no money from her. There were no witnesses to the handing over of the money but the victim's testimony and the pleas of Garrow were sufficient for the jury to find Waine guilty and he was sentenced to be transported for seven years.

Subsequently, in the case of *R. v. Patch* in 1806,[20] Garrow was able as prosecutor to speak to the jury and he cast aside all restraint by indulging in 'a virtuoso display of forensic power to prove to them that the prisoner was guilty.'[21] He told the jury that the motive for murder was to be found in:

> the bad and corrupt passions of the human heart; that envy, jealousy, long-conceived hatred; above all, Gentlemen, I am afraid the love of inordinate gain, which can be obtained only by putting another to death, are found In the history of the depravity of the human heart, to be the causes that produce these dreadful events. I shall shew that these causes, up to a most alarming degree, were certainly operating upon the Prisoner at the Bar.[22]

In the words of Cairns,

> He reasoned from facts, doubtful facts and pejorative interpretations of the facts; from suppositions, suspicions, probabilities, and the exclusion of possibilities; from anticipated defences, commonplaces, common experience, anecdotes and the conduct of a hypothetical innocent man; and from his own observation and opinion. This argumentative inventiveness was enhanced by a rich array of rhetorical embellishment. Garrow makes particularly effective use of questions—repeated questions, sequential questions, self-answered questions and rhetorical questions.
> Patch is painted in dark murderous tones, the victim in a benevolent light, God and providence are thanked for revealing the murderer, judge and jury are fawned upon, and in one extraordinary passage the victim, Isaac Blight, is introduced to confirm Patch was his murderer ... Contemporaries called the opening in Patch a 'hanging speech' for its effect was to make the result of the trial a foregone confusion.[23]

In the debate on the Prisoners' Counsel Act 30 years later Garrow's opening remarks in this case were again said to constitute a 'hanging speech'[24] as well as revealing the power of prosecution counsel to influence a jury. It is little wonder that over time the Bar introduced rules of etiquette and professional standards of conduct to restrain prosecuting counsel from endeavouring to secure convictions whatever the cost. After all, in a trial in 1791 Garrow asked a witness, 'What do you shake so for?' and continued:

Garrow: You were never in this court before?
Witness: Not as a witness.
Garrow: No! A witness! No; how long was it since you was here?
Witness: Six years, eight years, I was tried here.
Garrow: God bless me! What for pray?
Witness: Tried, I was arraigned, there was no witness against me.
Garrow: What was you tried for?
Witness: A charge of house-breaking.
Garrow: God bless me! House-breaking![25]

However, as we have seen, Garrow was not usually aggressive to defendants when he was prosecuting. Indeed, he played a considerable part in inducing the Bar to accept rules of etiquette along lines that led to its modern form. In a case in 1790, in his opening address to the jury as prosecuting counsel, he concluded:

Gentlemen, I shall lay before you the evidence. On the one hand, the growing experience of the times shews us that these accusations, which are very easily made, which are extremely difficult to be refused, which may be made by the worst of men against the best members of society, have grown to an amazing height, and it is a duty you owe to the publick to make the prisoners the sacrifices of their own delinquency, if you believe them guilty; but on the other hand, however much you may abhor and detest the crime you ought not to involve innocent persons in the consequences of guilt. Gentlemen, I have no doubt but you will attend to the evidence with the care and impartiality which must always, and which, thank God, always does, characterize an English jury. I shall call the witnesses with no anxiety about the result of the case, having no doubt but public justice will be satisfied.[26]

Moreover, when he was prosecuting Garrow was not above using his frequent appearances for prisoners to suggest to juries his understanding of the position of the defendant.

DEATH ON THE HUSTINGS

An interesting case in which Garrow and Erskine both appeared for the defence occurred in 1784 when a Patrick Nicholson was tried, with three others, named Ward, Shaw and Murray, for murder.[27] The alleged offence was said to have occurred during an election in the city of Westminster when the candidates were the Whig leader, Charles James Fox, Lord Hood and Sir Cecil Wray. In Parliamentary elections at the time, Westminster had one of the largest electorates in the country and the elections, which took place over several weeks, were frequently riotous. The hustings were held in the portico of St. Paul's Church, Covent Garden.[28] On the occasion that led to the trial the local police were present but there was also a considerable force of constables brought in from Tower Hamlets in east London. One of them, Nicholas Casson, was knocked down in a scuffle and died shortly afterwards from his injuries. An attempt to close the polls was unsuccessful, athough polling was stopped an hour early on the day of the funeral of the slain man,[29] and the election lasted for 40 days.

The prosecution alleged Casson was killed by the four accused men but, except in the case of Nicholson, they conceded that they had some difficulty in establishing who had hit him. Their problem was added to by skilful examination and cross-examination of witnesses by Garrow and Erskine. The first prosecution witness was a Thomas Davy whose lengthy cross-examination by Erskine led the judge, Mr Baron Perryn, to say in his summing-up to the jury, that he was contradicted by almost every other witness and that his evidence was not material to the charge.

The thrust of the prosecution case was that butchers armed with marrow-bones and cleavers had attacked the police and in a pitched battle Casson was killed. Eleven prosecution witnesses were called by the Crown but only one had been examined before the coroner or the Grand Jury and most of them could say little as to the actual killing. The judge himelf suggested that there was no case to answer for Ward, Shaw and Murray.

Another of the Crown witnesses was a constable from Tower Hamlets named Henry Harvy. He was cross-examined by Garrow and when asked if he was not one of a gang armed with tattoos and bludgeons in order to beat 5,000 demonstrators, he managed to avoid answering the question. The next Crown witness, a Joseph Gilmore, admitted to Erskine that he had seen Casson struck but that when questioned earlier by an examining justice he had not indicated by whom. 'I never was asked,' he declared. Another witness, Edward Arnold, denied he knew there was a reward for giving evidence despite it being widely advertised in newspapers and handbills.

When the prosecution endeavoured to produce the widow of the deceased constable to prove what he was wearing when he was killed (and about which some witnesses had given evidence) Garrow and Erskine objected that she had been in the gallery of the court throughout the trial and she was not allowed to testify.

Once the prosecution had completed their case, the defence produced a number of independent witnesses who swore under examination that they had seen a considerable body of constables bear down on the crowd and without provocation attack them with long staves. Indeed, it was constables and not bystanders who were crowded around the body of Casson when he lay injured and at least one witness said he was hit on the head by a fellow constable. The playwright, Richard Brinsley Sheridan, gave evidence confirming the attack by the constables on Mr Fox's supporters and, introducing hearsay without objection by counsel, stated that he had heard there was considerable feeling that they had themselves struck Casson his fatal blows.

In summing-up to the jury, the judge made the criticism of the prosecution witnesses already remarked upon and added that apart from John Joseph none of the other witnesses were known to be such until the trial had commenced. On the other hand, 'every one of the witnesses that have been examined on the part of the prisoner, and not contradicted at all, own, that the first attack was given by the constables; if so, what the people did, may be said to be in their own defence.' If, the judge continued, one of them gave an accidental blow, it had to be manslaughter but he thought, on the variations and contradictions that appeared on the part of the witnesses for the prosecution, it was for the jury to determine whether they would not acquit the prisoners. This they duly proceeded to do, giving us another example of the powerful influence of counsel in examination and cross-examination even with no opportunity to address the jury.

The election resulted in the Whig candidates Fox and Lord Hood defeating Pitt's nominee. Despite, or because of, the result the government forced a prolonged scrutiny of the votes which prevented Fox from representing Westminster with all its prestige, although he was in the House of Commons as member for a Scottish constituency. Fox accused Pitt of conspiring to injure him but for nine months Pitt ignored his reproach and supported the scrutiny which kept the city of Westminster unrepresented.[30] By 4 March 1785 Pitt's delaying tactics were finally brought to an end and Fox and Hood were returned as the MPs for Westminster.[31]

During this time Garrow appeared as counsel at the Bar of the Commons on behalf of the friends of Fox. The *Parliamentary History* shows he spoke for nearly two hours but gives us none of his words. It does say, however, that 'although Mr Garrow had been but newly called to the Bar, and never pleaded before the Commons of England till that night, he acquitted himself in a manner equally tending to the advantage of his clients and to his own honour and credit.'[32]

JURY NULLIFICATION AND PIOUS PERJURY

Nullification occurs where a jury act according to their consciences or where they appear to nullify the law or the evidence in a case. Pious perjury was where the jury reduced the value of goods stolen, sometimes substantially, in order to circumvent the death penalty when it was considered to be too harsh a punishment and out of proportion to the offence.

One such case of the latter occurred in 1784 when Garrow defended Elizabeth Jones and Mary Smith on charges of shoplifting goods valued at 14 shillings.[33] A witness named Lewis who helped to apprehend the two women swore that when arrested they begged for mercy. Garrow cross-examined him.

Garrow: I believe you have some reason to know some of the rules of evidence?
Lewis: Why, Sir?
Garrow: I believe you have been here pretty often in the character of prosecutor and witness?
Lewis: Frequently, and if I have an opportunity I may appear against more; but I never came without a safe conscience to this Court.
Garrow: You have a good deal of leisure time on your hands I take it for granted?
Lewis: I could perhaps fill up my time sometimes better than I do.
Garrow: Answer my question, Sir, you have heard it?
Lewis: I have sometimes leisure time upon my hands.
Garrow: It so happened you had a good deal of leisure at this time?
Lewis: I was attending these women in my shop the day before.
Garrow: Now you have told us, that when they [the prisoners] were carried back to Mr Gray's shop, they put their hands together and asked for mercy and acknowledged the fact; I wish you to state the very expression?
Lewis: They wrung their hands, and hoped for mercy.
Garrow: Was that all they said?
Lewis: I cannot recollect every word.
Garrow: Then that is what you meant when you said they acknowledged the fact?
Lewis: I consider that as an acknowledgment.
Garrow: Then when you told my Lord, that these women had acknowledged the fact, you meant to refer to their having said that they desired mercy?
Lewis: They begged for mercy.
Garrow: That is what you call acknowledging the fact, Sir, is it? That is a little extraordinary.

There was too much evidence against them for the prisoners to be acquitted but the jury found them guilty of stealing fans worth 4s. 10d. By putting the value of the stolen fans below five shillings the jury, in a fine example of 'pious perjury' avoided the women being sent to the gallows and they were each sentenced to be privately whipped and confined to hard labour for 12 months in a house of correction. When capital punishment existed for many property crimes juries would frequently reduce the charge and thus lessen the sentence, often from death to transportation or, as in this case, to whipping and imprisonment. The term 'pious perjury' was coined by Sir William Blackstone who wrote that 'the mercy of juries often made them strain a point, and bring in larceny to be under the value of 12 pence, when it was really of much greater value ... a kind of *pious perjury*.'.[34]

Another case where the jury appeared to have decided according to conscience was that of Elizabeth Adams on 26 April 1786.[35] She was charged with stealing clothes which belonged to her landlady and were hanging out to dry in some upper stairs of the house. The evidence of the landlady and her husband was that after the prisoner had gone upstairs it was discovered that the clothes were missing. A constable was called and he went to the prisoner's room where she handed him the clothing. Garrow's questioning of the landlady and her husband suggested that either they had taken the clothes away themselves or, alternatively, and more likely, they had promised that if the prisoner gave up the clothes she would not be prosecuted. The landlady, in fact, came close to admitting the truth of the latter and, after two witnesses gave the prisoner a good character the jury found her not guilty.

On 11 July 1787 Garrow appeared on behalf of William Carter who was charged with the murder of Elizabeth, his wife, only six days before.[36] The dead woman was 57 years of age and her husband was believed to be younger. At any rate, according to the evidence of her landlady, Margaret Currie, the prisoner had said, 'she was an old dry bitch, and he had no notion of spending his substance with such an old dry bitch as she was, and he wanted a young woman to have some children by.' One night Mrs Carter was not at home and, according to Margaret Currie, the prisoner told her that they would never see her alive again as 'she is hanged or drowned somewhere.' The next day she was found in a beer butt in the house where she had suffocated and drowned.

When the prisoner was confronted by Mrs Currie who called him a dirty scoundrel who had drowned his wife he declared he was innocent but said nothing further, which was unusual for a man who it was said frequently used obscene language and was violent. Indeed, another witness, Mary Harfield, testified that Carter had told her, 'with many shocking oaths, that if he saw his wife again he would chop off her arms and legs.' It appeared that the top of the butt was close to the ceiling and had no great aperture so that anyone forced into it would probably have suffered bruising and Garrow concentrated on the fact that there was no external bruising on the body. He also drew from some witnesses evidence that the deceased was very deaf, was badly treated by her husband and was likely to commit suicide.

Bearing this evidence in mind, and without any direct evidence of the circumstances of death, the jury found Carter not guilty. Discharging him, the recorder of London said that he was perfectly satisfied with the verdict as there was insufficient evidence that the prisoner was the immediate and actual cause of his wife's death. The only question, he added, that the jury had to try was whether he had occasioned her death himself or by his brutality was the means of her being the cause of her own death. 'The circumstances,' he concluded, 'perhaps in the sight of Him that will judge you hereafter, do not greatly differ; and I hope that the danger it has brought upon yourself [with the trial] will produce such a change in you mind, as to wipe off that guilt which you certainly lie under at present.'

In a case in 1789 the jury are seen to be asking if they have the power to find a partial verdict. John Merryman and William Pickering were charged with housebreaking and stealing goods to the value of 32 shillings, the penalty for which, if proved, was death.[37] Despite the main evidence coming from a witness who admitted to Garrow that he was an accomplice, the jury did indeed find the prisoners guilty. Garrow then addressed the judge and pointed out that before the verdict was recorded it should be noted that as to the capital part of the charge there was no evidence other than that of an accomplice. Without his evidence, although the house had been entered and theft occurred, there was no breaking and entering to make the case capital. Thanking Garrow for his remarks the judge told the jury it was his wish that they should have found the prisoners guilty of felony only but it was a matter for them to decide. The jury said it was their wish to leave out the capital part but they had had doubts about their power to do so.

'Certainly you have the power,' said the judge and Garrow urged the jury to alter their verdict as it had not yet been recorded. This the jury then did finding the prisoners guilty of theft of goods to a value of four shillings and ten pence and they were then sentenced to seven years' transportation.

On 13 January 1790 at the Old Bailey,[38] Garrow acted for William Hayward, a coachman employed by William Champion Crespigny, a gentleman of Cavendish Square in the City of Westminster. Hayward was charged with stealing from his employer in the previous August a chariot harness worth ten pounds. The accused did not speak on his own behalf or call witnesses and the defence rested entirely on the skills of Garrow who was persistent, and at times threatening, in his cross-examination of Crespigny and other prosecution witnesses. Undaunted by the social position of the gentleman prosecuting, Garrow set out to expose his spite against Hayward whom Crespigny had dismissed before the alleged theft of the harness arose. At one point he told Crespigny, 'I must trouble you to take time to reflect.' When Crespigny brushed aside a question, Garrow told him, 'Pray do not be in a hurry, Mr Crespigny.'

Hayward's defence was that he had been given certain perquisites such as boots, breeches and the harness to make up his wages and his employer went some way under sarcastic cross-examination to admitting this. As Garrow drew out, Hayward had openly disclosed his ownership of the harness by displaying it for sale. At one point a prosecution witness, Sarah Pitt, endeavoured to introduce something that Mrs Crespigny had told her but Garrow quickly pointed out that such evidence was hearsay and was inadmissible. Confident of his powers with the jury, Garrow declared, 'I shall call no witnesses in such a case; and I advise the coachman to say nothing.' At the end of the case the judge told the jury that servants had no right to 'lay hold of the property of their masters and keep it as wages' but the jury found the prisoner not guilty.

PRO BONO WORK

In a case heard on 10 December 1783 the record shows that two women, Sarah Slade and Mary Wood, charged with stealing clothing from a dwelling house, had no counsel and Garrow undertook to cross-examine the prosecution witnesses for them without fee. [39] The defendants were arrested by an officer of justice who said he recollected that they had been in his custody before. 'You know you are not to tell us that,' interrupted Garrow. 'I am telling you the reasons why I stopped them,' the officer replied. When Garrow told him he was not to give his reasons he responded, 'I am not talking to you, I am talking to my Lord.' Counsel immediately appealed to the judge who accepted his argument and allowed the witness to say merely that he knew the women before. But would the officer's reasons have been admitted if Garrow had not been acting for the women and objected? The judge said nothing until Garrow felt it necessary to appeal to him.

The witness also claimed to have found on one of the women a key to the door of the house where the theft was alleged to have occurred. How do you know it opens the door of the house, enquired Garrow, 'did you every try it?' When the officer replied that he had not Garrow turned to the question of whether the key he was producing was the same as the one he alleged he found on one of the accused, since it had changed hands before the trial. Yes, replied the witness, he knew it was a very remarkable key. 'By what was it remarkable, Sir?' asked Garrow. It was worn with rust, was the reply. 'Now I want to know,' said Garrow, 'whether in the whole course of your life, as a thief-taker, you ever knew a key identified in such manner; is it by the key being worn with rust, Sir, that you affect to identify it in a court of justice?'

'There is not a doubt in my mind', replied the witness. Garrow then said:

> It is not your saying bluntly here, that there is not a doubt in you mind, that will induce the Court or Jury to believe it: by what marks, Sir, will you make the Court and Jury believe that that is the key which you took on the woman, which key you gave to you do not know who, and have received a key from somebody you cannot describe. How will you make us believe it is the same key?

Court: (Looking at the key.) 'It is a very remarkable key.'
Garrow: Not, my Lord, because it has been eat up with rust.

When asked by the judge if he had examined the key carefully the witness could only repeat that it was much eaten with rust. At first the case against the accused had appeared to be a strong one and they must have been delighted that Garrow had offered to help them, and even more so when the jury found them not guilty and they were released.

Seven years later Garrow again served without fee *pro bono publico,* (i.e. for the public good). A Sarah Pearson was indicted for returning from transportation without lawful cause.[40] She gave evidence that she had been taken illegally to Jamaica where she served for six years but returned to England to seek a cure for her lame leg which prevented her from working. In response to a question from the judge, Mr Justice Grose, she said she had no witnesses. Garrow asked the court, 'My Lord, as this poor woman has no Counsel, will you permit me as *Amicus Curiae* to ask John Owen (the prosecution witness) a question or two?' The judge agreed and in reply to Garrow's examination Owen agreed that the prisoner was telling the truth. Garrow persuaded the jury who said, '[w]e think she was not at large without lawful cause' and acquitted her.

It is not apparent why Garrow undertook these cases without fee as it is clear that he worked in order to earn an income and he normally required a retainer before considering a case. It may have been a case of 'bread upon the water' or simply that he responded to the pathetic sight the prisoners presented and, certainly, in the Pearson case he more than once referred to her as a poor, pitiful woman. This would also explain his position in another case, where a young woman, Elizabeth Curtis, was charged on a coroner's inquisition with infanticide and Garrow opened the inquisition.[41] Apparently, he felt sorry for the young girl and asked her landlady, 'The poor woman has no Council, I will ask you what character she had?' To which she replied: 'I have had her six weeks, and I had a good character with her, and she deserved no other from me.' On the direction of the judge the jury found the girl not guilty.

DUELLING

A trial in which the two great barristers, Erskine and Garrow, appeared together for the defence was that of Richard England, charged with murder on 17 February 1796.[42] This case revolved around a duel at a time when to kill during a duel was legally held to be murder, although the courts often merely imposed a fine on the killer who was likely to be an army officer or a member of the gentry.[43]

In this case the accused and a William Rowlls had taken part in a duel on 18 June 1795 following a heated argument at the Ascot races. After a false start at the duel, Rowlls was hit by a bullet in the groin from which he died at the scene. A captain, George Donnisthorpe, was a second to one of the duellers and was called by the prosecution to give material evidence. But first he wished to be assured that he would not subsequently be prosecuted. The judges were inclined to promise to recommend him for a King's pardon if he gave evidence but both defence counsel demurred. Erskine argued that many witnesses stood in the same position as the captain and the court could not lawfully make such a promise.

Garrow took the view that there were no precedents for such indemnity as was being offered whereas there were many against it and he proceeded to quote from memory a number of them, in some of which the witness was a second in a duel. The judges then told captain Donnisthorpe that he would be able to claim the mercy of the Crown only in the same manner as all other men could and he would be cross-examined if he gave evidence. Faced with the prospect of questioning by Erskine and Garrow the witness, probably wisely, decided to withdraw and not give evidence.

At one point in the trial Erskine intervened successfully to secure the rejection of proposed evidence of other proceedings involving England in respect of which the prosecution were unable either to produce evidence or to prove. England put in a written statement to the court in which he said he acted solely from honour and without malice. The Marquis of Hertford appeared as a witness for him and, being questioned by Garrow, spoke of England's good character, as did Samuel Whitbread who was examined by Erskine. Other witnesses who spoke in the same vein included Colonel Bishop, Colonel Wollaston and the Earl of Derby.

In summing-up to the jury the presiding judge declared the law was that when two parties met together deliberately, and not in the heat of blood, for the purpose of seeking each other's lives, it was murder if one was killed. This was long-standing law, he declared, laid down in cited cases by Lord Coke, Lord Hale, other judges, Serjeant Hawkins, Mr Justice Foster and Blackstone. The duel, he said, took place the day following the dispute at Ascot which occasioned it and if England was cool and in possession of himself during the duel the law was strict. Only if England met with provocation on the morning of the duel, of which there was no evidence, could they find him guilty only of manslaughter. Despite these words, the jury retired for only 25 minutes and brought in a verdict of not guilty of murder but guilty of manslaughter.

Mr Justice Rooke then passed sentence, telling England, 'the Court think it proper to set you forth as an example in future, to let the world know, that they cannot commit even the crime of manslaughter in a duel, without subjecting themselves to very considerable punishment.' He then declared the sentence of the court upon him to be a derisory fine of one shilling and imprisonment for 12 months. Once again, defence counsel had exercised their skills to preserve the life of a prisoner.

CONCLUSION

As the assize court for London, the Old Bailey dealt with more crime than other such courts and being at the heart of the metropolis it dealt almost exclusively with urban crime. Even the streets of London were designated as highways to enable theft from the person upon them to be classified as highway robbery.

Here were brought not the high in the land charged with treason or other political offences but the ordinary poor of the capital with whom Garrow appears to have had a close empathy. Some of them knew him, would use his name and sometimes banter with him during the course of the trial. His fame spread rapidly and he flourished at the Old Bailey where he was engaged for prisoners far more frequently than any other barristers whose reputations were generally low. Some were regarded as 'ruffians' but not all were[44] and it was they who made secure the adversary system of trial.

Reading through the trials in which he appeared, it is clear that Garrow was extemporizing the art of cross-examination. Other trials reveal that his example was followed by both his contemporaries who pleaded alongside him and those who came after him. Nevertheless, no barrister at the Old Bailey before him, or during his time, achieved anything approaching his success or exhibited his pugnacity, aggression and tenacity despite the fact that his tactics were often successful with juries. He was astute enough to understand the strong feelings among the population against bounty hunters, who often prosecuted innocent men for their own financial benefit, and the reluctance of juries to sentence men to death for minor offences. Both his style and his rapport with juries were the soil in which adversary trial grew and flourished.

Garrow started as a Whig in politics but turned Tory, took office under Tory governments and sometimes acted for the Crown in criminal prosecutions. It is clear from his position in debates in the House of Commons that he was opposed to law reform which would have assisted prisoners but there can be no doubt as to his sympathy with many of those he defended, sometimes without fee. Which raises the question of income. He was among the early group of counsel who were able to appear for defendants in criminal cases and the usual fee of two or three guineas a brief was not comparable with fees paid in civil cases. Hence the widespread feeling at the Bar that the relatively few counsel at the Old Bailey were hacks. Even Garrow's character was impugned. Baron Charles Hompesch denounced him to the Prince [of Wales] as a 'liar, coward and poltroon, but only after Garrow had insulted him in court.'[45]

Despite the normally low fees paid to Old Bailey counsel Garrow was a byword for prosperity in his profession. He appears to have obtained the fee of 200 guineas mentioned above for one case and by 1808 he was 'netting 300 guineas a case at assizes.'[46] James Scarlett wrote that the business in the Lancashire sessions was so great, 'that when in a few years I came to be the decided leader [there], the profits were as great to me as those of the Home Circuit to Mr Garrow or Serjeant Best.'[47]

The sheer scale of Garrow's work, his high fees and the many hundreds of cases he undertook, must have made the work extremely profitable for him and certainly, when he died he left a considerable estate. This would have provided the motivation for his hard-hitting and persistent advocacy that unwittingly helped firmly to establish adversary trial and a prisoners' rights ethos.

In this context it is surely wrong to argue, as Cairns does, that modern scholars have made an 'over-hasty identification of the late eighteenth century criminal trial as adversarial.' He contends that this occurred only with the Prisoners' Counsel Act 1836[48] and the title of his book covers only the period 1800 to 1865. Indeed, Allyson May claims that his history of advocacy is weakened by his dismissal of the eighteenth century developments that preceded the 1836 Act.[49] But, although in the eighteenth century defence counsel could not address the jury at the end of a trial, the extracts from Garrow's cases set out in this (and the preceding) chapter surely confirm that the criminal trial in that century was already adversarial in the sense set out earlier in *Chapter 1*.

Nevertheless, May argues that 'the legal profession did not engage theoretically with the adversarial criminal trial until the 1840s'—an unjustified view shared by Langbein.[50] This leads her to add that, 'that engagement thus postdated significant developments in its history.'[51] But, this ignores the debates on the Prisoners' Counsel Bill in 1836 and the significant report at that time of the criminal law commissioners, both of which will be considered in *Chapter 9*. And, in any event, without those 'significant developments' and the role of Garrow there would have been no Prisoners' Counsel Act and English criminal procedure would be very different today from what it is.

ENDNOTES for *Chapter 7*

1 Ante. pp. 91-2.
2 D.J.A. Cairns. (1998) *Advocacy and the Making of the Adversarial Criminal Trial 1800-1865*. Oxford, The Clarendon Press. p. 177.
3 OBP Online. (www.oldbaileyonline.org, 5 December 2004). 26 May 1784. Trial of James Wingrove. Ref: t17840526-117.
4 OBP Online. (www.oldbaileyonline.org, 7 April 2005) 22 October 1788 Trial of William Akers for theft. Ref: t17881022-76.
5 OBP Online. (www.oldbaileyonline.org 26 July 2005) 24 February 1790 Trial of John Jones and Thomas Wix. Ref: t17900224-78.
6 OBP Online. (www.oldbaileyonline.org. 4 May 2005) 24 April 1790 Trial of George Bathurst and James Buchanan. Ref: t17900424-41.
7 OBP Online. (www.oldbaileyonline.org, 7 December 2004) 8 December 1784 Trial of Lewis Duroure. Ref. t17841208-194.
8 OBP. (www.oldbaileyonline.org, 12 January 2005) 29 June 1785 Trial of John Henry Aikles. Ref: t17850629-107.
9 OBP. Online. (www.oldbaileyonline.org, 12 January 2005) 14 September 1785 Trial of John Henry Aikles. Ref: t17850914-181.
10 OBP. Online. (www.oldbaileyonline.org, 3 March 2005). 22 February 1786 Trial of Samuel Higby. Ref: t17860222-61.
11 J.F. Stephen. (1883) *A History of the Criminal Law of England*. London, Routledge/Thoemmes Press. vol. i. p. 284.
12 OBP Online. (www.oldbailey.org, 1 December 2004) 9 December 1789. Trial of D'Arcy Wentworth. Ref: tr17891209-1.
13 Ibid.
14 OBP Online. (www.oldbaileyonline.org, 7 April 2005) 3 June 1789 Punishment Proceedings. Ref: s17890603-1.
15 J.M. Beattie. (1991) 'Scales of Justice: Defense Counsel and the English Criminal Trial in the Eighteenth and Nineteenth Centuries.' 9(2) *Law and History Review*. Univ. of Illinois Press. p. 238.

[16] OBP Online. (www.oldbaileyonline.org, 14 Jan. 2005) Trial of William Cook. Ref: t17850914-126.

[17] OBP Online. (www.oldbaileyonline.org, 7 April 2005) 9 September 1789 Trial of William Power. Ref: t17890909-109.

[18] OBP Online. (www.oldbaileyonline.org, 7 April 2005) 9 September 1789 Trial of Richard Pitham. Ref: t17890909-93.

[19] OBP Online. (www.oldbaileyonline.org, 17 May 2005) 7 December 1791 Trial of Jordan Waine for Fraud. Ref: t17911207-46.

[20] J. Gurney. (1806) *The Trial of Richard Patch for the Wilful Murder of Isaac Blight etc.* London.

[21] D. J. A. Cairns. *Advocacy and the Making of the Adversarial Criminal Trial.1800-1865.* Op. cit. p. 41.

[22] J. Gurney. Op. cit. p. 7.

[23] D.J.A. Cairns. Op. cit. pp.41-3.

[24] *Parliamentary Debates.* [11] (1824) col. 210.

[25] OBP Online. (www.oldbaileyonline.org, 7 January 2005) 14 September 1791 Trial of Thomas Plata and Thomas Colliss for Animal Theft. Ref: t17910914-47.

[26] OBP Online. (www.oldbaileyonline.org, 7 January 2005) 8 December 1790 Trial of George Platt and James Templeman for Highway Robbery. Ref: t17901208-28.

[27] OBP Online. (www.oldbaileyonline.org, 1 December 2004) 1 June 1784. Trial of Patrick Nicholson, James Ward, Joseph Shaw and James Murray. Ref: t178440601-1.

[28] Ibid.

[29] L. Reid. (1969) *Charles James Fox: A Man for the People.* London, Longmans, Green & Co. Ltd. p. 204.

[30] L. Reid. *Charles James Fox.* Op. cit. pp.205-213.

[31] *Journal of the House of Commons.* xl. 588.

[32] *Parliamentary History.* (1794) London, Longman and Others. vol. xxiv. cols. 857-8.

[33] OBP Online. (www.oldbaileyonline.org, 27 October 2004) 15 September 1784 Trial of Elizabeth Jones and Mary Smith. Ref: t17840915-68.

[34] Sir W. Blackstone. (1830) *Commentaries on the Law of England.* London, Thomas Tegg. vol. vi. p. 248.

[35] OBP Online. (www.oldbaileyonline.org, 3 March 2005) 26 April 1786 Trial of Elizabeth Adams. Ref: t17860426-57.

[36] OBP Online. (www.oldbaileyonline.org, 14 January 2005) Trial of William Carter. Ref: t17870711-88.

[37] OBP Online. (www.oldbaileyonline.org, 8 April 2005) 3 June 1789 Trial of John Merryman and William Pickering. Ref: t17890603-66.

[38] OBP Online. (www.oldbaileyonline.org, 7 January 2005) 13 January 1790. Trial of William Hayward. (t17900113-104).

[39] OBP Online. (www.oldbaileyonline.org, 24 October 2004) 10 December 1783. Trial of Sarah Slade and Mary Wood for Theft. Ref: t17831210-44.

[40] OBP Online. (www.oldbaileyonline.org, 24 October 2004) 24 February 1790. Trial of Sarah Pearson. Ref: t1790224-75.

[41] OBP Online. (www.oldbaileyonline.org, 27 October 2004) 15 September 1784 Trial of Elizabeth Curtis. Ref: t17840915-149.

[42] Old Bailey Proceedings Online. (www.oldbaileyonline.org, 23 October 2004) 17 February 1796. Trial of Richard England. Ref: t17960217-27.

[43] P. Johnson. (1991) *The Birth of the Modern: World Society 1815-1830.* London, Weidenfeld and Nicolson. pp. 462-72.

[44] A.N. May. (2003) *The Bar and the Old Bailey 1750-1850.* Chapel Hill, The University of North Carolina Press. p. 2.

[45] R.G. Thorne (ed.) (1986) *The History of Parliament. The House of Commons 1790-1820.* London, Secker and Warburg. p. 6.

[46] Ibid.

[47] P. C. Scarlett. (1877) *A Memoir of the Right Honourable James, First Lord Abinger.* London, pp. 61-2.

[48] D. J.A. Cairns. *Advocacy and the Making of the Adversarial Criminal Trial, 1800-1865.* Op. cit. p. 177.

[49] A.N. May. (2001) 'Review of Cairns' *Advocacy and the Making of the Adversarial Criminal Trial.'* 19(3) *Law and History Review.* Illinois, University of Illinois Press. p. 676. And see correspondence between Cairns and May (2002) in 20(2) *Law and History Review.* pp. 445-8.

[50] See post. p. 158.

[51] A. N. May. *The Bar and the Old Bailey, 1750-1850.* Op. cit. p. 241.

CHAPTER 8

Rules of Criminal Evidence

INTRODUCTION

According to legal historian T. A. Green, a 'great watershed in the history of trial practice was the increasing recourse to counsel and the development of a true law of evidence in the late eighteenth and early nineteenth centuries.'[1] Indeed, criminal law of evidence grew along with adversary trial and changes in trial procedure as defence lawyers grappled to secure maximum protection for their clients.

A contrary view is held by Langbein, however. He considers that the rules of criminal evidence were devised by the Bench, although he accepts that they played into the hands of the lawyers[2], saying '[t]he law of evidence may have been a judicial creation, but it had the effect of empowering counsel.'[3] And he concedes that, '[a]lthough the rules of evidence crystallized out of the judge's discretion over the conduct of trials in his courtroom, in the new setting of adversary combat the quest for advantage in the particular case would cause counsel to press to extend such potentially expansive principles as the hearsay rule.'[4] He also agrees that counsel gave more structure to criminal trials, as the 'rambling altercation' between the accused and witnesses was replaced by distinct prosecution and defence 'cases', which in turn encouraged evidential objections and the recognition of burdens of proof.

Thus, Langbein accepts that the increasing use of defence counsel in criminal trials contributed to the growth of evidential rules. But it is more than that. Despite the fact that some judges did admit new rules, he indicates no reason why the Bench as a whole and *ab initio* should want to introduce them. Although he claims his view is borne out by a study of the Old Bailey cases of the eighteenth and nineteenth centuries, this is not clearly established. Garrow, and other defence counsel, constantly raised questions of evidential rules many of which, in the words of Beattie, were referred by the court to the 'judges in their post-circuit meetings at Serjeant's Inn' which helped to form 'what amounted to a law of evidence in criminal trials.'[5] He adds that, '[i]n 1700 there were few treatises on this subject; by the early nineteenth century there was a substantial literature, a market having formed among lawyers at the criminal bar.'[6]

Sir Geoffrey Gilbert, Thomas Peake, William David Evans and S.M. Phillips all extolled exclusionary and adversarial rules of evidence. Gilbert, for example, wrote that, '[t]he attestation of the witness must be as to what he knows, and not to that only which he hath heard, for a mere Hearsay is no Evidence.'[7] And Peake included in his *Compendium of the Law of Evidence* an appendix of some leading cases on the law of evidence, confirming that by the opening of the nineteenth century evidential rules were contained in such cases.[8] They included civil actions in which Erskine and Garrow appeared and, indeed, the law of evidence owed a good deal to developments in such actions.[9] Nevertheless, it is possible, with Landsman, to see evidential rules as the 'impetus' for the lawyers taking over the criminal trial.[10]

This reflects that the 'best evidence' rule; the rule against hearsay evidence; the inadmissibility of previous convictions; the character rule, which prevented the introduction of evidence of the defendant's bad character except in rebuttal; and the corroboration and confession rules were all insisted upon by defence counsel to avoid an influence on jurors that was unfair and adverse to their clients. And it is confirmed by some of Garrow's cases outlined in this book, which indicate that although some of the judges formulated these rules it was usually after following counsel's insistence upon them as aids to the defence. And at times the judges actually refused to accept them and overruled the barristers, although this occurred less frequently as the eighteenth century advanced.

This growth of a concept of rules of evidence is in sharp contrast to the European situation where rules of procedure were more precise and largely reliant upon confessions. The system of roman-canonical proof, 'encouraged and, indeed, often required, the torture of the accused in order to produce a confession, which was considered of particularly high evidential value'[11] but regarded with much distaste in England.

However, as the distinguished American jurist, John Henry Wigmore, indicated, the purpose of the rules was to determine whether a given piece of evidence should be considered, not to establish the precise probative value to be attached to it. They were needed, he said, because adversary proceedings gave rise to dangers flowing from facts being the subject of controversy between human beings moved by strong emotions and tempted to gain their cause by deceiving the court.[12]

INVIOLABILITY

In one case, in September 1787,[13] the testimonial status of a witness, John M'Daniel, who was a convicted felon but had been granted a royal pardon, was in issue. In a statement which the judge, the recorder of London, described as 'ingeniously and forcibly put upon specious principles', Garrow claimed that, '[t]he King cannot break down, or infringe, or invade any one of the rules of evidence; he has no prerogative to say that innocence shall not be protected.'[14] Describing the case as of huge public importance he argued at length (and no doubt speciously) that a royal pardon meant that the man was acquitted of his offence and this restored his credibility and ability to give evidence. Saying that the matter could be decided later by all the judges, the recorder allowed the witness to give evidence. Clearly, Garrow believed the rules existed to support counsel and their clients without interference from any, even the King, and he was also in the forefront in endeavouring to gain acceptance of a presumption of innocence for defendants in all cases.

PRESUMPTION OF INNOCENCE

The gradual recognition of the advantage to defendants of being represented by counsel was of great significance, heralding the beginning of the concept of prisoners' rights, with adversariality its main catalyst. Prisoners were beginning to demand the right to be defended fully and alongside this grew the idea, largely the creation of defence counsel, that they were deemed to be innocent unless the prosecution proved guilt beyond reasonable doubt. As defence counsel became more involved in the courtroom, the judges and juries took a less active part in proceedings and, except in cases of murder, the presumption of innocence and the beyond-reasonable-doubt standard began to be forcefully applied.[15] The presumption, or something akin to it, may have existed for some time before the eighteenth century[16] but, if so, it was by no means applied generally and Beattie records that in Surrey in 1739 where a prisoner claimed he was not a thief the judge told him, 'You must prove that.'[17] Moreover, in summary proceedings, many defendants had to struggle against a statutory presumption of guilt.[18] Indeed, Bruce Smith says that cases of suspected petty theft were sent for summary trial precisely because of 'the challenges of securing convictions in the higher courts for the felony of simple larceny.'[19]

In a prosecution in 1790 Garrow told the jury:

> Let the prisoner have the advantage of the doubt; it is better, as has often been said, that guilty men should escape from the difficulty of proof, and the doubt that hangs over that proof, than that you and the sacred administrators of justice sitting on this bench, should run the risk of dooming to death a fellow creature, on precarious or uncertain evidence.[20]

However, it was not until a year later, in 1791, that Garrow was the first counsel to express the presumption clearly in an English court.[21] In the trial of George Dingler for murder, he told the judge, that it should be 'recollected by all the bystanders, (for you do not require to be reminded of it) that every man is presumed to be innocent till proved guilty.'[22] However, judges were not yet bound to accept the principle and it was certainly not accepted by the judiciary in murder trials. For instance, in a trial at the Old Bailey in 1787, Mr Justice Heath told the jury that with murder 'the law presumes it [the killing] is done with malice aforethought and it behoves the prisoner to give a reasonable excuse for his actions, and if he does not it is the duty of the Jury to find him guilty.'[23] The presumption was not established in such cases until the landmark trial of *Woolmington* in 1935.[24]

Nevertheless, one or two judges had already expressed similar sentiments to Garrow's in his day. For instance, in the trial of 17-year-old Richard Corbett for arson in July 1784, after a lengthy hearing the judge told the jury, 'If there is a reasonable doubt, in that case that doubt ought to decide in favour of the prisoner.[25] Corbett was found not guilty. Two months later a young man, Alexander Gregory, was charged with assaulting and robbing William Cole in a field and interesting comments were made by the judge.[26] Cole had some difficulty in identifying his assailant but he was accompanied by his daughter, Margaret, who claimed to know Gregory and identified him. As Margaret was only eight years old Garrow, for the prosecution, asked her what would happen to her if she told a lie? 'I will go to Hell and the Devil will burn me,' she replied. Asked what would happen to her if she told the truth she said 'God Almighty will love me.' On these replies the judge, Mr Baron Hotham allowed her to be sworn and give evidence.

When he came to sum up to the jury, the judge referred to the positive evidence of the child saying that 'she swears positively and seems to do so with great innocence and great ingenuity.' But at the same time, he warned the jurors, 'you will make great allowance where a man's life is concerned for a mistake or misapprehension of a child of that age.' During the hearing of the case, witnesses for the defence had not always agreed on points of detail but the judge told the jury that 'if any doubt at all hangs on your minds … any balance at all, you know it is much the safest way, and it must be most pleasant to you, to lean on the merciful side and acquit the prisoner.' And, indeed, the jury did so.

This case was followed by another in the same session of the Old Bailey at which Mr Baron Hotham was again the judge.[27] Joseph Nash and William Pearman were charged with assault and robbery that very nearly turned to murder. The victim positively identified the two accused and they were seen close to the scene by two witnesses. However, Garrow called a number of witnesses who gave them a good character and in his address to the jury the judge said, ' In such a doubtful case as this, a character as you had ought to stand them in some stead, and as from the cruelty of their behaviour, if they were convicted they could not hope for pardon, therefore we should be uncommonly cautious in such a case'. Despite their cruelty, once again the jury gave the prisoners the benefit of the doubt and they were acquitted. After all, under the principle a jury is not meant to decide the likelihood of guilt but to resolve all reasonable doubt in favour of the prisoner. And, the presumption had become commonplace by 1820 when it was placed as sixth in Sir Richard Phillips's *Golden Rules for Jurymen.*[28]

In the realm of theory, Shapiro asserts that, '[t]his appreciation for the rights of the innocent reflects the priorities of the new political theory. As the place of the individual in the political system became more central, the legal system was forced to treat the individual with greater deference.'[29] This was clearly a consequence of counsel appearing for the defence in adversarial style trial.

THE HEARSAY RULE

Prior to the 1730s, although hearsay evidence, i.e. an out-of-court statement as a form of proof, was always unpopular there had been little restriction upon its introduction in criminal trials. For example, in a case in 1721, it was alleged that the prisoner, Christopher Atkinson, had beaten Alice Peak to death. In a non-verbatim Old Bailey report it is said that one prosecution witness, a Mrs Hart, testified that 'the Deceased told her, that the Prisoner threw her down a pair of Stairs in his own House ... that the Deceased said, the Prisoner stampt on her Belly in the Coach, and that she laid her Death to him.' Since counsel could not appear for the defence at the time no objection was raised to this evidence, but fortunately for the prisoner a surgeon who had examined the body found that it had suffered no injuries at all. An apothecary testified that Alice had died of a fever and another witness declared that 'all the Evidences for the deceased were scandalous Persons and particularly that Mrs Hart was a wicked, abandoned wretch.' One of the serious problems arising with hearsay evidence was exposed and, not surprisingly, the prisoner was acquitted.[30]

It was different a year later, in a briefly reported case in which a 15-year-old boy, James Booty, was accused of raping a five-year-old girl. She was not competent to give oral evidence in court but it appears that her out-of-court remarks were deemed admissible. However, the boy was said to have confessed, although in court he claimed he had done so 'in a fright', which if the later rule about confessions had been operative might have invalidated the admission if someone had frightened him with threats. Without that protection, and with the girl's words admitted, the jury found him guilty.[31]

By the 1730s, there were a number of cases at the Old Bailey where hearsay evidence was no longer allowed by the judges, usually because it was not given on oath to which great importance was attached. For example, in the trial of Joseph Pearson, aged 17, on a charge on 6 December 1732 of rape of a nine-year-old child the judge told the mother of the girl, 'what another told you is not evidence.'[32] Despite strong medical evidence supporting the prosecution case the prisoner was acquitted after lack of evidence on oath, a revealingly different result from that in the case of James Booty ten years earlier. And in the case of Christian Brown and Sarah Thursby, charged in December 1734 with theft of clothing, the judge said, 'you must not swear what the Mother-in-Law told ye—Tis no Evidence.'[33] In neither case did the report show that defence counsel was present, but, as already noted, this is not conclusive. On the other hand, in 1744 Chief Justice Lee said that despite the exclusion rule it was notorious that from necessity hearsay evidence was sometimes allowed.[34]

The exclusion of hearsay meant an out-of-court statement was inadmissible since it was not 'best evidence', and as the jurist, Serjeant Hawkins, put it, was 'in Strictness no Manner of Evidence either for or against a Prisoner, not only because it is not upon Oath, but also because the other Side hath no Opportunity of a cross Examination.'[35] At the time the missing oath would have been the more important factor, and, in the case of George Mason charged with theft in 1731, the judge said, 'What was said by the Man or Woman at the Cow's Face [presumably a public house] is no Evidence on either side, except they were here to swear it themselves.'[36] Similarly, a year later in the trial of William Flemming for highway robbery, when witnesses wanted to repeat what two men not in court had said the judge interrupted to say, 'What they said is no Evidence, they should have been here to have sworn it.'[37]

Nevertheless, the second point made by Hawkins, on cross-examination, supports the idea that it was counsel rather than the judges who saw the important utility of excluding hearsay evidence. And, in fact, although the value of the Old Bailey reports varies, in that they were longer or shorter at different periods of time, Langbein himself has accepted that it was defence counsel who not only took advantage of the rules of evidence but also used the exclusionary principle as one of the levers that would help them to wrest control of the criminal trial.[38] Such exclusion can be considered to be of the essence of a trials system that protects defendants entitled to a presumption of innocence and it was welcomed as such by defence lawyers.

It was once barristers began appearing for prisoners that the dangers of hearsay were fully appreciated, since it precluded cross-examination which was counsel's strongest weapon in securing a not guilty verdict when an accused person was not competent to give evidence on oath. Although the rule was not fully accepted until the nineteenth century it was frequently adopted earlier and Garrow invoked it repeatedly.

With serious consequences, often death, flowing from a criminal conviction it takes little imagination to see the dangers in so-called 'second-hand' evidence. Repeating what another person has said may involve changes of emphasis or intended meaning or even miscomprehension of what was expressed and towards the end of the eighteenth century the rule was being applied more commonly. A case involving Garrow's objection to hearsay was that of William Jones charged on 10 December 1783 with receiving stolen goods.[39] Here a Mr Isaacs said he saw a quantity of locks and asked Mrs Dunn whose they were. When Garrow, acting for Jones told him he must not tell the court what she said, counsel for the prosecution, Mr Silverster who at times also acted for prisoners, intervened to say, 'He must tell his story.' Garrow appealed to the court and was upheld by Mr Baron Hotham who appears to have viewed evidential rules with favour. Nevertheless, in this case the evidence against Jones was very strong and he was found guilty and transported for 14 years.

Silvester was the leading counsel at the Old Bailey before the arrival of Garrow. Born the son of a physician in London, he was educated at the Merchant Taylor's School before going up to Oxford and being called to the Bar in the Middle Temple in 1771. He was, however, in no way equal to Garrow as an advocate and on the whole he appeared for the prosecution far more often than for the defence.

In the trial of George Dingler, heard at the Old Bailey in 1791, a magistrate took a statement from a patient in hospital who did not appear in court. Garrow objected that it was hearsay as the patient was not deceased or under imminent danger of death at the time, either of which would have made the introduction of the statement in the trial lawful. There was, he said, no oath and no possibility of cross-examination. The prosecution argued that the statement was on oath and should be admissible. Garrow dealt at length with the position under statute,[40] citing many precedents and claiming that the statement was outside its provisions since, although the deponent was not dead, he could not be cross-examined. In the face of Garrow's onslaught prosecuting counsel conceded that the 'best evidence' was required and the court ruled that the statement was inadmissible as evidence.[41] Nevertheless, at the end of the case justice was done by the jury and Dingler was found guilty of the cold-blooded murder of his wife and executed.

The 'best evidence' rule meant that evidence had to be original and not derivative and must have had a clear connection with the fact to be proved. Clearly this covers hearsay but such evidence was not excluded consistently until the nineteenth century.[42]

SELF-INCRIMINATION AND PRISONERS' SILENCE

The essence of the self-incrimination rule is that neither a prisoner nor a witness should be required to accuse himself of a crime. This also grew into a principle, when defence counsel began to appear in criminal trials although, ironically, sometimes as a protection against their aggressive cross-examination.

In a trial in 1784 where Garrow was defence counsel, he asked a prosecution witness, 'How long at times have you been a smuggler?' Opposing counsel, John Silvester, objected, saying, '[t]hat is certainly an improper question' to which Garrow responded, 'He has told us already that he is a smuggler.' The judge then pointed out that, 'If he was asked as to any act of smuggling, the question would be contrary to law.' In other words the manner in which Garrow posed his question was in order, although, later in the same cross-examination when Garrow put another question the judge told him, 'I must stop you in that question; a question that can be answered only one way without accusing himself, is not to be put.'[43]

Several times in the next few years Garrow had to be restrained by judges from aggressive cross-examination likely to lead the witness into self-incrimination. For example, in the trial of Uziel Barrah in April 1785 he asked the recorder if he might ask a witness if in his evidence he had perjured himself. The judge replied, 'No, you may prove it but not ask it of himself.'[44] In a case of burglary in 1787 Garrow was reprimanded by both the judge and prosecuting counsel for a self-incriminating question[45] and in another case he was told he could not ask witnesses whether they had received stolen goods.[46]

Alongside the protection against self-incrimination grew the idea that the accused should remain silent and allow his counsel to do the work.[47] Of course, before the Criminal Evidence Act 1898 [48] a prisoner was not competent as a witness but could make an unsworn statement to the court. In one case, in 1784, Garrow told his clients, after the prosecution had concluded its case, '[p]risoners, if you take my advice, I advise you to leave the case where it is, it is in perfect good hands.' The defendants took the advice and were acquitted by the jury.[49] Some five years later in the trial of D'Arcy Wentworth, the case in which the victim left Garrow at the mercy of a highwayman, the judge, Mr Baron Perryn, asked Garrow as defending counsel, 'Would the prisoner say anything?' to which Garrow responded, 'No, my lord, I would not advise him to say anything on this occasion.' This prisoner too was found not guilty.[50] Garrow knew that a prisoner could be his or her own worst enemy when speaking in a criminal trial. In a handwritten note made in the margin of a copy of the 1784 Old Bailey Proceedings where he had prosecuted in a forgery trial, he wrote, '[t]his prisoner was one of the innumerable Instances of Persons who by making a Speech occasion their own conviction.'[51]

Along the way, judges themselves, as well as defence counsel, sometimes advised prisoners to refrain from actively participating in their trial. In an Old Bailey trial in 1783 of Jacob Thompson who was charged with theft from a dwelling house, the prisoner, in answering a question, said 'I leave it to my council.' Garrow told him, 'You understand we cannot say any thing to the Court or Jury in your defence, we can only examine witnesses.' When the prisoner then asked a question the judge, Mr Baron Hotham, said, 'God forbid that you should be hindered from saying anything in your defence, but if you have only questions to ask, I would advise you to leave them to your counsel.'[52] The prisoner said no more but had read out to the court a written statement which reads as if Garrow had a hand in its preparation—an action that would once have seen him arrested, as was the solicitor in the trial of Stephen Colledge.[53] Ultimately, when counsel were allowed to address the jury after the Prisoners' Counsel Act 1836, it was held that if counsel did so the prisoner could not also make a statement to the court.[54] Equally, if he or she did make a statement he or she lost the benefit of a speech from their counsel and was thus encouraged to remain silent throughout the trial.[55]

INVOLUNTARY CONFESSIONS

Prior to the 1730s confessions were allowed to be given in evidence against the party who made the confession. As put by Serjeant Hawkins in 1721, '[t]he confession of the Defendant himself, whether taken upon an Examination before Justices of Peace … or in Discourse with private Persons, hath always been allowed to be given in Evidence against the Party confessing.'[56] An example was the case of Margaret Wilson at the Old Bailey, a year after those words were published, when her confession was admitted despite her claiming at her trial that the prosecutor 'told her if she'd confess they'd forgive her.'[57]

The confession exclusion rule dates from the late 1730s. In a case in Surrey in August 1738 an employer persuaded a servant named Ann Wilcox to confess a felony on a promise of impunity. She did so and he used the confession to prosecute her. Denouncing the employer's behaviour Chief Justice Willes declared that the confession should, 'have no Weight with the Jury.'[58]

On 9 July 1740, Tobias and Rachael Isaacs were charged at the Old Bailey with theft from a dwellinghouse. According to the prosecutor, Rachael denied her guilt 'with Earnestness for two hours, but upon my promising to be a Friend to her, and that I would not hurt [her] she confessed.' The Old Bailey report records that, 'The Prosecutor was not allowed to proceed; and another Witness afterwards offering to give an Account of what she had confessed to him, was likewise stopped; because a Confession obtained on a Promise of Friendship, or by false Insinuations (which was the latter Case) ought not to be given in Evidence against a Prisoner.'[59]

Nevertheless, there are cases in the Old Bailey Sessions Papers of the time where judges took different attitudes, either excluding confessions altogether, or admitting them or doing so with a caution about their reliability. In contrast with the Wilcox case there was that of Richard Hill in 1742 where the judge merely issued a warning saying that if the prisoner had 'any promises of Indulgence before he confessed … the Jury will consider that.'[60] And in the case of Samuel Moses in 1743 a confession was admitted without comment. Moses had been told that if he confessed to some robberies 'he should have Favour.' He did confess and, without any caution or direction to exclude by the judge, he was convicted by the jury.[61]

By 1775, however, Lord Mansfield was able to say in *Rudd's Case,* '[t]he instance has frequently happened of persons having made confessions under threats or promises; the consequence as frequently has been that such examinations and confessions have not been made use of against them on their trial.'[62] As stated by Baron Eyre in the case of Jane Warrickshall in 1783,[63] the rule excluded evidence that the prisoner had confessed his crime unless the confession had been given voluntarily. This meant that it had not to be obtained by a promise or a threat or, as put in the *Warickshall* case, 'forced from the mind by the flattery of hope, or by the torture of fear.'[64]

In the trial on 7 July 1784 of John Hinxman on a charge of theft from his employer the question again arose as to whether his confession was admissible in evidence and whether it had been induced by a promise.[65] As the alleged confession was not reduced to writing, Garrow objected to it being referred to, on analogy with something that was told to an examining magistrate which he did not record. He understood, said Garrow, 'that it was the duty of a Justice to reduce everything into writing, for that the neglect of the magistrate should not operate against the prisoner at the Bar, who may have said something, which, if reduced into writing, might appear in a different light, but which the witness keeps back, or part of it, and therefore monstrous mischief to prisoners might happen.'[66]

Garrow suggested that the prisoner might have been sold the goods it was alleged he had stolen from his employer by another employee or had sold them to himself and paid for them. When the employer said he knew his servants never sold the goods to the accused Garrow exploded: 'For God's sake, Sir, have a little regard to your oath and character,' only to receive the reply, 'I do, I have as much regard to my oath and character as you have.' As to the second suggestion of selling to himself, the employer said that it was not right to do so to which Mr Justice Ashurst added, 'it is very odd that he should.' 'But it is no theft,' exclaimed Garrow, and continued, 'it may perhaps be an impeachment of the prudence of the prisoner, but not of his honesty.' After four witnesses gave the prisoner a very good character the jury found him not guilty.[67]

A more complicated case was heard on 22 February 1786.[68] Three prisoners were charged with feloniously breaking and entering the dwellinghouse of John Chancellor and stealing watches and other silver to a considerable value. With Chancellor out for a meal, the prisoner Armstrong, who was a workman in the house and not a lodger, was with a maid, Elizabeth Johnson, when there came a knock on the door. Armstrong answered it. The maid gave evidence that Burdett entered, pointed a pistol at her and threatened to blow her brains out if she resisted. She was then blindfolded and tied up. Burdett was then joined by Armstrong and another but she admitted to Garrow that the only person she actually saw was Burdett apart, of course, from Armstrong who was clearly present. However, Garrow suggested to her that Armstrong was also tied up, to which she replied that as she was blindfolded she could not see if he was or was not.

It appears that Armstrong later made a confession of the theft to an officer but under cross-examination by Garrow the officer was ambiguous about whether he had made any promise to Armstrong to extract the confession. After that Garrow objected to the confession being received and was upheld by the judge. Another confession by Armstrong, this time to a magistrate, was similarly not admitted as evidence. One witness gave evidence that a watch she produced in court, and which Chancellor identified as his, was given to her by Burdett.

At the conclusion of the trial the jury found Burdett guilty and he was sentenced to death. Since Garrow had secured the non-admission of Armstrong's confessions as evidence his client was found not guilty but the judge told him: 'It will be happy for you, if the escape you have had should be effectual to your amendment; but there is too much reason to fear that it will only operate to the commission of fresh crimes, in which case you can expect no mercy. In the present instance, a strict adherence to justice, on the part of the jury, has saved your life'. Brown was also found not guilty but since there is no reference to him in the report the reason is unclear.

A clear case occurred on 9 January 1788 despite the prisoner being found guilty. Samuel Cheshum was indicted for stealing an iron chain valued at £1 from Archibald Campbell.[69] After the theft a witness, Joseph Kirkman, had taken hold of the young prisoner and told him that if he told the truth he would be as favourable to him as possible and he then confessed. Prosecuting counsel argued that no promise had been made that would induce a person to admit to a crime of which he was not guilty.

Addressing the court at some length, Garrow's central point was that the principle was that if anything operated by threat, menace or promise to induce a party to accuse himself or herself the confession would be excluded in favour of liberty and life. The judge, the lord chief baron, agreed that the evidence could not be received, although it is significant that he thought the principle had been extended too far but that it was no longer prudent to attempt to vary it. In the event the prisoner was found guilty on other evidence.

In another case at the Old Bailey in 1789, Garrow appeared on behalf of a prisoner who had confessed his crime to a constable. He argued that the confession was inadmissible as being made in hope of a favour. He said the words of the constable fell within 'the language I remember of Mr Justice Gross on our last circuit that the suspect, "must neither be influenced by hopes nor awed by fears".' Garrow's effort on this occasion was, however, too wide being based on a 'hope' of a favour and the judge allowed the confession to be admitted. Nevertheless, there remained, of course, a fear of induced false confessions and unscrupulous prosecutors interested in rewards,[70] and the rule remained in force.

CHARACTER

In modern times the situations in which evidence of an accused person's bad character have been admissible have been closely restricted, until the Criminal Justice Act 2003 which abolished existing legal rules in favour of a new code. Nevertheless, prior to the period under consideration in this book, it was not considered improper to adduce evidence of a defendant's bad character. As Stephen wrote of a trial for perjury in 1653, 'at this time it was not considered irregular to call witnesses to prove a prisoner's bad character in order to raise a presumption of his guilt.'[71] There are also a number of cases reported in the Old Bailey Sessions Papers in which evidence of bad character was admitted and determined the outcome against the prisoner. An example is the case in December 1684 of Anne Gardener charged with obtaining silk by fraud. She pleaded not guilty, 'but being known to be a notorious cheat and shoplift' she was found guilty, fined ten pounds and imprisoned for one month in the Bridewell.[72]

Bad character was clearly revealed when a prisoner was visibly seen to have been branded as a consequence of having pleaded benefit of clergy to avoid the death penalty for a former capital crime. In the case of William Sims, charged with grand larceny on 16 July 1685 it was reported that, 'The prisoner appearing to be an old Offender, and Burnt in the Hand, having no evidence in his defence, was thereupon brought in Guilty by the jury.'[73] No burden of proof on the prosecution there. In the following year, John Thacker, George Drury and William Clark were charged with grand larceny on 24 February 1686.[74] Here, it was reported that, 'The prisoners giving a slender account of themselves, and Clark and Thacker having been formerly Branded in the Hand they were all found Guilty,' — which appears to have been even harder on Drury than on the other two.

The situation had not changed much by 1732 as the trial of John Waller for perverting justice testifies.[75] Waller had brought a prosecution against two men at Cambridge who were sentenced to death but his bona fides came under suspicion. As a consequence the assize judge, Baron Cummins, ordered the under-clerk of the Norfolk Assizes, Daniel Bolton to enquire into Waller's character. Giving evidence at the Old Bailey, Bolton said, 'I enquired of a Gentleman at Thetford; "Waller, says he, "Why, he's the vilest fellow living; He makes a Trade of swearing away Men's Lives for the Sake of the Reward, granted for convicting Robbers".' On the basis of this hearsay and character assassination the jury found Waller guilty of perverting justice and the lives of the two men at Cambridge were saved.

Clearly it was in the interests of counsel, once they were allowed to appear for defendants, to prevent evidence of their clients' bad character being adduced on the ground that it was prejudicial to the accused and irrelevant to the facts in the case being argued. Langbein claims that the initiative for the rule against character evidence must have come from the judges, rather than in response to demands from defence lawyers.[76] Indeed, he goes on to say that 'the rule against character evidence was a safeguard for criminal defendants that predated the lawyerization of the felony trial' although he produces no evidence to back this statement which is contrary to what is shown above. Moreover, he concedes that judges at the Old Bailey sometimes committed errors in allowing character evidence and concludes that, '[u]nless defence counsel had been engaged ... there was nobody to detect, deter, or protest error. In this sense, although the early rules of criminal evidence developed without counsel, the presence of counsel may have been needed to complete the work of transforming rules of practice into rules of law.'[77]

CORROBORATION OF ACCOMPLICE EVIDENCE

Another rule that came into operation in the 1740s, shortly after prisoners were allowed counsel, was the exclusionary rule of corroboration by Crown witnesses. From January to May 1744 no corroboration rule was operating in the Old Bailey and there are four well-reported cases in which uncorroborated accomplice testimony seems to have been sufficient to convict.[78] The theory was put by Hawkins that, 'if no accomplices were to be admitted as witnesses, it would be generally impossible to find evidence to convict the greatest offenders.'[79] Then, in December 1744 there are three acquittals in which the only ground mentioned for the verdicts is lack of corroboration. In one of them the report concludes, '[t]here being no other evidence upon this indictment but the accomplice, the prisoners were acquitted.'[80] This situation was not to the liking of Henry Fielding who, in a partisan view arising from his position as chief magistrate at Bow Street, wrote of highway robbers in 1751:

Unless therefore the Robbers should be so unfortunate as to be apprehended in the Fact, (a Circumstance which their Numbers, Arms, &c. renders ordinarily impossible) no such Corroboration can possibly be had; but the Evidence of the Accomplice standing alone and unsupported, the Villain, contrary to the Opinion, and almost direct Knowledge of all present, is triumphantly acquitted, laughs at the Court, scorns the Law, vows Revenge against his Prosecutors, and returns to his Trade with a great Increase of Confidence, and commonly of Cruelty.[81]

Fielding's lawyer son, William, was subsequently involved as prosecutor in the trial of Joseph Dunbar who, in May 1784, was accused of forging a Bank of England banknote. When he proposed to call an accomplice as his first witness the judge, the recorder of London, said that whether to do so or not had, 'always been considered as discretionary.' 'Different Judges,' he continued, 'hold different practices, but I am clearly convinced that the better way is not to examine the accomplice first, for this reason: the jury ought not to receive impressions from evidence of which ultimately they may not be at liberty in point of law to believe.' Garrow, acting for Dunbar, immediately added, 'My Lord, I am not fond of the jury hearing what they are afterwards told to forget.'[82] The accomplice's evidence was excluded although this example was not always followed since, as the recorder of London indicated, different judges upheld different practices.

On 19 October 1785 Francis Hill, William Nicholson and Margaret Cadwell were charged at the Old Bailey with burglary from a dwellinghouse.[83] The main evidence against the prisoners was given by William Kendrick, an accomplice who claimed that he took part in the burglary with the three accused. When he was called upon to give evidence, Garrow submitted that there was no evidence against Nicholson but the judge held that it was regular to hear an accomplice in any stage of the prosecution and added that, 'whether afterwards it deserves credit, will turn out upon the whole evidence, in which, to be sure, care will be taken to separate, but I cannot at present, cut the evidence to pieces in the course of the narration.' So, again, a judge was permitting evidence and not taking the initiative in creating an exclusionary rule of evidence.

After Kendrick had given his evidence in chief he was questioned by Garrow.

> **Garrow:** Mr Kendrick, you tell your story as easily as a man can read a chapter in the Bible, as if it was to your honour; how long have you been engaged in this business?
> **Kendrick:** About a twelvemonth, as far as I can recollect.
> **Garrow:** How often have you been in custody?
> **Kendrick:** I cannot tell, that is an odd question to ask.
> **Garrow:** You are as often in custody as out?
> **Kendrick:** No, not quite, I cannot tell.
> **Garrow:** Give a random guess, we will not quarrel for a dozen times?
> **Kendrick:** I cannot give no random guess.
> **Garrow:** Do not you know that you have been much oftener at Bow-street than once?
> **Kendrick:** No.

Later in cross-examination Kendrick said, 'I did not squeak after I was taken, I stood out a week, and then I should not have squeaked if it had not been for other people.' The prisoner Hill was identified by a person in the house when the burglary took place and he was found guilty and sentenced to death. Nicholson and Cadwell were acquitted by the jury and the judge told Kendrick, 'I discharge you without any exhortation, because it will be thrown away, I have no hopes of you, I have no doubt but you will come to the gallows.'

In the case of John Langford and William Annand respectively accused of grand larceny and receiving stolen goods in 1788, Garrow poured scorn on a Crown witness accomplice, named Robert Kimber, when he interrupted examination in chief by the well-known Old Bailey counsel, Newman Knowlys, to say, 'The gentleman says you have been a bad boy, therefore, begin to amend.' Kimber testified that he had the stolen goods from Langsford and disposed of them to Annand. In subsequently cross-examining Kimber, Garrow addressed him as his 'honest friend' and remarked that it was 'an unexpected pleasure to get you into this part of the Court'. He got him to confirm that he had been out of Newgate for about a week and that there had been talk of sending him to Botany Bay for seven years. So, exclaimed Garrow, 'you are swearing now to get yourself out of the scrape.'[84]

Since he had turned King's evidence Kimber could not be prosecuted for participating in the theft and freely admitted taking part in the robbery. Alluding to transportation Garrow told him, 'If you do not go this time, you will go soon.' When Kimber replied, 'I will take care not to do anything to go,' the judge said, 'Take care, if ever you are caught tripping, you will certainly forfeit your life, and expect no favour.' Both prisoners were found guilty with Langford being sentenced to transportation for seven years and Annand, who the judge indicated was a persistent receiver, for 14 years.

In 1787 the corroboration rule was reduced to merely a caution to the jury by the case of *Atwood and Robbins*.[85] An accomplice was allowed to give evidence that he and two others had committed a robbery and on that testimony the jury found them guilty. The judge, Mr Justice Buller, then referred the matter to the twelve judges at Serjeants Inn who decided that an accomplice alone was a competent witness and that if the jury, weighing the probability of the testimony, found him or her believable a conviction supported only by such testimony was perfectly legal.[86] Buller was the judge of whom it was said he was 'always to hang for sheep-stealing, avowing as a reason that he had several sheep stolen from his own flock.'[87]

In December of the same year the case of *Atwood and Robbins* was applied in another case, against the protests of Garrow. In the trial of John Durham and Edward Crowther for burglary Garrow addressed the judge about a witness, Francis Fleming, who was an accomplice.[88] Garrow argued that though a man may describe the circumstances of a robbery, he should not be permitted to say others are partners in his guilt. 'My Lord,' he pleaded, 'the law has been frequently laid down in the most luminous manner by your lordship, and also by other Judges, that such a witness should not be received against any man.' The judge, Baron Perryn, replied that, '[o]n the very first day of this term, Mr Justice Buller, tried a person for a felony and he was convicted on the evidence of the accomplice only; he referred the case to the twelve Judges and the ten judges who were present were unanimously of the opinion that it only went to his credit, and not to his competency.'[89] Fleming's evidence was admitted, the judge told the jury that the case depended entirely on his credit, the jury found both prisoners guilty and they were sentenced to death.

In the light of the *Atwood* and *Durham* cases it is difficult to see the judges and not defence counsel as taking the initiative in securing the rules of evidence as Langbein, with qualifications, maintains.

CONCLUSION

Generally speaking, the rules of criminal evidence were unknown before the early eighteenth century. Something vaguely like them appeared in the works of Hale or Hawkins in a very rudimentary form but certainly not as binding rules. Nevertheless, on occasion their substance would be invoked by judges and there were conscious efforts to protect prisoners at the end of the seventeenth century and the beginning of the eighteenth century. Sometimes a prisoner, such as Sir Richard Grahme in 1691, would explicitly refer to his right to procedural safeguards during his trial and have his rights upheld by the judges.[90] Shapiro concludes that out of the legacy of the Whig victory in the Revolution of 1688,

> there slowly emerged a realignment of political priorities in favour of the citizen, creating in turn an appreciation for the defendant as an individual worthy of protection. In the interest of self-preservation, the individual demanded security, safety, certainty, and a presumption of innocence. These themes of criminal law, which would grow in importance throughout the eighteenth century, found embryonic expression in the Trials Act of 1696.[91]

However, it was only during the eighteenth century that such became established as rules to be strictly observed. Of course, it was the judges who had to impose them. But there is no evidence that judges introduced them to protect juries from lawyers or for any other reason. Although, as we have seen, Langbein considers that the rules of evidence were the work of the judges, even he concedes that, 'the presence of counsel may have been needed to complete the work of transforming rules of practice into rules of law.'[92] To which may be added the assessment in the mid-nineteenth century of William Best who referred to counsel's influence in the development of the rules of evidence:

> The necessary consequence of allowing defence counsel was hat objections to the admissibility of evidence were much more frequently taken, the attention of the judges was more directed to the subject of evidence, their judgments were better considered, and their decisions better remembered.[93]

Numerous cases show Garrow, and others, insisting, frequently that the hearsay and other evidentiary rules be applied and although they were sometimes unable to persuade the judges they often did so. By the end of the eighteenth century it was their efforts that had secured the status of the rules that helped transform felony trial in England.

It can be conjectured that continental jurisprudence, which was highly rule-based might have influenced the development of evidential rules in England but there is no evidence for this and, indeed, Langbein himself asserts that the transformation to adversary trial in England occurred without the least attention to the continental model which long into the eighteenth century was disgraced by the law of torture.[94]

ENDNOTES for *Chapter 8*

[1] T.A. Green. (1985) *Verdict According to Conscience. Perspectives on the English Criminal Jury Trial 1200-1800*. Chicago, University of Chicago Press. p. 267.

[2] J.H. Langbein. (2003) *The Origins of Adversary Criminal Trial*. Oxford, Oxford University Press. p. 179.

[3] Ibid. p. 243.

[4] Ibid.

[5] J.M. Beattie. (1991) 'Scales of Justice: Defense Counsel and the English Criminal Trial in the Eighteenth and Nineteenth Centuries.' 9(2) *Law and History Review*. Illinois. University of Illinois Press. p. 233.

[6] Ibid.

[7] G. Gilbert. (1754) *The Law of Evidence*. Dublin, Sarah Cotter. p. 107.

[8] T. Peake (1801) *A Compendium of the Law of Evidence*. London, E & R Brooke and J.Rider

[9] See ibid.

[10] S. Landsman. (1990) 'From Gilbert to Bentham: The Reconceptualization of Evidence Theory.' 36 *Wayne Law Review*. University of Oregon School of Law. p. 602.

[11] G. Fisher. (1997) 'The Jury's Rise as Lie Detector.' New Haven, 107 *Yale Law Journal*. p. 587.

[12] William Twining. (1985) *Theories of Evidence: Bentham and Wigmore*. London, Weidenfeld & Nicolson. p. 157.

[13] OBP Online. (www.oldbaileyonline.org, 23 October 2004) 12 September 1787 Trial of Thomas Reilly and Abraham Davis for Fraud. Ref: t17870912-111.

[14] Ibid.

[15] J.H. Langbein. (1978) 'The Criminal Trial before the Lawyers.' 45 *The University of Chicago Law Review*. p. 266. Contrast the view of B. Shapiro that the beyond-reasonable-doubt test in effect existed in the seventeenth century as a 'satisfied conscience' standard. (1983) *Probability and Certainty in Seventeenth-Century England: A Study of the Relationships Between Natural Science, Religion, History, Law and Literature*. New Jersey, Princeton University Press. p. 168.

[16] Perhaps in the seventeenth century. See B Shapiro. (1991) *'Beyond Reasonable Doubt' and 'Probable Cause': Historical Perspectives on the Anglo-American Law of Evidence*. Berkeley, University of California Press. p. 40.

[17] J. M. Beattie. (1986) *Crime and Courts in England 1660-1800*. Oxford, The Clarendon Press. p. 349.

[18] B.P. Smith. (2005) 'The Presumption of Guilt and the English Law of Theft, 1750-1850.' 23(1) *Law and History Review*. University of Illinois Press. p. 135.

[19] Ibid. p. 136.

[20] OBP Online. (www.oldbailey online.org. 16 June 2005) 8 December 1790. Trial of George Platt and Philip Roberts. Ref: t17901208-35.

[21] Interestingly, the presumption appears in the French *Declaration of the Rights of Man* in 1791.

[22] OBP Online. (www.oldbaileyonline.org, 27 October 2004) 14 September 1791. Trial of George Dingler for Murder. Ref: t17910914-1.

23 OBP Online. (www.oldbaileyonline.org, 19 March 2005) 12 December 1787. Trial of James Carse for Murder. Ref: t1787 1212-3.

24 *Woolmington v. DPP.* [1935] AC. 462.

25 OBP Online. (www.oldbaileyonline.org, 27 October 2004) 7 July 1784. Trial of Richard Corbett for Arson. Ref: t17840707-10.

26 OBP Online. (www.oldbaileyonline.org, 27 October 2004) 15 September 1784 Trial of Alexander Gregory. Ref: t17840915-10.

27 OBP Online.(www.oldbaileyonline.org, 27 October 2004) 15 September 1784 Trial of Joseph Nash and William Pearson. Ref: t17840915-78

28 Cited by J.M. Beattie. 'Scales of Justice:' Op. cit. p. 249.

29 A.H. Shapiro. (1993) 'Political Theory and the Growth of Defensive Safeguards in Criminal Procedure: The Origins of the Treason Trials Act of 1696.' 11(2) *Law and History Review*. Illinois, American Society of Legal History. p. 243.

30 OBP Online. (www.oldbaileyonline.org, 24 October 2004) 6 December 1721. Trial of Christopher Atkinson for Murder. Ref: t17211206-9.

31 OBP Online. (www.oldbaileyonline.org, 1 November 2004) 10 May 1722 Trial of James Booty for Rape. Ref: t17220510-34.

32 OBP Online. (www.oldbaileyonline.org, 23 October 2004) 6 December 1732 Trial of Joseph Pearson. Ref: t17321206-69.

33 OBP Online. (www.oldbaileyonline.org, 27 October 2004) 4 December 1734 Trial of Christian Brown and Sarah Thursby. Ref: t17341204-72.

34 *Omychund v. Barker.* [1744] 26 *Eng. Rep.* p. 31.

35 Serjeant W. Hawkins. (1716) *Treatise of the Pleas of the Crown.* London, J. Walthoe. vol. ii. p. 431.

36 OBP Online. (www.oldbaileyonline.org, 22 October 2004) 8 December 1731 Trial of George Mason. Ref: t17311208-38.

37 OBP Online. (www.oldbaileyonline.org, 23 October 2004) 6 September 1732 Trial of William Flemming. Ref: t17320906-67.

38 J. H. Langbein. *The Origins of Adversary Criminal Trial.* Op. cit. pp. 178-79.

39 OBP Online. (www.oldbaileyonline.org, 24 October 2004) 10 December 1783. Trial of William Jones for Theft. Ref: t17831210-105.

40 2 & 3 William and Mary, c. 32.

41 OBP Online. (www.oldbaileyonline.org, 27 October 2004) 14 September 1791 Trial of George Dingler for Murder. Ref: t17910914-1.

42 A. N. May. (2003)*The Bar and the Old Bailey, 1750-1850.* Chapel Hill, The University of North Carolina Press. p. 109.

43 OBP. Online. (www.oldbaileyonline.org, 1 December 2004) 26 May 1784 Trial of Joseph Dunbar for Forgery. Ref: t17840526-132.

44 OBP Online. (www.oldbaileyonline.org, 3 December 2004) 6 April 1785 Trial of Uziel Barrah. Ref: t17850406-86.

45 OBP Online. (www.oldbaileyonline.org, 28 November 2004) 12 December 1787 Trial of Thomas Duxton for Burglary. Ref: t17871212-78.

46 OBP Online. (www.oldbaileyonline.org, 15 October 2004) 12 December 1787. Trial of John DunBar. Ref: t17871212-34.

47 This is a revolutionary change from Langbein's 'accused speaks' type of trial.

48 62. Vict. C. 36.

49 OBP Online. (www.oldbaileyonline.org, 1 December 2004) 7 July 1784 Trial of Thomas Isham and Others for Theft. Ref: t17840707-74.

50 OBP Online. (www.oldbaileyonline.org, 1 December 2004) 9 December 1789. Trial of D'Arcy Wentworth. Ref: t17891209-1.

51 OBP Online. (www.oldbaileyonline.org, 1 December 2004) 20 October 1784 Trial of Thomas Freeman. Ref: t17841020-70. The note is cited by John H. Langbein. (2003) The *Origins of Adversary Criminal Trial.* Oxford, Oxford University Press. p. 268.

52 OBP Online. (www.oldbaileyonline.org, 12 October 2004) 10 December 1783. Trial of Jacob Thompson. Ref: t17831210-148.

53 See ante. p. 28.

54 See D. J.A. Cairns. (1998) *Advocacy and the Making of the Adversarial Criminal Trial, 1800-1865.* Oxford, The Clarendon Press. pp. 118-9, for decisions on the point.

55 Ibid. p. 124.

56 Serjeant W. Hawkins. *Treatise on the Pleas of the Crown.* Op. cit. vol. ii. p. 429.

57 OBP Online. (1722) Trial of Margaret Wilson for Theft from a Dwelling House. Cited by Langbein. *The Origins of Adversary Criminal Trial.* p. 218.

58 J.M. Beattie. (1986) *Crime and Courts in England 1660-1800.* Oxford,The Clarendon Press. p. 346-7.

59 OBP Online. (www.oldbaileyonline.org, 27 November 2004) 9 July 1740 Trial of Tobias and Rachael Isaacs. Ref: t17400709-34.

60 OBP Online. (www.oldbaileyonline.org, 27 November 2004) July 1742 Trial of Richard Hill. Ref: t17420714-8.

61 OBP Online. (www.oldbaileyonline.org, 27 November 2004) 7 December 1743 Trial of Samuel Moses and Simon Emanuel. Ref: t17431207-61.

62 *R. v. Margaret Caroline Rudd.* [1775] *Eng. Rep.* pp. 160-61.

63 OBP Online. (www.oldbaileyonline.org, 27 November 2004) 30 April 1783 Trial of Jane Warickshall. Ref: t17830430-9.

64 See [1783] 168 *Eng. Rep.* p. 234.

65 OBP Online.(www.oldbaileyonline.org, 27 November 2004) 7 July 1784. Trial of John Hinxman for Theft. Ref: t17840707-62.

66 Ibid.

67 Ibid.

68 OBP. Online. (www.oldbaileyonline.org, 3 March 2005) 22 February 1786. Trial of Thomas Burdett, Samuel Armstrong, William Brown. Ref: t17860222-45.

69 OBP Online. (www.oldbaileyonline.org, 21 March 2005) 9 January 1788 Trial of Samuel Cheshum. Ref: t17880109-38.

70 S. Landsman. (1990) 'The Rise of the Contentious Spirit: Adversary Procedure in Eighteenth Century England.' New York 75 *Cornell Law Review.* p. 527. note 147.

71 J. F. Stephen. (1883) *A History of the Criminal Law of England.* London, Routledge/Thoemmes. vol. i. p. 368.

72 OBP Online. (www.oldbaileyonline.org, 28 October 2004) December 1684 Trial of Anne Gardner. Ref: t16841210-35.

73 OBP Online. (www.oldbaileyonline.org, 28 October 2004) 16 July 1785 Trial of William Sims. Ref: t16850716-8.

74 OBP Online. (www.oldbaileyonline.org, 28 October 2004) 24 February 1686. Trial of John Thacker, George Drury and William Clark. Ref: t16860224-20.

75 OBP Online. (www.oldbaileyonline.org, 28 October 2004) 25 May 1732 Trial of John Waller. Ref: t17320525-69.

76 J.H. Langbein. *The Origins of Adversary Criminal Trial.* Op. cit. p. 202.

77 Ibid. p. 196.

78 .Ibid. pp. 203-5.

79 Serjeant W. Hawkins. (1716) *Treatise on the Pleas of the Crown.* Op. cit. p. 432.

80 OBP Online. (www.oldbaileyonline.org, 28 November 2004) 5 December 1744 Trial of James Leekey and William Robinson. Ref: 17441205-6.

81 H. Fielding. (1751) *An Inquiry into the Causes of the Late Increase of Robbers.* London, A. Millar. p. 160.

82 OBP Online. (www.oldbaileyonline.org, 28 November 2004) 26 May 1784 Trial of Joseph DunBar. Ref: t17840526-132.

83 OBP Online. (www.oldbaileyonline.org, 18 January 2005) 19 October 1785. Trial of Francis Hill, William Nicholson and Margaret Cadwell. Ref: t17851019-14.

84 OBP Online. (www.oldbaileyonline.org, 29 November 2004) 9 January 1788 John Langford and William Annand. Ref: t17880109-40.

85 *R. v. Atwood and Robbins.* [1788] 168 *Eng. Rep.* 334.

86 Ibid.

87 Lord J. Campbell. (1868) *Lives of the Lord Chancellors.* London, Murray. vol. 8, p. 55.

88 OBP Online. (www.oldbaileyonline.org, 15 March 2005) 12 December 1787 Trial of John Durham and Edward Crowther. Ref: t17871212-34.

89 Ibid.

90 12 *State Trials* pp. .661-2.

91 A.H. Shapiro. 'Political Theory and the Growth of Defensive Safeguards in Criminal Procedure.' Op. cit. p. 255.

92 J.H. Langbein. *The Origins of Adversary Criminal Trial.* Op. cit. p. 196.

93 W. M. Best. (1849) *A Treatise on the Principles of Evidence and Practice as to Proofs in Courts of Common Law.* London, p. 133. Case and treatise cited by Langbein. *The Origins of Adversary Criminal Trial.* Op. cit. p. 244.

94 J.H. Langbein. *The Origins of Adversary Criminal Trial.* Op. cit. pp. 339-40.

CHAPTER 9

Counsel Finally Address the Jury

INTRODUCTION

In the early nineteenth century, when the efforts of Garrow and others had produced the great changes seen above, it appeared more of an anomaly than ever that defence counsel could not address the jury on behalf of their clients. By this time they had come to dominate the courtroom in criminal cases but the final step in consolidating adversary trial remained elusive.

Paradoxically, to a large extent this was due to the Bar itself, and particularly its members who were in Parliament. Many of them were largely involved in civil courts and aspiring to gentrification they looked at the Old Bailey with distaste. According to May, the Bar had mixed feelings about the Old Bailey which in the early nineteenth century they 'regarded as a forum for dishonest hacks' with even its outstanding advocates being regarded with a degree of suspicion.[1] And not only members of the Bar. Calling for reform at the Old Bailey in 1834, *The Times* newspaper in an editorial complained of barristers being 'veteran brawlers and bullies', and 'irritable and foul-mouthed.' 'The Old Bailey,' it said, 'has long been a scandal to the country, and a by-word expressive of everything coarse and indecent in the business of advocacy.'[2]

Nevertheless, from 1821 to 1834 liberal and radical Members of Parliament had introduced Bills into the House of Commons to enable counsel to address the jury but they were all defeated. Then, in 1836 William Ewart, the radical barrister MP for Liverpool, introduced a Bill which passed the Commons with a large majority but still faced the hostility of the lawyers and landed interests in the House of Lords.

Lord John Russell, who had become Home Secretary in April 1835, was determined to break the deadlock. In 1833, following the passing of the Great Reform Act 1832 in which Russell had played a principal part, criminal law commissioners had been appointed to codify the entire criminal law and by 1836 they were busy at that task. Nothing daunted, Russell asked them to turn their minds to the Prisoners' Counsel Bill before Parliament. They did so and produced a powerful report in favour of the concept[3] which was published just prior to the decisive speech for the Bill in the House of Lords by Lord Lyndhurst.

Once the Bill became law the size of the Bar grew rapidly both on the civil and criminal sides. In fact so rapidly that some barristers began to bring the name of the Bar—particularly at the Old Bailey—into even more contempt than before, but eventually this led to the strict rules of etiquette that changed the perception of barristers and still obtain today.

JURORS' PETITION

In regard to the question of counsel addressing the jury there had been an interesting petition calling for 'the full benefit of counsel' presented to the House of Commons by George Lamb, the brother of Lord Melbourne, on 6 April 1824. Lamb was a barrister and a contributor to the influential *Edinburgh Review*. He had won Westminster for the Whig interest after a bitter election following the death of Sir Samuel Romilly in 1818. The petition was submitted by several jurymen in the habit of serving on juries at the Old Bailey and it read, in part, as follows:

> With every disposition to decide justly, the Petitioners have found, by experience, in the course of their attendances as Jurymen at the Old Bailey, that the opening statements for the prosecution too frequently leave an impression more unfavourable to the Prisoner at the Bar, than the evidence of itself could have produced, and it has always sounded harsh to the Petitioners to hear it announced from the Bench that the Counsel to whom the Petitioner has committed his defence, cannot be permitted to address the Jury on his behalf, nor reply to the charges which have, or have not, been substantiated by the witnesses. The Petitioners have felt their situation peculiarly painful and embarrassing when the Prisoner's faculties, perhaps surprised by such an intimation, are too much absorbed in the difficulty of his unhappy circumstances to admit to an effort towards his own justification against the statement of the Prosecutor's Counsel, often unintentionally aggravated through zeal or misconception.[4]

No doubt with Lamb's help the jurors had produced a succinct statement of the whole case for prisoners' counsel.

THE PRISONERS' COUNSEL ACT 1836

The struggle for the right of prisoners to have counsel address the jury reached its climax 12 years later with the Prisoners' Counsel Bill 1836, but the task of securing its passage through Parliament was not an easy one. Although this right is of great importance, and is today regarded as inalienable, the Prisoners' Counsel Act was a long time in gestation owing to the strong opposition to the Bill in the legal profession, including barristers acting at the Old Bailey. According to May, many members of the Bar were 'vehemently opposed' to implementation of the Act, and

> while the reasons for their resistance were various, mistrust of professional advocacy was prominent among them. In the 1830s strong doubts about the utility of advocacy in the criminal courts were entertained within the Bar as well as without.[5]

This is confirmed by the *Law Magazine* in 1836 when it claimed that large sections of the legal profession were opposed to permitting counsel for the defence to address the jury.[6]

The issue of prisoners' counsel had been raised in the House of Commons by Richard Martin supported by Sir James Mackintosh in 1821 and 1824, and again on 25 April 1826 when George Lamb asked leave to bring in such a Bill, called the Counsel for Persons Prosecuted for Felony Bill.[7] After opposition from both the Attorney-General, Sir Charles Wetherell, and the Home Secretary, Sir Robert Peel, the Bill received only 36 votes, with 105 against.[8] It is interesting that in the 1821 debate, Sir James Mackintosh, in an attempt to win public support, had stressed that allowing defence counsel to address the jury would result in an increase in convictions of the guilty. In the House of Commons, he said:

> He did not seek this privilege to enable criminals to have a better chance of escaping; for their escape he thought the greatest slur upon the practice of the law. His object was, not that these should escape, but that the innocent should have a better protection. The utmost that could result from agreeing to this measure would be a greater number of guilty persons would be convicted, which must be regarded as a good and not as an evil.[9]

Why this should be so was not apparent and his view was not generally supported. On the other hand, support for the principle was growing and in 1834 a similar Bill was successfully steered through the House of Commons only to be dropped when it reached the Lords. It was then reintroduced in the following year when, after receiving its second reading, it was referred to a select committee where it sank without trace.

The period after the defeat of the long-surviving Liverpool and Wellington Tory governments saw a spate of reforming legislation by the Whigs including the Great Reform Act 1832, important Factory Acts, the Municipal Corporations Act 1835 and the setting up of county courts and police forces across the country.[10] These statutes aroused considerable public debate, and this was particularly so around the discretion exercised by prosecutors, jurors and judges in criminal trials.[11] The extensive statutory reduction in the incidence of capital punishment brought about by Sir Robert Peel when he was Home Secretary also encouraged the support for full defence by counsel.

CRIMINAL LAW COMMISSIONERS—REPORT

In 1836 yet another Bill, known as the Prisoners' Defence by Counsel Bill was introduced into the House of Commons by William Ewart, who also supported the total abolition of the death penalty, and on this occasion a select committee reported favourably. The Bill, which included provision for the establishment of a form of legal aid by the assignment of counsel to poor prisoners without the prisoner paying a fee, passed the full house with a large majority, but still faced the opposition of the Lords. It was at this stage that a report on the topic by the criminal law commissioners was requested of them by the Home Secretary, Lord John Russell.[12] Appointed in 1833 by Lord Chancellor Brougham to reform and codify the criminal law, the commissioners were: John Austin, Henry Bellenden Ker, Andrew Amos, William Wightman and Thomas Starkie. They were all eminent lawyers and liberal reformers, well suited to the task and more than willing to innovate and act as a pressure group for law reform.[13]

The bias of the commissioners in favour of prisoners' counsel was clear from the beginning. They began by setting themselves guidelines and limiting the principle of their inquiry to two questions. First, whether allowing counsel to address the jury would tend to the discovery of the truth? And secondly, if so, whether there were any counterbalancing factors? They then immediately let it be known that they had no doubts on the first point and, indeed, argued that it would also tend to the advancement of justice.

They expressed the view that the criminal justice system should not only be moderate and just, but should also appear to be so to the jurors who carried out their vital duties. Yet, they said, the law so far as counsel addressing the jury was concerned, 'closed the lips of the prisoner's advocate in every case of felony, and told the prisoner so whenever he said he left his defence to his counsel.' This, they concluded, appeared to people to be harsh and unreasonable and they argued strongly that prisoners' counsel should be allowed to address the jury.[14]

The commissioners also explained that in their view statements and explanations of the parties were as important to a court as the necessity to hear both sides of a case. In many instances an accused, but innocent, person was incompetent to conduct his own defence. Though in possession of all his faculties he often, from a sense of the disgrace and danger to which he was exposed, and from ignorance of the forms of law, conducted his defence to his own disadvantage. It frequently happened, they said, that hardened villains possessed more coolness and composure than the innocent, who could exhibit a degree of confusion which seemed only to indicate guilt.

'It will hardly, we think, be disputed', declared the commissioners, 'that the permitting the advocate to speak for the client tends, generally, to the discovery of truth and the consequent advancement of justice, since', they added, somewhat inaccurately, 'the practice has obtained in every civilized age and country.' On stronger ground they further argued that, 'The principles of legal investigation ought not to differ from those suggested by every man's experience in the ordinary transactions of life … Such experience would seem to require that some statement and explanation should accompany the proof of the facts in dispute without which the truth may not suggest itself to the inquirer.' And this required the involvement of a professional advocate.

The commissioners took evidence from selected witnesses, most of whom supported their stand, but some idea of the feeling against the proposal may be gauged from a letter[15] written to the commissioners by R. Spankie, a serjeant-at-law. He believed it was the duty of the judge not merely to sum up the facts to the jury, but to state the fair result of the evidence with an indulgent leaning in favour of the accused. This resulted, according to Spankie, in a trial being a dispassionate inquiry into the truth, relieved from the 'obstreperous contention of counsel' with more unaccountable acquittals than unexpected verdicts of guilty.

Another effect of change he foresaw was that a profession which taught caution and discretion would become, for its younger members, a 'school of vicious eloquence.' The whole temper in which criminal justice was conducted would be altered with a Bar corrupted by the temptation to address speeches to the audience and, through the press, to political parties all over the country. Counsel for the prosecution would follow the example and the jury would be placed in opposition to the judge. Jurors, he concluded, would be 'flattered, or threatened, or deceived into the usurpation of an irresponsible power, subversive of the laws, and formidable equally to innocence and guilt.' The moderation and sobriety of the administration of criminal justice would be totally destroyed.

Another barrister, Frederic Calvert, took a similar view and claimed that, although the arguments in favour of the Bill were all of a 'catching, popular and easily-intelligible' sort, a large proportion of the profession, including three-quarters of the judges, were still unconvinced.[16] He also followed Spankie in suggesting that the 'absurd distinction' between felony and misdemeanour (where counsel could address the jury) should be cured by taking away counsel's speech in trials for the latter, although he produced no evidence that any awful consequences were to be found in such trials. And, whilst he believed transactions involving landed property would be unintelligible to jurors without explanation by counsel, the 'subject-matter of criminal trials is almost always familiar to their minds.'[17]

The commissioners rejected all such arguments and accepted those of witnesses favourable to the project. Alderman Harmer was one. A solicitor with 23 years' experience in practice at the Old Bailey, his success was revealed when, in order to become an alderman of London for the ward of Farringdon Without, he gave up legal practice worth the huge sum of £4,000 a year. Giving evidence, he said that he generally found that innocent men were the least capable of defending themselves as 'their mind is so agitated by the falsehood of the testimony that they are in confusion.'

As an attorney, he added, he had met many a thief who would recall every point of evidence against him, and what every man had said before a magistrate; but an innocent man would often hardly be able to tell him anything at all of what had passed. He had sometimes prepared for a client a written defence to be read to the jury, but circumstances could arise in the course of a trial which would render the defence mischievous instead of beneficial.[18] This led to situations such as that in the trial of Francis Parr for deception and fraud in 1787. Parr was about to read his own defence to the court when his counsel interjected, 'Hand it here first that we may see if it is proper to be read.'[19]

Sir Frederick Pollock, former Attorney-General to Sir Robert Peel, made an impressive witness with his profound knowledge of the common law and experience of juries. He believed the existing position was quite unprincipled. On several occasions, he said, he had known great injustice done for want of counsel.

He instanced cases of rape and murder where convictions given had been doubted by many members of the Bar present. He was a strenuous advocate for allowing counsel to address the jury, particularly where the prosecution case was based upon circumstantial evidence which a prisoner was usually unable to deal with fully.

The commissioners thought it necessary also to have a counter-balance to the opening speech of the prosecution. Occasionally, even on trials for murder, the whole skill of an expert advocate was allowed to be exerted on his opening statement, 'as was seen so often with the celebrated speeches of Sir William Garrow.' As for a written defence prepared before the trial, this was of no use to the illiterate, it was often irrelevant and in any event the practice was not at all general. At no time did the commissioners specifically refer to the adversarial system as such but they advocated it in the concept of reaching the truth through forensic battle with counsel on each side.

The view of Coke and Hawkins set out in *Chapter 2* of this book that the prisoner did not require counsel because the proof of a crime should be clear and manifest was described by the commissioners as 'strange and unreasonable' and a relic from earlier times. And as for the argument that the judge was the prisoner's counsel, they considered that it was impossible for the judge properly to be so. Furthermore, it was unfair to him. At assizes, they submitted, the attempt to finish the list of causes and deliver the gaol often occasioned late sittings and produced a degree of mental and bodily fatigue which impaired the energies of even the most powerful mind. As an example they referred to the remarks of the judge in the celebrated trial of Spencer Cowper for murder.[20]

Another serious objection to the Bill was that it would cause a great increase in expenditure by defendants. The commissioners accepted that this would be so but did not agree that trials would be protracted to twice or three times their former length. They thought the opportunity of addressing the jury would have the effect of reducing cross-examination. Earlier, in 1826, Brougham had made a similar point that many artificial questions of law were raised in order to reach the ears of juries which would no longer be taken if counsel could address the jury.[21]

Finally, the commissioners submitted their conclusions:[22]

1. That, as a general position, the right of an accused to be heard prior to condemnation was founded upon principles of reason, humanity and justice recognized by the law of England.
2. That it was essential to this right that it should, at the option of the accused, be exercised through counsel.
3. That no reasonable distinction as to the exercise of the right could be made between felonies and other classes of crime.
4. That the existing practice was in many respects detrimental to the interests of justice in regard to the conviction of the guilty, as well as the protection of the innocent.
5. Considerable inconvenience might follow a change, but the arguments urged in favour of the anomaly, were insufficient to warrant its continuance.
6. Prisoner's counsel was in all cases to be entitled to the concluding address and this was also to be extended to trials for misdemeanours.

LEGISLATION

When the report was published the Bill had already passed the House of Commons and on 23 June 1836 Lord Lyndhurst, a commanding figure in the House of Lords, accepted the difficult task of winning over its members on their second reading of the Bill.[23] Repeating many of the arguments in support of the Bill contained in the commissioners' report, which he described as 'most elaborate and learned', he cast the existing law as 'remnants of a barbarous code of laws relating to felons.' Castigating the views of Sir Edward Coke and Serjeant Hawkins mentioned earlier, he declared that it was absurd to say that it was better for uneducated prisoners with anxious minds, who could lose their lives from a mere phrase of speech, were better off defending themselves.

And what injustice it was, he continued, to allow counsel for the prosecution to address the jury, but not counsel for the party accused. An ingenious counsel for the prosecution could collect all the little facts of the case and so arrange them that, interspersed with occasional observations, they would lead the minds of the jury to the conclusion that the accused was guilty. This was particularly true when accompanied by counsel's expression of great mercy towards the prisoner, with a hope that he would be able to extricate himself from the foils in which he had entangled himself. Reasonable men, he thought, could not sanction a system so partial as to deny a reply.

He dismissed the argument that the tranquility of the courts would be destroyed by the warmth and zeal of counsel on both sides arguing a case, on the ground that this had not happened with cases of misdemeanour or in other countries. And he did not like the suggestion that the judge was, or should be, counsel for the prisoner. The judge stood high and independent and was looked up to by the jury. He had to be wise, experienced and, above all, impartial.

In the Lords debate one Member challenged the Bill on the ground that to allow defence counsel to address the jury would inhibit prosecutions since, 'it is not every man who has the firmness to stand a speech with the power that Mr Garrow could exert, and which he always did exert in defence of his clients.'[24]

Lyndhurst's long speech was undoubtedly effective and for the first time a Bill on this question received a second reading in the House of Lords and was quickly enacted. However, the Lords had insisted on deleting from the Bill not only legal aid but also clause 1(2) which gave defence counsel the final right of reply. The clause read,

> That in all such cases of Felony, and likewise in all cases of Treason, Misprison of Treason and Misdemeanour, if after the close of the case for the person or persons accused, the Counsel for the prosecution shall make any reply, the Counsel for the person or persons accused shall be admitted to answer it.

In consequence of the deletion, on 17 August an unusual conference was held between the Members of the two Houses of Parliament on this proposed clause.

And, to avoid defeat on the entire Bill, the Commons finally capitulated with Lord John Russell and Ewart promising to raise the matter again later.[25] The measure was then quickly enacted with section 1 allowing persons indicted for felony 'to make full Answer and Defence thereto by counsel.' Thus was adversary trial finally given Parliamentary approval.

The judges, however, were not immune from bouts of mind-changing. Lord Campbell revealed that 12 out of 15 judges (three were ill), curiously including Mr Baron Garrow who as counsel had often complained about not being able to address the jury, had strongly condemned the Bill, out of fear of having to listen to boring speeches. Moreover, Mr Justice Allan Park had written a letter to Campbell saying that if he, as Attorney-General, allowed the Bill to pass he (Park) would resign his office.[26] In the event he did not do so and, once the statute was enacted, the 12 judges quickly issued a Practice Note on the Act clarifying points of detail to the detriment of defendants.[27]

In 1834, Lord Brougham, who had appointed the commissioners, ceased to be Lord Chancellor and two years later he took no part in the debate on the Prisoners' Counsel Bill in the House of Lords. Then, after the Act came into force, he replied to a letter from Lord Lyndhurst asking about its effect on criminal trials. Brougham's reply was that at the Old Bailey the Act had been found to increase acquittals against the evidence, but he considered that this could not be attributed to the Act but to the absence of prosecution counsel in court. He said:

> There is a general belief & I think from all I can learn a well founded one that it [the Act] has led to acquittals in no small number against the truth of the case. This is the fault, however, not of the Bill but of there being no council for the prosecution. The judge cannot (if he chose) do the business of the Prosecution & he ought not to choose to place himself in so odious a position. Tho' the Bill had never passed, I should have said a prosecution without council ought not to be but the Bill makes it quite clear Something must be done to remedy this glaring defect … I need hardly add (after what I have said) that there has been no instance of wrong conviction, owing to the Bill. It has been all the other way.[28]

If this was correct in showing how the absence of prosecution counsel could affect the verdict, it must also indicate that the absence of defence counsel was equally a disadvantage.

It has been said that the Act helped only professional thieves who could afford counsel and not members of the 'honest poor'.[29] That may have been true in the sense that many of the poor would have been unable to afford to pay counsel's fees before the introduction of legal aid in the twentieth century. There was, however, the 'dock brief' whereby a prisoner in the dock could pick out any barrister who happened to be in court and robed at the time to defend him and, by the etiquette of the Bar, the barrister had to accept the brief for a fee of £1. 3s. 6d., which sum was to be paid in cash on the spot. This remained the rule many years later when the famous, and highly paid, barrister, Norman Birkett, found himself frequently chosen by prisoners who were struck by the red hair protruding from his wig. 'I'll 'ave the bloke with the red 'air', the man in the dock would say more often than not when Birkett was in court.[30] And, of course, Birkett accepted the 'brief'.

But for the suggestion that the Act helped only professional thieves it is significant that by 1843—only seven years after the Act—David Phillips finds that, in cases reported in the newspapers in the Black Country for all non-larceny cases, 63 per cent of all prosecutors were represented by counsel and 49 per cent of defendants. With the more serious offences of homicide, assault occasioning grievous bodily harm, burglary and robbery tried at assizes, almost all prosecutors had barristers acting for them and most prisoners had defence counsel.[31] It is difficult to believe that such high percentages would not also obtain in larceny cases where they would refer only to professional thieves.

THE LEGAL PROFESSION

Such was the opposition of large parts of the profession to the growth in adversary trial in the early nineteenth century that it is reasonable to assume that the more academic members of the Bar writing in legal journals, the judges and the barrister MPs had all underestimated the opportunity for more work and fees for members of the legal profession that was to follow defence counsel being allowed to address the jury. Nevertheless, the turning point did not come until *Courvoisier's Case* in 1840 which raised the question of Bar ethics in an acute form and was a further stage in the development of adversary trial. François Courvoisier was a Swiss valet accused of murdering his master, Lord William Russell, a younger brother of two dukes of Bedford, whilst asleep by slashing his throat so violently as to almost sever his head from his body.

The trial took place at the Old Bailey in June 1840 and Courvoisier pleaded not guilty. On the Bench sat Lord Chief Justice Sir Nicholas Tindal and Mr Baron James Parke. John Adolphus led the prosecution assisted by William Bodkin and Montagu Chambers. Courvoisier was represented by Charles Phillips, the 'Old Bailey Garrow' of the day who had appeared in over 2,300 cases at the Old Bailey between 1825 and 1834.[32] According to *The Times* when the trial opened, 'the anxiety to witness the proceedings, particularly by those who compose the higher classes of society, was beyond all precedent.'[33] The evidence was all circumstantial, which might have led the jury to acquit the defendant but in fact he was convicted and sentenced to death.[34]

Trouble arose when it was subsequently revealed that halfway through the trial Courvoisier had called Phillips, who had been defending him for eight hours, over to the dock and told him he had committed the murder but would not change his plea of not guilty. He asked Phillips to continue to defend him 'to the utmost.' Phillips felt inclined to withdraw from the case but consulted Baron Parke who advised him that if the prisoner insisted that he wanted Phillips to continue to defend him Phillips was bound to do so, 'and to use all fair arguments arising on the evidence.' Phillips decided to continue, saying later in November 1849,

> I had no right to throw up my brief, and turn traitor to the wretch, wretch though he was, who had confided in me. The counsel for a prisoner has no option. The moment he accepts his brief, every faculty he has becomes his client's property. It is an implied contract between him and the man who trusts him.[35]

This decision was widely criticized and led to a lengthy debate on the ethics of criminal advocacy and standards of professional conduct for defence counsel.[36] The outburst in the press and among public figures was considerable with a good deal of criticism of Phillips' conduct, including the suggestion that he was unfit for judicial office to which he was aspiring. In his speech to the jury he had pleaded, 'I beseech you to be cautious how you imbrue your hands in this man's blood. The Omniscient God alone knows who did this crime.' This has caused one writer to exclaim that, 'there were those who thought that God had company.'[37] Nevertheless, the Bar accepted that Phillips was 'justified in testing the strength of the prosecution evidence, even if he would not have been justified in suggesting his client's innocence.'[38] By this time the presence of defence counsel and his 'role in securing procedural fair play for his client was no longer questioned.'[39]

Subsequently, on 20 November 1849, Phillips defended himself by publishing in *The Times* his correspondence with the legal writer Samuel Warren. He wrote of the 'wretched night' before the final day of the trial when, 'If I slumbered for a moment, the murderer's form arose before me, scaring sleep away, now muttering his awful crime, and now shrieking to me to save his life!'[40] Yet, Phillips had never been happy with the Prisoners' Counsel Act and had told the jury in the *Courvoisier* trial 'It is no new notion of mine, that the consequences of an Act of Parliament which is now in operation would be to make the courts of criminal justice the arena of angry passion, and to place the lives of our fellow-creatures in peril, or in safety, just in proportion to the skill and talent of the advocate.'[41] In his correspondence with Warren, Phillips made public for the first time that he had consulted the presiding judges who confirmed that he had not indicated during the trial any personal opinion on the case.[42]

The legal press was divided on the issue of whether counsel should act for a prisoner he knew to be guilty but eventually with the continued growth of the concept of the presumption of innocence it became easier for a barrister to avoid prejudging his client. However, Phillips was widely believed to have gone too far and there was held to be moral limits to counsel's advocacy of a cause, such as not browbeating or confusing a witness, which form part of the modern etiquette of the Bar.[43]

Despite the criticisms of the 1836 Act, a new determined and aggressive self-expansion of the Bar gradually occurred and some members quickly seized the opportunities arising to make money, even at the expense of their conduct in court. Certainly, *The Law Review* was later to condemn in strong terms those barristers who, it claimed, put financial rewards before professional integrity, although it fancied that making money was 'agreeable.'[44]

Later, it pointed to continuing in-fighting between the two branches of the profession.[45] And barristers practising at the Old Bailey were particularly criticized by the *Law Times* which wrote that, 'practices unrecognized by the Bar have existed and do exist to a great extent at the Old Bailey. The world also knows, and long has known, that 'An Old Bailey Practitioner' is a byword for disgrace and infamy.'[46] *The Examiner* claimed that the 'indiscreet conduct of a part of the Bar has called attention to its morality, which we consider most vicious and mischievous.' It complained that barristers were 'advocates of falsehood for a guinea' and that in the very temple of justice, 'they glory in procuring the triumph of the wrong-doer.'[47]

By 1867 the position had not greatly improved and the *Law Magazine*, in an article on the high standard required of practitioners, attacked what it called 'scandalous offendings.' It referred to the Bar having increased in numbers rather than quality and complained that many could not be restrained by the discipline of the profession from 'a laxity of practice closely akin to dishonesty.'[48]

What seems beyond doubt is that the by that time unquestioned control of the courtroom by the lawyers had improved their status and opportunities for enhanced incomes, and led to the rapid rise in the size of the Bar already noticed, with a consequent lowering of standards for the time being. Perhaps Lord Chief Justice Erle best summed up the role of barristers in an interesting case which confirmed that they could not sue for their unpaid fees. Speaking of the profession in 1863 he pointed out that at times clients had to trust them with their fortune, character and even life:

> The law trusts him [the Barrister] with a privilege in respect of liberty of speech which is in practice bounded only by his own sense of duty, and he may have to speak upon subjects concerning the deepest interests of social life and the innermost feelings of the human soul. The law also trusts him with the power of insisting upon answers to the most painful questioning ... only controlled by his own view of the interests of truth.[49]

As it was clearly thought that not all members of the Bar lived up to this standard, Erle declared it to be of great importance that their sense of duty be 'in active energy proportioned to the magnitude of these interests.'[50] It is expressed in the present *Code of Conduct of the Bar*, which upholds adversary trial, by the words that the advocate must, 'promote and protect fearlessly and by all proper and lawful means his lay client's best interests and do so without regard to his own interests or to any consequences to himself or to any other person.'[51]

In effect, a new style of adversarial advocacy, controlled by practice rules and in sharp contrast to Garrow's, was developed in the nineteenth century which made the final steps in entrenching adversary trial possible.

CONCLUSION

The growth of adversary trial was brought to a near-conclusion by the Prisoners' Counsel Act 1836 which permitted counsel to address the jury. Support for the principle came from law reformers and opponents of the death penalty like Lamb and Ewart, whilst the public were on the whole indifferent to the concept and the Bar largely opposed. The struggle in Parliament took over a decade and was finally successful when Lord John Russell sought the aid of the criminal law commissioners. In a sense the time was right anyway as the measure was linked with the general reform of the law that followed the Great Reform Act 1832, and, crucially, in particular with the considerable restrictions placed on the use of the death penalty as a punishment in 1837 with its removal from 21 of the 37 offences still capital and reduced use in the 16 remaining.

The 1836 Act was followed by a steep rise in the numbers of the Bar (although by no means all in criminal practice) and a consequent defining of the ethics of counsel in acting in adversarial proceedings, particularly after the squalls over the role of Phillips in the *Courvoisier* trial. Significantly, in consequence, a new style of advocacy, controlled by practice rules and in sharp contrast to Garrow's, was developed in the nineteenth century.

The right of defence counsel to make a final speech without foregoing defence evidence which the House of Lords had deleted from the 1836 Act was restored in 1865 by the Criminal Procedure Act of that year.[52] And, at the end of the nineteenth century, in the drawn out saga of adversary trial, prisoners were permitted to give sworn evidence in their own defence by the Criminal Evidence Act 1898.[53] Even this measure was strongly opposed in Parliament for some years, however, before it was finally enacted. And, outside Parliament there was also opposition with the *Edinburgh Review,* for example, arguing that the effect of the Bill would be to, 'apply a species of terrorism to the accused to extort a confession.'[54] Although the Act was clearly desirable, it cannot be known, however, how many prisoners convict themselves out of their own mouths under penetrating cross-examination by counsel. What is crucial is that it enhanced adversary trial by including the defendant as a full participant. As Vogler has put it, 'the post-1898 trial must be acknowledged as the maturation of adversariality, which had survived the powerful attacks which had been mounted throughout the latter part of the nineteenth century by continental positivist jurisprudence.'[55]

Other developments in adversary trial procedure included the appointment of a Director of Public Prosecutions in 1878 and, finally, in the twentieth century the Criminal Appeal Act 1907[56] which brought in an appeals procedure, the abolition of the Grand Jury and the granting of state legal aid to defendants. These lifted adversary trial, with counsel appearing in all defended cases, to its apex. The old system of trial was now merely a memory, totally eclipsed by modern style adversariality.

ENDNOTES for *Chapter 9*

[1]   A. N. May. (2003) *The Bar and the Old Bailey, 1750-1850*. Chapel Hill and London, The University of North Carolina Press. p. 133. The words in quotation marks are cited from R. Cocks. (1983) *Foundations of the Modern Bar*. London, Sweet & Maxwell. p. 22.

[2]   4 November 1834. p. 2.

[3]   Parliamentary Papers. (1836) Second Report, 'Defence of Prisoners by Counsel'. vol. xxxvi. Shannon, Irish University Press. p. 91.

[4]   Ibid. pp. 91-2.

[5]   A.N. May. *The Bar and the Old Bailey 1750-1850*. Op. cit. p. 5.

[6]   *Law Magazine*. (May 1836) vol. 15. p. 394.

[7]   *Hansard*. (1826) New series. [15] col. 589.

[8]   Ibid. col. 633.

[9]   *Hansard*. (1821) [4] cols. 1513-14.

[10] E.L. Woodward. (1954) *The Age of Reform: 1815-1870*. Oxford, The Clarendon Press.

[11] P. Handler. (2004) Review of Langbein's *The Origins of Adversary Criminal Trial*. *The Cambridge Law Journal*. Cambridge, The Cambridge University Press. p. 518.

[12] Parliamentary Papers. (9 June 1836) vol. xxxvi. p.123. All the extracts which follow are taken from this report.

[13] See J. Hostettler. (1992) *The Politics of Criminal Law: Reform in the Nineteenth Century*. Chichester, Barry Rose Law Publishers Ltd.

[14] Ibid.

[15] 28 May 1835. Reproduced in Appendix 2 of the commissioners' report.

[16] *The Law Magazine*. (May 1836) vol. 15. p. 394.

[17] Ibid.

[18] Parliamentary Papers. Op. cit. vol. xxxvi.

[19] OBP Online. (www.oldbaileyonline.org, 7 January 2005) 15 January 1787 Trial of Francis Parr. Ref: t17870115-1.

[20] See *ante*. pp. 24-25.

[21] *Hansard*. New series. [15] col. 627.

[22] Parliamentary Papers. Op. cit. vol. xxxvi.

[23] *Hansard*. 3rd series. [34]. col. 760.

[24] House of Lords Sessional Papers. (130) (1835) xlvi. 317)App. iv) 52.

[25] *Hansard*. 3rd series. [35]. col. 1275 and the *Annual Register* (1836) p. 167.

[26] M. S. Hardcastle (Campbell's daughter). (1881) *Life of John Lord Campbell, Lord High Chancellor of Great Britain consisting of a Selection from his Autobiography, Diary and Letters*. London, Murray. vol. 2. pp. 106-7.

[27] *Law Magazine*. (1837) vol. 17. p. 470 which published the Note in full.

[28] Lord Brougham to Lord Lyndhurst, (20 December 1836) *Lyndhurst Papers No. 121*. Cited by Cairns. *Advocacy and the Making of the Adversarial Criminal Trial*. Op. cit. p. 117.

[29] J. J. Tobias (1967) *Crime and Industrial Society in the 19th Century*. London, B.T. Batsford. p. 230.

[30] H. Montgomery Hyde. (1964) *Norman Birkett. The Life of Lord Birkett of Ulverston*. London, Hamish Hamilton. p. 72.

[31] D. Phillips. (1977) *Crime and Authority in Victorian England, the Black Country 1835-60*. London, Croom Helm. p. 105.

[32] A. N. May. (2005) 'Advocates and Truth-Seeking in the Old Bailey Courtroom.' 26(1) *The Journal of Legal History*. London, Routledge. p. 74.

[33] 19 June 1840.

[34] I. Townsend. [1850] *Modern State Trials*. p. 244.

[35] Correspondence between S. Warren and C. Phillips. Cited by May *The Bar and the Old Bailey.1750-1850*. Op. cit. p. 214.

[36] Ibid.

[37] D. Mellinkoff. (1973) *The Conscience of a Lawyer*. Boston, Little Brown. p. 222.

[38] P. Handler. (2005) 'Review of May's *The Bar and the Old Bailey, 1750-1850'*. 26 *The Journal of Legal History*. P. 110.

[39] Ibid.

[40] *The Times*. 20 November 1849.

[41] *Morning Chronicle*. 22 June 1840.

42 A.N. May. *The Bar and the Old Bailey, 1750-1850.* Op. cit. p. 228.

43 Ibid. p. 235.

44 *The Law Review.* (Aug. 1845-May 1846). vol. 3. p.353.

45 Ibid. (Nov. 1848-Feb.1849) vol. 9.

46 *Law Times.* (1844) vol. 3. p. 501.

47 *The Examiner.* (17 August 1846).

48 *Law Magazine.* (August 1867) vol. 23. p. 101 (N.S.)

49 *Kennedy v. Brown* [1863] 32 L.J. Reports, 146-7.

50 Ibid.

51 *Code of Conduct of the Bar of England and Wales.* (27 January 1990). para. 207.

52 28 & 29 Vict. c. 18.

53 62 Vict. c 36.

54 *Edinburgh Review.* (October 1897) vol. 150. p. 549.

55 R. Vogler. (2005) *A World View of Criminal Justice.* Aldershot, Ashgate Publishers. p. 151.

56 7 Edw. VII, c. 23.

CHAPTER 10

Conclusion

INTRODUCTION

As we have seen, in the pre-modern criminal trial it was the judge who dominated the proceedings. Prisoners were not allowed to instruct counsel (except, rarely, on points of law) and so the judge was able to control the testimony of witnesses. The accused were usually held in prison in appalling conditions and had no facilities to prepare a defence which, in any event, they were usually incapable of doing. They could not compel witnesses to attend even if they could contact them and any who did appear were, unlike prosecution witnesses, not permitted to testify on oath. According to Vogler, 'It is not too much to see pre-trial incarceration (with the prisoners usually shackled in leg-irons up to the moment of arraignment) as a species of torture aimed at cowing the prisoner into passivity and submission.'[1]

All this changed in the eighteenth century when, for the first time in felony trials, counsel were permitted to cross-examine prosecutors and their witnesses on behalf of prisoners. With this onset of adversariality came a remarkable change which altered the relationship between the state and the individual. How the situation was transformed has been outlined above and it provided one of the first glimpses of a modern human rights culture in the civilized world.

PROCEDURAL REVOLUTION

Until recently legal historians, including Blackstone, Stephen and Holdsworth, were totally unaware of how and when adversary trial commenced in cases of felony. All that has changed as a consequence of research in the last 30 years by Langbein, Beattie, Landsman and others into the Old Bailey Sessional Proceedings in various libraries in Britain and North America.

These proceedings are now online thanks to the inspiration of Professor Tim Hitchcock of the University of Hertfordshire and Professor Robert Shoemaker of the University of Sheffield, and they contain reports of 100,621 trials from April 1674 to December 1834. As has been noticed earlier, these reports are not verbatim and, indeed, they are of varying lengths during different periods of time. Even more important, the reports were sold to the public and those writing them included only such elements as they considered necessary and thought would be found entertaining and instructive. What the judges said is often left out because there was no time to obtain their consent to what they were reputed to have said and the reports do not always indicate if counsel were involved in trials. However, the fact remains that some of them are of considerable length and they are exceptional and unique in the world, enabling us to see with certainty that defence counsel began to appear in felony cases in England about the year 1734. They thus cover the period when lawyers created the adversary trial in England and in the process produced a procedural revolution and a network of defence rights incorporated in the rules of criminal evidence. The influence of the lawyers secured a crisp division of testimony, instead of formless or wandering trial procedure, which was soon extended to all felony trials.[2]

RELAXING THE 'NO-COUNSEL' RULE

In not allowing defence counsel to make a full defence, even when gradually permitting them to cross-examine prosecution witnesses, it is clear that the judges had no intention of permitting the capture of the courtroom by the lawyers. But there is no consensus among academic lawyers as to how, and the reasons why, defence counsel were permitted to appear at all in cases of felony and no clear recognition of the significance of adversary trial in the development of a human rights culture. The latter is mentioned by Vogler but, significantly, not by Langbein, Beattie, Landsman or, of course, earlier legal historians.

The change was not effected by Parliament, or by the judges after due deliberation. Some reasons that contributed to the judges gradually relaxing the 'no counsel' rule have already been mentioned[3] and can be summarized as follows.

First, the advent in the early eighteenth century and before of professional prosecutions with the rapid growth of Associations for the Prosecution of Felons and the statutory introduction of payment for thief-takers which created a rewards culture for bounty hunters that was still very much in evidence in Garrow's day, late in the century.

Secondly, political campaigners such as John Wilkes used their trials for propaganda purposes and sought the assistance of defence lawyers,

Thirdly, the growth, under the impetus of lawyers, of rules of evidence.

To these should be added the growth of a prisoners' rights culture in a situation, following the Glorious Revolution of 1688, in which defendants were seen to be disadvantaged when prosecutions were more and more counsel based. There was also the fundamental shift in society brought about by the Enlightenment and the American and French Revolutions. At the same time, a rights-based trial process was, in many ways, 'inspired by the market [and] pioneered by the men who represented the new capitalists and was imbued with the ideologies of the industrial revolution.'[4]

THE ADVOCATE'S DUTY

As part of his attack on adversary trial, Langbein describes Brougham's assertion, in the proceedings in the House of Lords against Queen Caroline in 1820, that the duty of defence counsel was to his client, as 'self-serving prattle [which] became window dressing for a truth-be-damned standard of defensive representation that served the economic self-interest of the Bar.'[5]

Brougham's precise words were:

> An advocate, by the sacred duty which he owes to his client, knows, in the discharge of that office, but one person in the world, that client and none other. To save that client by all expedient means, to protect that client at all hazards and costs to all others, and among others to himself, is the highest and most unquestioned of his duties; and he must not regard the alarm—the suffering—the torment—the destruction—which he may bring upon any other. Nay, separating even the duties of a patriot from those of an advocate, and casting them, if need be, to the wind, he must go on reckless of the consequences, if his fate it should unhappily be, to involve his country in confusion for his client's protection.[6]

He back-tracked shortly afterwards, however, when he said the speech was 'anything rather than a deliberate and well-considered opinion on the general question of an advocate's duties.'[7]

Nevertheless, he later indicated that he had spoken so strongly of the advocate's duty in the particular case in order to let the government know he had evidence that the King had legally forfeited his right to the Crown when, as heir-apparent, he had married the Catholic Mrs Fitzherbert. That is hardly the same as 'self-serving prattle'.

Langbein's description of what he calls the 'accused speaks' approach is flawed in that, on his own showing, before the eighteenth century most prisoners were incapable of making a coherent defence in the circumstances of their trials and, in any event, were not permitted to give sworn evidence. And it is not correct to say that today defendants are often prevented by their counsel from giving evidence.[8] Since the Criminal Evidence Act 1898 it is unusual for defendants to decline to give evidence even thought they face the hazard of convicting themselves out of their own mouths. It is certainly fraught with the danger of what conclusions the jury might draw if they do so decline.

SEARCH FOR THE TRUTH

Langbein, who considers that the adversarial criminal procedure, 'harboured truth-defeating tendencies', argues that:

> to understand how a system so flawed could gain acceptance, we need to bear in mind the growing aversion to capital punishment that characterized [the eighteenth and early nineteenth centuries]. Contemporaries were peculiarly disposed to tolerate the truth-defeating consequences of adversary procedure, because in the realm of criminal trial too much truth brought too much death.[9]

However, the 'flawed system' was accepted only in part because of the death penalty.

More important were the considerations discussed above, in particular the need to question the evidence of the prosecution and hear the prisoner's case, and these factors were widely welcomed, not least by the judges.

Furthermore, making criminal investigation a public function, as Langbein wishes,[10] would have meant, in the words of May, 'making it a state function, and there is a strong argument to be made to the effect that those concerned with the administration of justice, and the English more generally, have quite simply feared the state more than they have feared criminals.'[11] She concludes that, "Disdain' is thus too weak a word to describe the English response to the European model of justice—horror would be more appropriate. An historic, deep-rooted mistrust of an authoritarian state, and fear of abuses of state power, explain why the English were disinclined to believe that state-instigated pre-trial inquiries would further either truth or justice.'

There is some force in Langbein's other argument that, 'adversary criminal procedure privatizes the investigation and presentation of evidence [and] is intrinsically skewed to the advantage of wealthy defendants, who can afford to hire the most skilled counsel and to pay for the gathering and production of defensive evidence.'[12] This is what he describes as the 'Wealth Effect'. He is on less secure ground, however, with his 'Combat Effect' which, he claims, subordinates truth-seeking. 'Because', he writes, 'adversary procedure remits to partisans the work of gathering and presenting the evidence, each side operates under an incentive to suppress and distort unfavourable evidence, however truthful it may be.'[13] But, in England at least, this is now far more difficult to achieve than before and counsel for the prosecution has a duty to put the whole case before the jury and strive to find the truth. If the ideal is not always attained neither does the inquisitorial system provide for a truly roving investigation into the truth.

In any event, as May indicates, '[t]hrough the exposure of false or malicious prosecution barristers did much to reveal the absolute truth, to uncover facts that prosecutors and witnesses had endeavoured to subvert or conceal.'[14] She adds,

But in the era of the 'Bloody Code' the 'truth' of the crime was only one issue at trial: the jury, that is, had also to decide whether what the defendant had done merited the death penalty. In the eighteenth century truth and justice were often competing interests and partial verdicts and down-charging, by which the accused was convicted of a lesser, non-capital charge, were not uncommon.[15]

Truth-seeking was not the main purpose of the early adversary trial lawyers and was not to be so until the death penalty was abolished for most crimes.[16]

Langbein says that defence lawyers could 'effectively shape some of what the defendant and the defence witnesses said,' and this is no doubt to some extent true although they were hardly likely to tell defendants to lie. Yet, he draws the conclusion that the tendency of the adversary system is to interfere with seeking the truth, overlooking that even in inquisitorial trials witnesses may invent or lie. He continues, 'As the adversary dynamic took hold, the court's access to the accused and to the witnesses was filtered through partisan lawyers whose interest was in winning, not in truth-seeking.' But what does that word 'access' involve? According to Lord Justice Sedley,

> There is no intelligible sense in which the old form of trial was more apt than the modern criminal trial to elicit the truth. It was directed to establishing, by largely unjust means, the guilt of the accused as a prelude to brutal punishment or, occasionally, ostentatious clemency. It was the jury, albeit composed entirely of male property-owners, which stood between the accused and his accusers, and not infrequently it acquitted. The fact that the record of the defendant's interrogation by a local magistrate was sent on to the trial court, and the fact that at trial he had to speak for himself or perish, hardly amounted to a collaborative search for the truth.[17]

Further, Langbein says, cross-examination was a 'hit-or-miss safeguard against the truth-bending and truth-concealing effects of placing partisans in charge of the production and presentation of the evidence.'[18]

But all this may be an academic approach to the work of practising lawyers which ignores several points. First, it was not the lawyers, partisan or otherwise, who denied accused persons the right to give evidence on oath. That was the situation they were faced with until 1898 and it is hardly surprising that they should wish to help prisoners in their voiceless situation in court. Secondly, is Langbein — an academic lawyer, albeit an outstanding one — assuming too much venality or incompetence on the part of practitioners? Cross-examination is intended to bring out the truth and what better system of doing so is there? Unless the judge intervened, largely unchallenged prosecution evidence, which was the alternative before defence counsel began to appear in felony cases, was far worse and quite unlikely to reveal the truth. And, the inquisitorial system, which Langbein prefers, is hardly foolproof. He regards adversary trial as a mistake which prevents truth-seeking and this defines his approach to it.

An alternative view is propounded by Cairns when writing of Lord Cockburn's prosecution of William Palmer who was found guilty in 1856 of murdering his friend, John Cook. According to Cairns:

> The adversarial criminal trial is seen to come of age with *Palmer*. Twenty years after the Prisoners' Counsel Act, this trial ... triumphantly realized the expectations of full defence by counsel ... The thoroughness of the trial manifested Palmer's guilt, and the opportunity of his representatives to say all that could be said in his favour eliminated all sympathy for him. In *Palmer*, adversarial procedure delivered the truth, and a verdict beyond reproach.[19]

Langbein also asserts that we live under 'a criminal procedure for which we have no adequate theory'.[20] This contention, however, ignores both the debates over the Prisoners' Counsel Act and the 1836 report of the criminal law commissioners which represented the first detailed and theoretical analysis of the benefits of the adversarial mode of trial and proposed, 'a theory of truth-finding which differed radically from the older "plain-facts" conception as well as the forensic investigation practiced in continental procedure'. [21] This clearly undermines Langbein's view about both lack of theory and truth-finding.

ADVERSARY VERSUS INQUISITORIAL TRIAL

It will be clear that Langbein is opposed to adversary trial and in his book on its origins he makes a strong attack on such a system of trial (and Garrow) when he says:

> Adversary procedure entrusts the responsibility for gathering and presenting the evidence upon which accurate adjudication depends to partisans whose interest is in winning, not in truth. A procedure that could make the trickster William Garrow into the dominant figure in the administration of criminal justice, which is what happened in England in the 1780s, was not a truth-serving procedure. The adversary dynamic invited distortion and suppression of the evidence, by permitting abusive and misleading cross-examination, the coaching of witnesses, and the concealment of unfavourable evidence ...
>
> The lawyer-dominated system of criminal trial that emerged in eighteenth-century England was not premised on a coherent theory of truth-seeking. Adversary procedure presupposed that truth would somehow emerge when no one was in charge of seeking it. Truth was a byproduct.[22]

But the reality is rather different, as extracts from trials cited earlier in this book have shown. Garrow was not a 'trickster' and his cross-examinations, far from suppressing evidence, often extracted the truth from prevaricating, and financially interested, prosecution witnesses. With regard to the alleged coaching of witnesses it is very rare to find defence witnesses speaking in Old Bailey trials of the time except briefly as to the character of the accused, although Langbein may be referring to prosecution witnesses. It is significant that on many occasions when acting for a prisoner, Garrow asked the prosecution witnesses to stay outside the courtroom until called in order that they might not adopt the testimony of earlier witnesses. Alternatively, Langbein may have had in mind the statement of William David Evans, an analyst of evidentiary questions, referring to the frequent turning of King's evidence of notorious thief-taker Jonathan Wild,

> The suspicion of fabrication rises highest, when the witness is one of those inferior retainers of the law, who are commonly attendant upon courts of judicature, who have a cunning acuteness in the observations of its proceedings, and who, from their occupation, are frequently in the habits of swearing to facts, in their own nature liable to misrepresentation, and placed beyond the reach of detection or contradiction.[23]

As for the 'concealment of unfavourable evidence', adversariality also enables counsel for the Crown to cross-examine defence witnesses and endeavour to extract the truth.

On the other side of the coin, Langbein favours what he says is on display across the English Channel namely, 'a highly visible alternative to adversary criminal procedure' which 'placed upon the court the responsibility to seek the truth, and gave it the investigative authority and resources to do so.'[24] Why then, he asks, did the English not adopt this superior model? He has to concede that there were profound flaws in the way the Europeans had implemented their system. In particular, torture used to restrict judicial discretion was 'the great European blunder.'[25] This, however, was swept away in the nineteenth century and he alleges that the Europeans avoided the further blunder of adopting the adversary system which does not seek the truth.[26] In contrast, Vogler sees the most essential characteristic of inquisitorial method is that it is authoritarian and says that the 'sanguinary and terrifying history of its long development should alert us to its shortcomings.'[27]

Against Langbein's views are a number of other important considerations. Landsman, for example, argues that adversariality was in part a response to the activities of professional thief-catchers against whom lawyers adopted adversary tactics that led to more robust defences.[28] Other factors included the 'rise of dynamic individualism and the growth of a market economy.'[29] He adds that the adversary method,

> was created by judges and lawyers who sought, through hundreds of incremental reforms, to build a more equitable court system ... Lawyers were allowed entry into the process in an apparent effort to secure a more reasonable balance between prosecution and prisoner.

Such developments suggested that 'the legal community of the day saw its task not simply as convicting the guilty, but as satisfying a profound social desire for fair play.'[30]

INQUISITORIAL TRIAL UNDER ATTACK

In countries using the inquisitorial system, cases are sometimes heard shortly after the alleged offence. This may not always be desirable, however, since it may give the defendant too little time to prepare his or her defence and find witnesses. On the other hand, in other cases *juges d'instruction* often work quite slowly and by law are permitted to keep suspects in custody for considerable lengths of time while investigations continue and before any claim for a breach of human rights can succeed in court. Equally, career judges who are young and have no experience of acting as counsel may not compare favourably with their counterparts in common law countries. And the relative absence of examination and cross-examination may be a decisive disadvantage in endeavouring to extract the truth.

In this regard it is interesting that in May 2004 the collapse of a trial in St Omar in France prompted heavy criticism of the institution of the powerful *juge d'instruction*. After the defendants were imprisoned, the chief witness admitted having made up the whole story on which the charges were based. One of the defence lawyers responded, 'It is time to close the book on an inquisitorial justice system that dates from the Middle Ages.' Another suggested that, 'we have now seen the total negation of any presumption of innocence.' The newspaper *France Soir* added that, 'In countries with old democratic traditions such as Britain, investigation is entrusted to professionals with long experience. In France, as at St Omer, it is done by young graduates from the School of Magistrature.'[31]

In January 2006 came another call for the abolition of France's 200-year-old Napoleonic system of criminal justice. On this occasion a 34-year-old judge at Outreau, near Boulogne, had detained 13 men and women defendants and sent them to trial as paedophiles on flimsy evidence. Another defendant committed suicide in gaol. Four of the defendants had made the accusations and remained in prison. The others were acquitted on appeal and alleged they were tormented and humiliated by the judge to obtain confessions. He had ruined their lives, they said, breaking up marriages and families.[32]

Of course these are individual cases, but the origins of the inquisitorial system seem still to influence its modern style to an unacceptable extent, with the European Court of Human Rights criticizing pre-trial detention that can last up to five years.

There is no certain way of ensuring that the truth is revealed in a trial but despite Langbein's contrary view, it can be argued that adversariality is more likely to do so than the inquisitorial system. After all, inquisitorial judges compile a dossier of evidence from which they question witnesses and may have a prosecution bias. Whether combining the best features of both is possible and desirable is open to debate.

'THE ACCUSED SPEAKS'

Langbein claims, as part of his argument against the adversarial system, that in the earlier system in England, 'the main purpose of the trial was to give the accused the opportunity to speak in person to the charges and the evidence adduced against him. Counsel was forbidden and the logic of this was to pressure the accused to speak in his own defence.[33] This is his 'accused speaks' concept. It is hard to agree with this 'logical' conclusion, however, when two points are considered.

First, how could prisoners who were 'dirty, underfed and often ill'[34] as well as illiterate, be considered capable of defending themselves adequately, or at all? Often they were taken up to the court from the cells in an entirely bewildered state and returned to the cells shortly afterwards, unaware of what had happened to them.[35]

Dealing with assizes in Surrey, Beattie found that on one occasion some 35 accused were dealt with in two days in addition to the court dealing with misdemeanours and administrative matters. And, in the Old Bailey 20 to 30 prisoners were often dealt with in a day.[36] The time allotted to each prisoner must have been minimal. J.H. Baker calculates that the average length of a trial was a few minutes, and 'full two thirds of the prisoners, on their return from their trials, cannot tell of any thing which has passed in court, nor even, very frequently, whether they have been tried.'[37]

Research in both courts a the Old Bailey by H.B. Andrews of Serjeant's Inn, showed the average time for each trial never exceeded eight-and-a-half minutes and was frequently less. There would be 50 to 60 prisoners in cells under the court. Seeing fellow prisoners return, having been tried and found guilty in a minute or two, they became alarmed and nervous, would try to re-arrange their ideas and plan of defence only to lose control and be taken up to be 'knocked down like Bulocks unheard.' Two-thirds knew nothing of what had happened in court and often thought their case had not been heard only that, as frequently occurred, they had been called up to be present when a fresh jury was empanelled.[38]

According to the *Westminster Review,* the chairman of one Old Bailey sessions tried 16 prisoners in an hour on one occasion and eight prisoners in 20 minutes on another with, in both cases, the majority being sentenced to transportation. In an understatement with no trace of irony the *Review* suggested that 'in these instances a little more time might have been taken, without being guilty of useless delay.'[39]

Most prisoners, says Beattie, put up only the weakest of defences, if any at all. Only a few had defence counsel and

undoubtedly many were overwhelmed by the occasion and by the speed of events and not a few betrayed obvious confusion when, at the conclusion of the prosecution case, the judge asked what they had to say about the evidence brought against them or if they had any questions to put to the Crown witnesses.[40]

And how was a judge to be seen as counsel for the prisoner, as suggested by Sir Edward Coke, when one was able to say without embarrassment that though he had serious doubts about a man's guilt, he had left him to be hanged because of the seriousness of the crime.[41]

And secondly in reply to Langbein, the whole history of criminal trial in England after the replacement of trial by ordeal with trial by jury in 1219 was adverse to the defendant's rights until the early eighteenth century, with not only the denial of defence counsel but also placing severe restrictions on the calling of defence witnesses. There appears to have been no total bar on defence witnesses[42] but they could not be subpoenaed and when they did attend court they could not give evidence on oath which placed them in an unfavourable position compared with prosecution witnesses who could. In any event, giving evidence was often out of the question. How could a prisoner contact a potential witness? And, if he or she managed to, it would frequently be the case that the witness would be unable to raise the fare for a lengthy journey to the seat of a trial or pay for lodgings when arriving there.[43]

Langbein has strongly confirmed his preference for the continental inquisitorial system, which he says seeks the truth, over the modern adversarial system which he considers suppresses or evades the truth.[44] He claims that 'in the European legal tradition the work of investigating and adjudicating cases of serious crime is treated as a public responsibility assigned to neutral professionals who bring the resources of the state to bear both for and against the accused.'[45]

In contrast, Vogler sees the English procedural transformation of the mid-eighteenth century as having far-reaching consequences affecting the whole relationship between the state and the individual. In the criminal trials of the period, he says, 'we have the very first sighting of a recognizable human rights culture in Western, if not global civilization. From this period, the trial chamber in England ... would slowly assume the character of an open and independent forum for the negotiation of rights by autonomous actors.'[46] He continues:

> The idea of a passive, undefended and right-less defendant, faced with the overwhelming power of the state ... was not unique to the common law. In fact it was universal in Europe and the western world at the beginning of the eighteenth century. What is extraordinary and what marks out the achievement of the English common lawyers, is that within a century, and for reasons that will be explored, they pioneered and then entrenched, the concept of a rights-centred process in which the defendant was no longer passive and defenceless against the state. In short, the common law trial became the crucible in which, for the first time in human history, a system was created for the practical and universal application of the doctrine of Human Rights.'[47]

HUMAN RIGHTS

Stephen, lawyer, jurist and judge, considered the differences between adversary trial and the inquisitorial system operating in France in his book, *A General View of the Criminal Law of England*.[48] He first argued, like Langbein, that the French approach was more suitable, saying, 'Upon the general merits of our mode of procedure, it must be observed that the inquisitorial theory of criminal procedure is beyond all question the true one. It is self-evident that a trial ought to be a public inquiry into the truth of a matter deeply affecting the public interest.' On the other hand, unlike Langbein, he saw that adversary trial was also likely to reveal the truth. He wrote, 'The general result may be fairly expressed by saying that an English criminal trial is a public inquiry, having for its object the discovery of truth, but thrown for the purpose of obtaining that end into the form of a litigation between the prosecutor and the prisoner.'[49] And, that was before the prisoner became competent to give evidence himself from 1898.

Adversary trial also resulted in a new role for the judge who ceased to participate actively in the trial as in earlier times. Instead he became an umpire to prevent excessive zeal by counsel during the trial and to sum up the facts of the case to the jury at its close. As Langbein complains, English judges have, 'no prior familiarity with the evidence and no investigative resources within the court'[50] but many other observers regard this as a strength of English criminal procedure.

Furthermore, article 6 of the European Convention for the Protection of Human Rights and Fundamental Freedoms[51] (agreed at Rome on 4 November 1950 and incorporated into UK domestic law by the Human Rights Act 1998, c. 42) provides a general right to a fair and public trial by an independent court of law in article 6(1) and also sets out certain minimum rights. In particular, article 6(3)(d) states that, 'everyone charged with a criminal offence has the following minimum rights ... (d) to examine or have examined witnesses against him.'

Brought to life in the period of social movements such as the Industrial Revolution and the Enlightenment, the adversarial system of trial transformed criminal procedure and gave meaning in criminal law to the Enlightenment legacy—a concept of human rights which included the right to a fair trial involving the concept of due process under the rule of law. The age of deference was being undermined and replaced with a better understanding of the rights of citizens—including prisoners on trial, usually for their lives.

One important example of such rights embedded in the social field was the growing recognition of the presumption of innocence. The birth and growth of adversary trial occurred gradually over a period of time with barristers like Garrow and Erskine having the clarity of mind and the determination to persist in establishing individual rights for prisoners. With adversary trial came the concept of the presumption of innocence and an early application of the doctrine of human rights. The significance in this of cross-examination of opponents' witnesses was profound in its effect in trials and, in particular, in wringing out the truth. Whether adversary trial is superior to inquisitional trial can be debated but Langbein's onslaught on the former appears to be unsustainable.

What is apparent is that in the eighteenth century a procedural transformation was taking place that was part of the first culture of human rights in the world and it preceded both the Constitution of the United States of 1787, with its right to a speedy and public trial by an impartial jury, and the French Declaration of the Rights of Man and the Citizen, with its assertion of man's free and equal rights, of 1789. It also had far-reaching consequences 'which would extend beyond criminal trial and impact upon the whole relationship between the state and the individual'[52] as well as the growth of personal freedom, democracy and the rule of law.

In philosophical terms, the theory behind what the English common law was achieving was the assertion of the rights of the individual following John Locke (1632-1704) in his *The Letter for Toleration* in 1689[53] and *Two Treatises of Government* the following year.[54] That such rights were not always acknowledged as self-evident as the American Declaration of Independence proclaimed is shown by the Hegelian Declaration of Rights in Germany in 1848 which spoke not of the rights of man but of the rights of the German people.[55]

The right to cross-examine witnesses is an intrinsic part of the Anglo-American adversary system of trial and the wonder of it is that it came about not by legislation but by the efforts of Garrow and other barristers in their concern not with developing the law (a process which 'as establishment men' did not occur to them) but simply to win cases by the best means available. That they did so in the favourable environment of a growing human rights culture in no way diminishes their achievement.

ENDNOTES for *Chapter 10*

[1]   R. Vogler. (2005) *A World View of Criminal Justice*. Aldershot, Ashgate Publishers. p. 134.

[2]   J.H. Langbein. (2003) *The Origins of Adversary Criminal Trial*. Oxford, Oxford University Press. pp. 257-60.

[3]   Ante. pp. 51-3.

[4]   R. Vogler. *A World View of Criminal Justice*. Op. cit. p. 131.

[5]   J.H. Langbein. *The Origins of Adversary Criminal Trial*. Op. cit. p. 309.

[6]   Speeches of Lord Brougham. (1838) Edinburgh, vol. i. p. 105.

[7]   W Forsyth. (1849) *Hortensius; the Advocate*. p. 389. Cited by D. J.A. Cairns. (1998) *Advocacy and the Making of the Adversarial Criminal Trial*. Oxford, Clarendon Press. p. 139.

[8]   J.H. Langbein. *The Origins of Adversary Criminal Trial*. Op. cit. p. 267.

[9]   Ibid. p. 334.

[10] J.H. Langbein. *The Origins of Adversary Criminal Trial*. Op. cit. p. 342.

[11] A.N. May. (2005) 'Advocates and Truth-Seeking in the Old Bailey Courtroom.' 26(1) *The Journal of Legal History*. London, Routledge. p. 76.

[12] J. H. Langbein. *The Origins of Adversary Criminal Trial*. Op. cit. p. 103.

[13] Ibid.

[14] A. N. May. 'Advocates and Truth-Seeking in the Old Bailey Courtroom.' Op. cit. p. 73.

[15] Ibid.

[16] Ibid. p. 74.

[17] S. Sedley. (25 September 2003) '"Howzat?" A Review of Langbein's *The Origins of Adversary Criminal Trial*.' London, London Review of Books. p. 15.

[18] J. H. Langbein. *The Origins of Adversary Criminal Trial*. Op. cit. p. 270.

[19] D.J.A Cairns. (1998) *Advocacy and the Making of the Adversarial Criminal Trial 1800-1865*. Op. cit. p.163.

[20] Ibid. p. 9.

[21] R. Vogler. *A World View of Criminal Justice*. Op. cit. p. 146.

[22] Ibid. pp. 332-3.

[23] W. D. Evans. (1826) *On the Law of Evidence*. Cited by S. Landsman 'The Rise of the Contentious Spirit: Adversary Procedure in Eighteenth Century England.' Op. cit. p. 85, note 406.

[24] J. H. Langbein. *The Origins of Adversary Criminal Trial*. Op. cit. p. 338.

[25] Ibid. p. 339.

[26] Ibid. pp. 342-3.

[27] R. Vogler. *A World View of Criminal Justice*. Op. cit. pp. 19 and 21.

[28] S. Landsman. 'The Rise of the Contentious Spirit:' Op. cit. pp. 502-3.

[29] Ibid. pp. 602-3.

[30] Ibid. pp. 603-4.

[31] These details are taken from the report of C. Bremner in Paris in *The Times* of 27 May 2004. p. 21.

[32] *The Times*. 20 January 2006. p. 43.

[33] J. H. Langbein. *The Origins of Adversary Criminal Trial*. Op. cit. p. 2.

[34] J. M. Beattie. (1986) *Crime and the Courts in England 1660-1800*. Oxford, The Clarendon Press. pp. 350-51.

35 Anon. (1833) *Old Bailey Experiences.* pp. 59-60. Cited by J.H. Baker. *An Introduction to English Legal History.* (1979) London, Butterworths. p. 417.

36 J.M. Beattie. (1977) 'Crime and Courts in Surrey 1736-1753.' In *Crime in England 1550-1800.* (ed J.S. Cockburn) London, Methuen & Co. Ltd. p. 165.

37 Anon. *Old Bailey Experiences.* Op. cit.

38 H.B. Andrews. (1833) *Criminal Law: Being a Commentary on Bentham on Death Punishment.* London, Charles Reader.

39 'Old Bailey Experience'. (1834) 20 *Westminster Review.* London, R. Heward. p. 147.

40 J.M. Beattie. 'Crime and Courts in Surrey 1736-1753.' Op. cit. p. 167.

41 Public Record Office. SP 36/116, f. 107. Cited by Beattie. Ibid. p. 185.

42 J. H. Langbein. *The Origins of Adversary Criminal Trial.* Op. cit. p. 55.

43 See article by Sydney Smith in the *Edinburgh Review* vol. xlv. p. 76-7.

44 J.H. Langbein. *The Origins of Adversary Criminal Trial.* Op. cit. pp. 342-3.

45 Ibid. p. 9.

46 R. Vogler. (2005) *A World View of Criminal Justice.* Aldershot, Ashgate Publishing. p. 131.

47 Ibid. p. 135.

48 J. F. Stephen. (1863) *A General View of the Criminal Law of England.* London, Macmillan & Co.

49 Ibid. pp. 166-7.

50 J.H. Langbein. *The Origins of Adversary Criminal Trial.* Op. cit. p. 338.

51 www.hri.org/docsECHR50.html

52 R. Vogler. *A World View of Criminal Justice.* Op. cit. p. 51.

53 (1689) London.

54 (1690) London, Awnsham Churchill.

55 M. Cranston. (1962) *Human Rights Today.* London, Ampersand Books. p. 10.

Glossary 1

Judicial and Historical Terms

Adversary trial: A criminal trial in which there is a clash of proofs presented by the parties and their counsel. The decision is reached by an independent, randomly chosen, jury with a judge who sums up the evidence to the jury and rules on points of law but otherwise takes no part in the proceedings. It is often contrasted with the **inquisitorial system of trial** where the judge conducts both the pre-trial proceedings and the case in court.

Assizes: Originally regional criminal courts throughout England and Wales that dealt with the most serious crimes. They were abolished by the Courts Act 1971 and replaced by the Crown Court in 1972.

Associations for the Prosecution of Felons: Voluntary societies whose members' contributions were used to pay the expenses of criminal investigations and fees to counsel for prosecutions. They also offered rewards for information and thereby often induced perjury and false prosecutions by thief-takers and bounty hunters.

Attorney-General: The principal law officer of the Crown and head of the Bar. He or she is usually a member of the House of Commons and changes with the ministry.

Benefit of clergy: Device concocted by the Church in the reign of Henry II whereby a convicted prisoner would be set free from the jurisdiction of the lay courts if he or she could read the first verse of psalm 51 (the so-called 'neck verse'). The benefit was not available to women until 1624 and treason was never 'clergyable'. In Tudor times it was provided that the benefit could not be claimed more than once, leading to branding for the purposes of future identification. Abolished by statute in 1827.

'Best evidence' rule: This provides that evidence must be original and not derivative and must have a clear connection with the fact to be proved. Under it **hearsay** was normally excluded once rules of evidence were established in the eighteenth century.

'Bloody Assizes': In 1685 the Duke of Monmouth unsuccessfully attempted a rebellion in the West Country. Lord Chief Justice Jeffreys presided at the assizes in the major towns of the area where alleged rebels were prosecuted. He constantly browbeat accused and witnesses alike and sentenced large numbers of people to death or transportation without a fair trial.

Capital crimes: Crimes punishable by death.

City of London: The oldest part of London. Governed by the lord mayor and city officials independently of the surrounding county of London.

Common Law: That part of the law formulated, developed and administered by the judges of the common law courts as distinct from statute law. It is not written down in any one place but survives in law reports.

Confession: An admission of guilt made by a person charged with a crime. It became inadmissible in the eighteenth century if made in response to an inducement or threat.

Corruption of the blood: A feudal doctrine under which a person found guilty of treason or felony could not hold or inherit land or, more importantly since the penalty for these offences was frequently death, transmit a title by descent. Abolished by the Forfeiture Act 1870.

Counterfeiting: Forgery, usually of money.

Cross-examination: The right of defence counsel to question prosecution witnesses after examination in chief is closed. It is not confined to matters alleged in examination in chief and may include leading questions. Once permitted to counsel in the early eighteenth century it assisted the development of adversary trial.

Dock: The box in which a prisoner stands in court.

Dock brief: A prisoner in the dock who could not afford to pay counsel's fees was allowed to choose from their number in court a barrister to act for him or her on payment of a fee of £1. 3s. 6d.

Either-way case: A case that could have been tried at assizes (now the Crown Court) by a jury or alternatively before magistrates. Such cases still exist subject to a preliminary procedure known as mode of trial.

Enlightenment: A rationalistic philosophy in the period preceding the outbreak of the French Revolution which looked to reason for the answer to all human problems and demanded a ` revaluation of all social institutions. It highlighted human rights which it linked with a questioning of tradition and authority.

Ex officio: By virtue of office.

Examination in chief: Oral examination by prosecuting counsel of his witnesses. It may not include leading questions. After his witness is cross-examined by the defence counsel he may **re-examine** on matters arising out of the cross-examination.

Gaol delivery: A court which heard accusations against prisoners in gaol and decided their guilt or innocence. The Old Bailey was the court of gaol delivery for the adjacent Newgate Prison.

Glorious Revolution: To avoid Roman Catholic succession to the throne as plotted by James II, the Whigs and the Tories invited William, Prince of Orange, to replace James and enforce the Protestant religion. William landed in Devon in 1688, secured a non violent revolution and ended the so-called 'divine right of kings'.

Guinea: A coin first minted in 1696 and worth twenty-one shillings.

Habeas Corpus: A prerogative writ used to produce before the courts persons detained illegally. It is Latin for 'You have the body'.

Hearsay: So called 'second hand evidence.' Statements made out of court and not subject to cross-examination. Generally permitted before the eighteenth century and subsequently disallowed after pressure for its exclusion by defence counsel.

House of correction: A prison where offenders found guilty of minor offences were put to hard labour.

Indictment: Formal written accusation charging one or more persons with a serious crime and reciting the charges in technical language. If the accused could find a flaw in the wording of the indictment it failed and for this reason, until modern times, a prisoner was not allowed to see the indictment prior to the commencement of his trial.

Industrial Revolution: The development in the eighteenth and early nineteenth centuries of industrial capitalism which transformed Britain into the first industrial nation on the globe and for a time the 'workshop of the world'.

Justices of the peace: They heard criminal complaints brought to them by victims and constables and decided if the suspects should be sent for trial or released. They also acted as judges at quarter sessions.

King's evidence: Where a person confessed his guilt of a crime and offered evidence against his co-accused on condition of the charge against him being dropped he was said to have turned King's evidence. (Currently, 'Queen's evidence').

Magistrate: Another name for a Justice of the Peace.

Misdemeanour: A minor crime, not punishable by death. Most were tried at quarter sessions and only a few at the Old Bailey.

Nullification: The jury's power to acquit a defendant on the basis of conscience even when, on the evidence and the law, the defendant would technically be guilty.

Old Bailey: The assize court for London and Middlesex.

Pardon: Either a **free pardon** by the Crown under which the convict would receive no punishment or a **conditional pardon** whereby a sentence would be reduced as, for example, from the death penalty to transportation.

Partial verdict: The reduction by the jury of the value of money or goods stolen. The reduction in value was often considerable and this **pious perjury** was invoked to prevent widespread use of the death penalty for theft and was largely supported by the public and the judiciary.

Popish Plot: A fake plot instigated by Titus Oates alleging a Jesuit plan to murder Charles II, put the Roman Catholic Duke of York on the throne and bring a French army into Britain. The 'plot' raged from 1678 to 1681 and produced a public outcry that fostered the judicial murder of many Whig leaders after biased trials. In response, when the Whigs came to power they introduced the

Treason Trials Act 1696 to allow, for the first time, those charged with treason to be represented by counsel.

Presumption of innocence: The fundamental rule of criminal procedure that the prosecution is obliged to prove the case against an accused person beyond reasonable doubt.

Pro bono publico: Counsel appearing for a defendant without fee 'for the public good'.

Quarter Sessions: Courts presided over by justices of the peace where misdemeanours were tried. Outside London they met four times (hence their name) and in London eight times a year.

Recorder of London: Chief legal officer of the city of London and one of the judges who heard cases at the Old Bailey. He forwarded reports to the King about all the cases where convicts were sentenced to death, in order that the King could decide whether or not to pardon them.

Respite: A postponement of a punishment. Some punishments which were respited were never carried out.

Royal Pardon: After someone was convicted of a capital offence, if the judge (or sometimes the jury) considered that for sound reasons he or she should be shown clemency they could petition the monarch for a royal pardon. This was often done to avoid capital punishment.

Rye House Plot: An actual, but unsuccessful, plot to murder Charles II on his journey from Newmarket to London in 1683.

Shilling: Equivalent of 12 old pence – now five new pence.

Solicitor-general: Second law officer of the Crown after the **Attorney-general**. He is a member of the House of Commons.

Statute: An Act passed by Parliament and approved by the monarch.

Thief-taker: A person who received payment from the government for arresting thieves or arranging the return of stolen goods. Also known as a bounty hunter who, to obtain a reward, would often accuse an innocent person of committing a crime and securing his or her arrest and prosecution. In trials in which Garrow appeared for the defence he mercilessly cross-examined them.

Transportation: Sending convicts to serve their sentence overseas, first the West Indies, then North America and later Australia. By the Transportation Act 1718 a felon guilty of a capital offence subject to benefit of clergy could be transported instead of being sentenced to death.

Treason Trials Act 1696: The statute which, *inter alia*, allowed prisoners accused of treason to have counsel appear for them fully and not merely on points of law. It formed the first step in the birth of adversary trial.

Glossary 2

Crimes Tried Frequently at the Old Bailey

In the period under review serious indictable offences (which were punishable with death) were dealt with at the Old Bailey and included the following:[1]

Assault: Physical attacks on others and included cases where there was no physical attack but the victim was terrified by gestures or shouting.

Assault with intent to rape: Arose where an attempted rape was unsuccessful or it was thought impossible to prove an actual rape.

Bigamy: Marrying a second spouse while the first spouse was still alive.

Burglary: Breaking into a dwellinghouse at night with intent to commit a felony or actually doing so. Such breaking during the hours of daylight was **Housebreaking** if the inhabitants of the house were put in fear.

Coining: Counterfeiting or interfering with the currency of the realm, either coin or paper. The offence included the possession of moulds for the manufacture of coins.

Constructive treason: A doctrine—invented by the judges—that a conspiracy to do some act in regard to the monarch which might endanger his, or her, life was itself treason, even though not defined as such by statute until the Treason Act 1795.

Customs offences: Included smuggling, seizing goods from customs and excise officers and obstructing or shooting at the officers when performing their duty.

Embezzlement: Thefts committed by clerks, servants or employees of goods belonging to, or in the security of, their employers.

Forgery: The fraudulent making or altering of a written document (usually money but also bonds and wills) to the detriment of another.

Fraud: Criminal deceit or false representation, usually obtaining goods under false pretences.

Highway robbery: A robbery on or near the King's highway which included London's streets.

Infanticide: The killing of a new born child. If the accused was an unmarried mother and the death of the baby was concealed the mother had by statute to rebut a presumption of guilt. Generally, however, a mother would be acquitted if she could demonstrate that she had prepared for the birth of the baby, for example by acquiring clothing for it.

Larceny: Was either **Simple grand larceny** (see below), which was theft of goods of a value exceeding 12 pence without aggravating circumstances, such as assault or breaking and entering, or **Petty larceny** which was theft of goods valued at less than 12 pence and was not a capital crime. **Grand larceny**, where the goods were valued at 12 pence or more, was a capital offence whilst petty larceny was punishable with whipping, imprisonment or transportation. But see **Transportation** in *Glossary 1*. The distinction between the different types of larceny was not abolished until 1827.

Libel: The malicious defamation of a person in print in order to expose that person to public hatred. Libels against the monarch were prosecuted as the more serious offence of **seditious libel**.

Manslaughter: An unlawful killing without premeditation or malice.

Murder: Unlawful homicide with malice aforethought. Where death is caused by an unlawful act done intending to cause death or bodily harm, or which is commonly known to cause death or bodily harm.

Perjury: Wilfully testifying falsely under oath in a judicial proceeding or procuring another to do so.

Perverting justice: Enticing thieves to commit a crime and then receiving rewards for their arrest and prosecution.

Pickpocketing: Stealing from the person of another, without his knowledge, goods worth more than one shilling. It ceased to be a capital offence in 1808.

Rape: Forced sexual intercourse with a woman against her will.

Receiving stolen goods: By a statute of 1691 a person receiving stolen goods, knowing them to be stolen, was guilty of being an accessory to a felony.

Returning from transportation: Doing so before the period of the sentence had expired was a felony punishable with death (as with Magwitch in Dickens' *Great Expectations*).

Riot: Where three or more persons assembled to carry out an unlawful act, usually to commit a breach of the peace, and then performed it. Where there was an assembly with the intent but no act was performed the charge was **Unlawful Assembly**.

Robbery: An open and violent assault to forcibly take property of any value from the victim and putting him or her in fear.

Simple grand larceny: The most common offence at the Old Bailey. It consisted of stealing goods or money valued at one shilling or more without aggravating circumstances.

Shoplifting: Stealing goods valued at five shillings or more from a shop. It was a capital crime.

Treason: Conspiring to overthrow the monarch or levying war against him or her. By the Treason Act 1352[2] an overt act and two witnesses were required.

ENDNOTES for *Glossary 2*

[1] See Internet. www.oldbaileyonline.org/history/crime/crimes.html
[2] Edw. 3. st. 5, c.2.

Bibliography

Primary sources

Old Bailey Proceedings. (www.oldbaileyonline.org). Original reports of 100,621 criminal trials from April 1674 to December 1834.

Annual Register, 1836.

Archives of the Honourable Society of Lincoln's Inn.

Atkyns, Sir Robert. *A Defence of the late Lord Russel's Innocency.* 1689.

Beccaria, Count Cesare. (1764) *Of Crimes and Punishments.*

British Library:
    Add. MSS. 25203, f. 569v
    Hardwicke Papers. *Add. MSS.* 35863.

Brougham, Henry. (1810) 'Speeches of Thomas Erskine when at the Bar, on Subjects connected with the Liberty of the Press, and against Constructive Treasons.' 16 *Edinburgh Review.*

—(1812) Speeches of Lord Erskine when at the Bar, on Miscellaneous Subjects. 19 *Edinburgh Review.*

—(1836) Review of *A Popular and Practical Introduction to Law Studies* by Samuel Warren. 64 *Edinburgh Review.*

—(1838) Speeches. Edinburgh.

—(1845) 'Mr. Baron Garrow. London,' 1 *Law Review.*

—(1864) Speech in Middle Temple Hall. *The Times.*

Campbell, Lord John. *Lives of the Lord Chancellors.* (1868)

Cobbetts *Parliamentary History.* 1696.

Code of Conduct of the Bar of England and Wales, 1990.

Coke, Sir Edward. (1797) 3 *Institute.*

Cottu, Charles. (1822) *On the Administration of Criminal Justice in England; and the Spirit of the English Government.*

Criminal Law Commissioners Report, 1836.

Dalton, Michael. *The Countrey Justice, Containing the Practice of the Justices of the Peace out of their Sessions.* 1619.

English Reports, 1588, 1744.

Farington, Joseph. *Diary.* (ed. Kathryn Cave) Vols. ii 1796, viii 1807, xi 1811.

Foster, Sir Michael. *A Report of Some Proceedings on the Commission of Oyez and Terminer and Gaol Delivery for the Trial of the Rebels in the Year 1746 etc.* 1792.

Gurney, J. *The Trial of Richard Patch for the Wilful Murder of Isaac Blight.* 1806.

Hardy, Thomas. *Memoir.* 1832.

Hague, Thomas. *A Letter to William Garrow, Esquire, in which the Conduct of Counsel in the Cross-Examination of Witnesses and Commenting on their Testimony is fully discussed and the Licentiousness of the Bar Exposed.* 1808.

Hale, Sir Matthew. *The History of the Pleas of the Crown,* 1736.

Hansard. 1806, 1810, 1813, 1814, 1816, 1817, 1821, 1826, 1836.

Hawkins, Serjeant William. *Treatise of the Pleas of the Crown,* 1716.

Hawls, Sir John. *A Reply to a Sheet of Paper, entitled The Magistry and Government of England Vindicated,* 1689.

Howell's State Trials, 1818.

Journals of the House of Commons. 1785.

Locke, John. (1689) *Letter for Toleration.* London.

—(1690) *Two Treatises of Government.* London, Awnsham Churchill.

Parliamentary History. 1794, 1824.

Parliamentary Papers 1809, 1810, 1813, 1836.

Pellew, George. *The Life and Correspondence of the Rt. Hon. Henry Addington, first Viscount Sidmouth.* 1847.

Public Record Office. SP 36/116, f.107.

Ridgway, James. (ed) *Speeches of the Right Hon. Lord Erskine When at the Bar, with a Preparatory Memoir by the Right Hon. Lord Brougham.* vol. i. 1810.

State Tryals. 1719.

Year Books 30 and 31. Edw. I. (Rolls Series).

Journals and newspapers

American Journal of Legal History, 1973.

Cambridge Law Journal, 2004.

Cornell Law Review, 1990.

Edinburgh Review, 1810, 1812, 1827, 1836, 1838,1884, 1897.

The Examiner, 1846.

History Today, 1991.

Irish Jurist, 1973.

The Journal of Legal History, 2005.

Law and History Review, 1991, 1993.

Law Magazine, 1836, 1837, 1867.

Law Review, Aug. 1845 – May 1846, Nov. 1848 – Feb. 1849.

Law Times, 1844.

The Law Quarterly Review, 1895, 1899, 1950, 1953.

The Modern Law Review, 2003.

Morning Chronicle, 1840.

The Times, 1786, 1789, 1800, 1840, 1849, 2004.

University of Chicago Law Review, 1978, 1983.

Wayne Law Review, 1990.

Westminster Review, 1834.

Yale Law Journal, 1997

Books and articles

Anon. (1833) *Old Bailey Experiences.*

Andrews, H.B. (1833) *Criminal Law: Being a Commentary on Bentham on Death Punishment.* London, Charles Reader.

Aspinall, A. (1963) (ed) *The Correspondence of George, Prince of Wales 1770-1812* London, Cassell.

Baker, J.H. (1973) 'Criminal Justice at Newgate 1616-1627. Some Manuscript Reports in the Harvard Law School.' *Irish Jurist.* Dublin, Periodical Publications.

—(1979) *An Introduction to Legal History.* London, Butterworths.

Barker, G.F.R. (1975) *Dictionary of National Biography.* Oxford University Press.

Beattie, J.M. (1977) 'Crime and Courts in Surrey 1736-1753.' In *Crime in England 1550-1800.* (ed. J.S. Cockburn) London, Methuen & Co. Ltd.

—(1986) *Crime and the Courts in England 1660-1800.* Oxford, Clarendon Press.

—(1988) 'London Juries in the 1690s.' In Cockburn & Green (eds.) *Twelve Good Men and True: The Criminal Trial Jury in England, 1200- 1800.* New Jersey, Princeton University Press.

—(1991) 'Garrow for the Defence.' *History Today.* History Today Ltd.

—(1991) 'Scales of Justice: Defence Counsel and the English Criminal Trial in the Eighteenth and Nineteenth Centuries.' 9(2) *Law and History Review.* University of Illinois Press.Blackstone, William. (1830) *Commentaries on the Law of England.* vol. iv. London, Thomas Tegg.

Cairns, David J.A. (1998) *Advocacy and the Making of the Adversarial Criminal Trial. 1800-1865.* Oxford, The Clarendon Press.

Chitty, Joseph. (1826) *A Practical Treatise on the Criminal Law etc.*

Clark, Sir George. (1955) *The Later Stuarts 1660-1714.* Oxford, The Clarendon Press.

Cockburn, J.S. (1972) *A History of the English Assizes 1558-1714.* Cambridge, Cambridge University Press.

—(1985) *Introduction to Calendar of Assize Records: Home Circuit Indictments Elizabeth I and James I.* London, HMSO.

Cole, G.D.H. and Postgate. R. *The Common People 1746-1938.* London, Methuen & Co. Ltd.

Cornish, W.R. (1968) *The Jury. London,* Allen Lane, The Penguin Press.

Cranston, Maurice. (1962) *Human Rights Today.* London, Ampersand Press.

Darbyshire, Penny. (2001) What Can the English Legal System Learn from Jury Research up to 2001? www.kingston.ac.uk/~ku00596.elsres01.pdf

Deane, Phyllis. (1979) *The First Industrial Revolution.* Cambridge, Cambridge University Press.

Dwyer, Déirdre. (2003) Review of Langbein's *The Origins of Adversary Criminal Trial.* 66 *The Modern Law Review.* Oxford, Blackwell Publishing.

Evans, W.D. (1826) *On the Law of Evidence.*

Fielding, Henry. (1751) *An Inquiry into the Causes of the Late Increase of Robbers.* London, A. Millar.

Fisher, George. (1997) 'The Jury's Rise as Lie Detector.' New Haven, 107 *Yale Law Journal.*

Foss, Edward. (1864) *The Judges of England: with Sketches of their Lives and Miscellaneous Notices Connected with the Courts at Westminster from the Time of the Conquest.* Vol. 9. London, John Murray.

Gilbert, Sir Geoffrey. (1754) *The Law of Evidence.* Dublin, Sarah Cotter.

Green, T.A. (1985) *Verdict According to Conscience: Perspectives on the English Criminal Trial Jury 1200-1800. Chicago, University of Chicago Press.*

Handler, P. (2004) 'Review of Langbein's *Origins of Adversary Criminal Trial.' Cambridge Law Journal,* Cambridge University Press.

—(2005) 'Review of May's *The Bar and the Old Bailey', 1750-1850.* London, *The Journal of Legal History.*

Hardcastle, Mary Scarlett. (1881) (ed) *Life of John, Lord Campbell Lord High Chancellor of Great Britain: consisting of a selection from his autobiography, diary and letters.* London, Murray.

Harding, A. (1973) *The Law Courts of Medieval England.* London, George Allen & Unwin Ltd.

Havighurst, Alfred. (1950) 'The Judiciary and Politics in the Reign of Charles II.' 66 *The Law Quarterly Review.* London, Stevens & Sons.

—(1953) 'James II and the Twelve Men in Scarlet.' *The Law Quarterly Review.* London, Stevens & Sons.

Hazlitt, William. (1998) 'Illustrations of the Times Newspaper' in *Selected Writings* (ed Duncan Wu). London, Pickering and Chatto.

Hobsbawm, E.J. (1962) *The Age of Revolution: Europe from 1789- 1848. London, Weidenfeld & Nicolson.*

Holdsworth, Sir William. (1938) *A History of English Law. vol.* 11. London, Methuen & Co. Ltd. and Sweet & Maxwell.

Hostettler, John. (1992) *The Politics of Criminal Law: Reform in the Nineteenth Century.* Chichester, Barry Rose Law Publishers

—(1996) *Thomas Erskine and Trial by Jury.* Chichester, Barry Rose Law Publishers.

—(2002) *The Red Gown – The Life and Works of Sir Matthew Hale.* Chichester, Barry Rose Law Publishers.

—(2004) *The Criminal Jury Old and New: Jury Power from Early Times to the Present Day.* Winchester, Waterside Press.

Hyde, H. Montgomery. (1964) *Norman Birkett. The Life of Lord Birkett of Ulverston.* London, Hamish Hamilton.

Ilbert, Sir Courtenay. (1895) *The Law Quarterly Review.* London, Stevens & Sons Ltd.

Jardine, David. (1836) 'A Reading on the Use of Torture in the Criminal Law of England Prior to the Commonwealth.' Delivered at New Inn Hall, London, Michaelmas Term. Published in 67 *Edinburgh Review* (1838)

Johnson, Paul. (1991) *The Birth of the Modern: World Society 1815-1830.* London, Weidenfeld & Nicolson.

Keeton, G.W. (1965) *Lord Chancellor Jeffreys and the Stuart Cause.* London, Macdonald.

King, Peter. (2000) *Justice and Discretion in England 1740-1820.* Oxford, Oxford University Press.

Landsman, Stephan. (1983) 'A Brief Survey of the Development of the Adversary System.' 44(1) *Ohio State Law Journal.*

—(1990) 'The Rise of the Contentious Spirit: Adversary Procedure in Eighteenth Century England.' New York, 75 *Cornell Law Review.*

'From Gilbert to Bentham: The Reconceptualization of Evidence Theory.' 36 *The Wayne Law Review* University of Oregon School of Law.

Langbein. John H. (1973) 'The Origins of Public Prosecutions at Common Law.' 17 *The American Journal of Legal History.* North Carolina University Press.

—(1977) *Torture and the Law of Proof: Europe and England in the Ancien Regime.* Chicago, University of Chicago Press.

—(1978) 'The Criminal Trial before the Lawyers.' Chicago, 45 *The University of Chicago Law Review.*

—(1983) 'Shaping the Eighteenth Century Criminal Trial: A View from the Ryder Sources.' Chicago, 50 University of Chicago Law Review.

—(2003) *The Origins of Adversary Criminal Trial.* Oxford, Oxford University Press.

Lemmings, David. (2002) *Professors of the Law. Barristers and English Legal Culture in the Eighteenth Century.* Oxford, Oxford University Press.

—(2005) 'Criminal Trial Procedure in Eighteenth-Century England: The Impact of Lawyers.' 26(1) *The Criminal Law Review.* London, Routledge.

Mackie, J.D. (1992) *The Earlier Tudors 1485-1558.* Oxford, The Clarendon Press.

Manchester, A.H. (1980) *A Modern Legal History of England and Wales 1750-1950.* London, Butterworth & Co. Ltd.

Mander, Nicholas. (1998) *Varnished Leaves; a Biography of the Mander Family of Wolverhampton 1742-1998.* Internet.

May, Allyson N. (2003) *The Bar and the Old Bailey, 1750-1850.* Chapel Hill, The University of North Carolina Press.

—(2005) 'Advocates and Truth-Seeking in the Old Bailey Courtroom.' 261) *The Journal of Legal History.* London, Routledge.

Milsom, S.C.F. (1981) *Historical Foundations of the Common Law.* London, Butterworths.

North, Roger. (1742) *The Life of the Lord Keeper Guilford.* London, J. Whiston.

Odgers, W. Blake. (1901) *A Century of Law Reform.* London, Macmillan & Co. Ltd.

Ogg, David. (1967) *England in the Reign of Charles II.* Oxford, Oxford University Press

—(1969) *England in the Reigns of James II and William III.* Oxford University Press.

Peake, Thomas. (1801) *A Compendium of the Law of Evidence.* London, E. & R. Brooke and J. Rider.

Phillips, David. (1977) *Crime and Authority in Victorian England, the Black Country 1835-60.* London, Croom Helm.

Pickard, Liza. (2005) *Victorian London.* London, Weidenfeld & Nicolson.

Pollock & Maitland. (1898) *The History of English Law.* Cambridge, Cambridge University Press.

Pope, A. (1714) *Five Cantos.* London, Bernard Lintot.

Radzinowicz. Leon. (1956) *A History of English Criminal Law and its Administration from 1750.* Vols. I and ii. London, Stevens & Sons Ltd.

Rawlings, Philip. (1999) *Crime and Power: A History of Criminal Justice 1688-1998.* Harlow, Wesley Longman Ltd.

Reid, Loren. (1969) *Charles James Fox: A Man for the People.* London, Longmans Green & Co. Ltd.

Rogers, Showell. (1899) 'The Ethics of Advocacy.' 15 *The Law Quarterly Review,* London, Stevens & Sons Ltd.

Romilly, Samuel. (1840) *Memoirs.* London, John Murray.

Scarlett, P.C. (1877) *A Memoir of the Right Honourable James, First Lord Abinger, including part Autobiography, Correspondence etc.* London.

Shapiro, Alexander H. (1993) 'Political Theory and the Growth of Defensive Safeguards in Criminal Procedure: The Origins of the Treason Trials Act of 1696.' 11(2) *Law and History Review.* Illinois, American Society of Legal History.

Shapiro, Barbara. (1983) *Probability and Certainty in Seventeenth-Century England: A Study of the Relationships Between Natural Science, Religion, History, Law and Literature.* New Jersey, Princeton University Press.

—(1991) *'Beyond Reasonable Doubt' and 'Probable Cause': Historical Perspectives on the Anglo-American Law of Evidence.* Berkeley, University of California Press.

Smith, Bruce P. (2005) *The Presumption of Guilt and the English Law of Theft, 1750-1850*. University of Illinois Press.

Steiner & Alston. (1996) *International Human Rights in Context: Law, Politics, Morals*, Oxford, Clarendon Press.

Stephen, James Fitzjames. (1863) *A General View of the Criminal Law of England*. London, Macmillan & Co.

—(1883) *A History of the Criminal Law of England*. London, Routledge/Thoemmes Press.

Stephen, Leslie. (1991) *Hours in a Library*. vol. iii. London, The Folio Society.

Stewart, Robert. (1986) *Henry Brougham 1778-1868: His Public Career*. London, The Bodley Head.

Thomas, Donald. (1999) *The Victorian Underworld*. London, John Murray.

Thompson, E.P. (1968) *The Making of the English Working Class*. London, Pelican Books.

Thorne, R.G. (ed.) (1986) *The History of Parliament: The House of Commons 1790 -1820*. London, Secker & Warburg.

Tobias, John Jacob. (1967) *Crime and Industrial Society in the 19th Century*. London, B.T. Batsford.

Twining, William. (1985) *Theories of Evidence: Bentham & Wigmore*. London, Weidenfeld & Nicolson.

Vogler, Richard. (2005) *A World View of Criminal Justice*. Aldershot, Ashgate Publishers.

Watson, J. Steven. (1960) *The Reign of George III: 1760-1815*. Oxford, The Clarendon Press.

Werkmeister, Lucyle. (1967) *A Newspaper History of England: 1792-3*. Lincoln, University of Nebraska Press.

Wharam, Alan. (1992) *The Treason Trials, 1794*. Leicester, Leicester University Press.

Wigmore, John Henry. (1974) *Evidence in Trials at Common Law*. Chadbourn.

Woodward, E.L. (1954) *The Age of Reform: 1815-1870*. Oxford, The Clarendon Press.

Appendix

The Old Bailey Sessions Papers

Apart from the fact that the Old Bailey was only one among many assize courts, it also needs to be borne in mind that, as we have seen, the reports in the Old Bailey Proceedings, which run from the year 1674 to 1834 and contain accounts of some 100,621 criminal trials, are not foolproof. To start with they have an urban slant but, nevertheless, they deal with far more cases each year than those of reports for any other single assize court. Moreover, they are not verbatim. They were sold as a form of entertainment on the streets of London, and, at least in the early days of adversarial trial, the reporters would have omitted to mention the presence of counsel if they considered it not to be relevant to what they were recording. Hence, it may be that the presence of counsel was significantly under-reported.[1]

At different periods, under different ownerships, the reports also varied in length and for a long time they did not publish remarks of the judges as there was not time to obtain their approval. Furthermore, for two years in the 1790s they ceased reporting acquittals because the city officials who subsidized publication feared the reports were schooling potential criminals in how to secure 'not guilty' verdicts.[2] However, most of the reports include the names of counsel and the judge, the evidence given by the prosecution, any cross-examination, the defence case, counsel's objections, the judge's observations and the verdict of the jury.

But another problem is that they were not always accurate. After the trial of Eliza Fenning in 1815 a pamphlet was issued correcting errors in the Old Bailey report which, the pamphlet claimed, omitted evidence, parts of the statement of the accused, the summing-up of the judge and exchanges between him and the accused.[3]

An even clearer example is given in the case of John Hawkins and George Simpson accused of robbing the Bristol Mail in 1785. The Old Bailey Proceedings report indicates that the trial concluded as follows: 'The prisoners insisted on their innocence; but the evidence being positive, and fortified by many concurrent circumstances, the Jury found them both guilty of the indictment.'[4] According to another source, however, the jury was indecisive, and it required the intervention of the judges before a conviction could be obtained. Hawkins rested his defence on a claim that he had been in London at the time of the crime and he attempted to demonstrate this alibi by producing a receipt written by a William Fuller. Questions about its authenticity arose, however, because the receipt appeared to be written in two different colours of ink. As reported in the *Malefactor's Register*:

> After staying out about an hour, the jury returned into court without agreeing on a verdict, saying they could not be convinced that Fuller's receipt was not genuine, merely on account of the different colours of the ink.

In answer hereto the court intimated that many witnesses had sworn that Hawkins was absent from London: to contradict all whom there was only the evidence of Fuller, which was at least rendered doubtful by the ink appearing of two colours; and it was submitted whether Fuller's single testimony ought to be of equal validity with that of all the opposing parties.

Hereupon the jury went out of court, and on their return, gave a verdict of 'guilty' against both the prisoners.[5]

A fine example of the influence the judges could have on juries at the time.

Nevertheless, in spite of some omissions and inconsistencies, Langbein who has tested the accuracy of the reports against the notes of Chief Justice Sir Dudley Ryder, as well as trial calendars and judicial memoirs, concludes that although the records of trials contain serious omissions they were never invented.[6] In other words, if the Old Bailey Proceedings report says something happened, it did; if the report does not say it happened, it still may have.[7] Moreover, the reports frequently provide more comprehensive accounts than their competitors who often copied their own texts from them. And most importantly, they are arguably the most extensive record in the world of criminal trials of the time.

ENDNOTES for the *Appendix*

[1] J.H. Langbein. *The Origins of Adversary Criminal Trial*. Op. cit. p. 185.

[2] Ibid. p. 190. Citing S. Devereuax. (1999) 'The Fall of the *Sessions Paper*: Criminal Trial and the Popular Press in Late Eighteenth-Century London.' *Criminal Justice History*.

[3] J. Watkins. ((1815) *The Important Results of an Elaborate Investigation into the Mysterious Case of Elizabeth Fenning*. London, J. Fairburn.

[4] www.oldbaileyonline.org/proceedings/value.html

[5] *The Malefactor's Register*. (1785) London, vol. i. p. 293.

[6] J.H. Langbein. (1983) 'Shaping the Eighteenth-Century Criminal Trial: A View from the Ryder Sources.' Chicago, 50 *University of Chicago Law Review*. pp. 126-7.

[7] Langbein. *The Origins of Adversary Criminal Trial*. Op. cit. p. 185.

Index